THE ACT YOU'VE KNOWN FOR ALL THESE YEARS

Also by Clinton Heylin

Babylon's Burning: From Punk to Grunge
Despite The System:
Orson Welles versus the Hollywood Studios
All Yesterday's Parties:
The Velvet Underground in Print: 1966–1971 (editor)
From the Velvets to the Voidoids:
The Birth of American Punk Rock
Can You Feel the Silence? Van Morrison: A New Biography
Bob Dylan Behind the Shades: The Biography – Take Two
Bootleg: The Rise and Fall of the Secret Recording Industry
Bob Dylan: A Life in Stolen Moments. Day by Day 1941–1995
Bob Dylan: The Recording Sessions 1960–1994
No More Sad Refrains: The Life & Times of Sandy Denny
Never Mind The Bollocks, Here's The Sex Pistols
The Penguin Book of Rock & Roll Writing (editor)
Rise/Fall: The Story of Public Image Limited
Form & Substance: A History of Joy Division (with Craig Wood)
Gypsy Love Songs & Sad Refrains:
The Recordings of Richard Thompson & Sandy Denny
Dylan's Daemon Lover: The Story of a 450-year old pop ballad

THE ACT YOU'VE KNOWN FOR ALL THESE YEARS

The Life, and Afterlife, of *Sgt. Pepper*

CLINTON HEYLIN

CANONGATE

Edinburgh · New York · Melbourne

To Paul Nelson (1936–2006)

First published in 2007 by
Canongate Books Ltd, 14 High Street,
Edinburgh, EH1 1TE

1

British Library Cataloguing-in-Publication Data
A catalogue record for this book is available on
request from the British Library

Every effort has been made to contact copyright holders
where appropriate, but please contact the publisher if there
are any errors or omissions.

Typeset by Palimpsest Book Production Limited,
Grangemouth, Stirlingshire

Printed and bound in Great Britain by
Creative Print & Design, Ebbw Vale, Wales

ISBN 978 1 84195 955 9

www.canongate.net

CONTENTS

CHAPTER ILLUSTRATIONS

CHAPTER 1

The famous endorsement of Dylan by the Beatles, which appeared in a March 1965 issue of *Melody Maker*, prior to Dylan's first UK tour in May.

CHAPTER 2

The first known use of the so-called 'Butcher cover', as photographed by Robert Whitaker, which appeared on the front page of a June 1966 issue of *Disc and Music Echo*, with the legend, 'What a carve-up', beneath.

CHAPTER 3

The front cover of the April 1966 issue of *Life* magazine that highlighted the dangers of LSD in a twelve-page feature that sent shock-waves through Middle America.

CHAPTER 4

The American advert for the double A-side, 'Strawberry Fields Forever b/w Penny Lane', proved a boon to the Liverpool Tourist Board for decades to come.

CHAPTER 5

The rarer of the two handmade posters that were produced to promote the Roundhouse bash that would launch *International Times* (and Rock at the Roundhouse) in October 1966. [Courtesy of Andrew Sclanders.]

CHAPTER 6

The infamous trade ad for the Rolling Stones' follow-up to 'Paint It Black', 'Have You Seen Your Mother . . . ?', in which they got the jump on the New York Dolls by a good six years in the dressing-in-drag department.

CHAPTER 7
The front page of the syndicated west-coast paper, KYA *Beat*, the week in January 1967 when the Monkees outsold the Beatles.

CHAPTER 8
The highly collectible 'Arnold Layne' music-sheet, featuring a still from the single's promotional video as illustration.

CHAPTER 9
The *Beat Instrumental* issue which asked the question on every popster's tongue, 'Is the new Beatles album the most expensive pop album ever made?'

CHAPTER 10
The one and only contemporary ad for the aborted *Smile* album, prematurely placed by an unduly optimistic Capitol Records in the March 1967 *TeenSet*.

CHAPTER 11
Disc and Music Echo again beat out their weekly rivals with a cover story on the imminent *Sgt. Pepper* LP.

CHAPTER 12
One of the more surreal adverts for the short-lived UFO club, from an early issue of *International Times*.

CHAPTER 13
The *New Musical Express Book of Rock* (1973) was one of the earliest and wittiest parodies of the fabled *Pepper* cover.

CHAPTER 14
To celebrate the twentieth anniversary of the Beatles, Capitol paid for a full-page ad in *Billboard*, using the opening line of 'Sgt. Pepper' to push the entire existing catalogue.

PREFACE
What Gives?

Forty years ago *Sergeant Pepper's Lonely Hearts Club Band* was issued on a suspecting world. It had been seven long months since first reports of the sessions for *Revolver's* supposedly psychedelic successor, and expectations were sky high. And the initial reaction seemed to suggest that the four lively lads from Liverpool had pulled off the most difficult trick in the book: re-inventing themselves as serious artists after four years at the beck and call of teenyboppers.

As it happens, for me 1967 was the year 'we' bought 'Franny' Lee, 'Big Mal' built a championship-winning side, and Liverpool (and Everton) were just another couple of football clubs 'we' rolled over on the way to the title. Yes, I was one of those children of the sixties, but a teenager of the seventies. The Beatles meant very little to me at the time. In fact, my first clear memory of them is watching a (long) news item reporting that they were breaking up. Which seems somehow appropriate, because I spent much of the first half of the seventies digesting an awful lot of received wisdom on the pop music of the decade just gone, my experience akin to one John 'Teenage Kicks' O'Neill of The Undertones recently imparted to me:

> I'd started getting into music at a time when The Beatles had just broken up, and it [all] read romantically about how great it would have been in the sixties . . . They just weren't making the same kinds of records.

Reading the English music papers in the early seventies, there seemed to be a secret subtext that only the Sergeant's recruits were expected to understand. Not surprisingly, I began to wonder what all the fuss was about, especially after I heard 'With A Little Help From My Friends', one of the most cathartic experiences of my young life. Imagine my disappointment when the gut-punch vocals of Joe Cocker, and the equally physical riffing of Jimmy Page, were replaced by the vaudeville vocals of Billy 'Ringo' Shears and the lads' unutterably jaunty accompaniment. For the first, but not last, time this esteemed platter asked of me, 'What gives?'

This mixed message had come to me courtesy of a major (month's pocket money) investment in a copy of the double-album Beatles anthology, 1967–70. It was here that I first heard four songs from *Pepper*. If the likes of the title-track, 'With A Little Help', 'Lucy in the Sky with Diamonds' and 'A Day in the Life' didn't convince me as to its (not yet benighted) stature, I wasn't a great deal wiser after my then-Maths teacher had dubbed me a cassette of the remaining nine songs.

I was experiencing *Pepper* removed of all context – cultural, technological, and, most importantly, musical – and without the least visual aid, much like someone hearing the songs randomly sequenced on an iPod today. I hadn't as yet learnt that with *Sgt. Pepper* – as with most pop culture artefacts – context is all. I wasn't even hearing the songs in their original mono (which, trust me, is how they should really be heard). When I finally did come to the album whole, and wholly mono, punk was already upon the land, and I wasn't at all sure how I was supposed to like both (so I didn't).

In 1977, 1967 seemed like a long way away (longer than that now, as it were). If 1967 can be seen as the year when a new order took over (witness the likes of *Surrealistic Pillow*, *Mr Fantasy*, *Piper At The Gates of Dawn*, *Are You Experienced?* and *Fresh Cream*), it had become the very order punk had a problem with. Strange as it seems, back in '67 the likes of Hendrix, Floyd, Airplane, Cream and Traffic had The Beatles, the Stones and The Beach Boys very much in their sights. And if albums like *Their Satanic Majesties Request* and *Smiley Smile* hardly enhanced their creators' reputations, for much of the first half of the year many doubted The Beatles' ability to hold their own.

That they did was, in and of itself, a triumph. At last The Beatles – and all dedicated followers of their flag – got to make albums on their own terms; for 1967 – with *Sgt. Pepper* leading the way – signalled the end of record labels randomly compiling collections of songs from what came out of the studio (*Their Satanic Majesties* and *Sgt. Pepper* were in fact the first albums by the Stones and The Beatles not to be bastardised for the US market). As artists began to choose their own producers, art-work, album-sequence and songs, the Album became potentially 'a thing of beauty and a joy forever'.

Hence *Pepper* signalled *not* the birth of Rock, but certainly its validation as a genre clear and distinct from pop. So on the one hand, this little red book is about something as ephemeral as an album of twelve songs (one of which is reprised), some truly great, most simply well-crafted, and a couple of fillers; on the other, it is about the emergence of the most important popular musical form (he says) of the twentieth century. And, just like the defining musical form of a previous Elizabethan renaissance – the popular ballad – it came largely from a localised part of the tiny isle of Albion, its heyday spanned barely a single generation, it was surrounded by a remarkable revival in all the popular arts, and one of its goals was to address the world at large.

It also took what was actually an appalling mish-mash of styles that *sold* – the one and only criterion for pop in the sixties – and separated the wheat from the naff. Prior to this, there was no distinct name for the kind of music made in the first half of the sixties by pop's most forward-thinking acts. File Under Popular was the way it was put to retailers. And though 'Pop' exemplified everything bright, modern, shiny and energetic to Britain's teenagers, it also meant anything played on the BBC Light Service, or on *Sunday*

Night at the London Palladium. So in this world of pop, Engelbert Humperdinck operated in the same universe (sic) as The Rolling Stones.

Rock was a necessary reaction to this. As a word it existed first as a hybrid form of folk (folk-rock), then as a lower-case variant on pop and/or shorthand for rock'n'roll – rock – and finally, post-*Pepper*, as pop's more serious cousin, Rock. In the interim, it would co-opt all new forms of pop and rebrand them in its own image. Thus, when Dylan got downright homey with *John Wesley Harding*, it was classed as country-rock (though it was a lot more folk than country). Psychedelia, or pyschedelic pop – certainly the happening sound in the months leading up to *Pepper* – was recast as acid rock. By the winter of 1968, there was an unspoken assumption that everyone knew the difference between pop and Rock, and that it was the difference between *For Sale* and *Sgt. Pepper*. *Pepper* was the codicil for an album-orientated, 'arty' kind of pop; hence both its importance, and its immediacy of impact.

The struggle for legitimacy may have begun when Dylan – that most illegitimate of pop artists, a poet – went full-on electric in CBS Studio A, New York, and then at the Newport Folk Festival. But if so, it ended with the perceived triumph of *Pepper*, having produced the most exciting period pop and/or Rock would ever know. Between 15 June, 1965 and 1 June, 1967 the pop world turned upside-down, its resultant sounds proving to be the shape of all things to come.

If June 1965 through May 1966 was the moment when, in Greil Marcus's memorable phrase, 'Bob Dylan seemed less to occupy a turning point in cultural space and time than to be that turning point', The Beatles reclaimed the baton in time, and just ran with it. As such, this book takes as its starting point that reclamation, at the Royal Albert Hall on 27 May, when an exhausted Dylan conjured up one last electrical storm for the benefit of the boys.

A year later, to the day, *Sgt. Pepper* appeared in the London shops (five days early). This account of the (second half of the) race to Rock aims to show how The Beatles upped the pace with *Revolver*, then, exhausted by their final live tour, were temporarily overtaken by the likes of The Who, The Kinks, The Move and Hendrix, and then set pop pulses racing again with a sublime double A-side single, before crossing the line – a nose ahead – with *Sgt. Pepper*. It is, in a sense, as much about their competitors as The Beatles themselves; those who fell off the pace and those who ran them very close, at a time when 'pop' bands indulged in the fiercest of friendly rivalries.

To the papers the pop world was all about conflict: Beatles vs Stones, Beatles vs Beach Boys, Beatles vs The Monkees, Beatles vs The Byrds. Yet The Beatles themselves were good friends with members of all those bands. And when the British underground chanced upon its own psychedelic sprinters in The Pink Floyd, the band had the blessing of the hippest Beatle from day one.

The nature of the Sergeant's triumph was such that the Beatles successfully turned the making of albums – not just theirs – into a marathon. Where *Pepper* did not instigate any great rush of blood from those hounds on their tail was in the conceptual stakes. An album like *The Who Sell Out* used an equally slight connecting device to link its largely disconnected songs, but the *material* hardly smacked of the Sergeant. The album-length rock opera was still a little way off, and all the talk of *Pepper* as a concept album quietly died a death after initial efforts failed to find what self-evidently wasn't there.

One could perhaps try – as indeed Ian MacDonald has – to suggest that it was with *Pepper* that The Beatles first conceived of Englishness as a perennial theme, but there are enough earlier English examples to kick the crutches away from this crippled claimant. Rather, like *Citizen Kane* – with which it shares a great deal in terms of immediacy of cultural impact, if not in critical longevity – it was precisely the fact that *Pepper* was a clever collage of all the most up-to-date innovations of others that made it sparkle so brightly.

Nineteen sixty-seven was also the year of the greatest albums that never were. Brian Wilson's *Smile* was an attempt to trump *Pepper* before it had even been started, but it collapsed around Wilson's ears in a requiem of recriminations. A somewhat greater claimant to the Greatest Album That Never Was, Dylan's own basement tapes, was an equal and opposite reaction to The Beatles' new *raison d'être*. However, he had no inclination to return to the race, and held back all the evidence of his own 'back to basics' one-band campaign until the following year, and then leaked it out only to the chosen few, on publisher acetates and mono composite reels. If hype was in, Dylan still wanted out.

Both *Smile* and *The Basement Tapes* were an attempt to turn back the clock – to the pop confection of *Pet Sounds* in Wilson's case; to the rootsy Americana of *The Anthology of American Folk Music* in Dylan's. Both albums appeared long after the fact, and in a form wholly unrepresentative of their original inspiration. Playing the Rock snob, one can't help but wonder what might have happened if *Pepper had* come after *Smile* and/or Dylan's successor to *Blonde on Blonde*. Or even The Pink Floyd's *Piper at the Gates of Dawn*, which was recorded across the Abbey Road hall from the Beatles album, and could well have come out first. For if *Pepper* seemed to change the world – and it certainly received enough plaudits for doing so – it was *Piper at the Gates of Dawn* that in fact set the place-mats for the form of Rock that would dominate the album charts for the next decade – Prog-Rock.

Yet it is *Pepper* which has retained its hold on the popular imagination, and *Piper* which remains a cult classic to the few, a curio on the road to the Dark Side for most. That *Pepper* has much to commend it, I have learnt to accept; that it should be called the best album of all time, I still find frankly risible. But its effect on me, and its effect on Rock, retains real resonance. And the critic in me can't help but rise to its bait.

Thankfully, because I accumulated my knowledge of sixties music in reverse, by buying up the records its survivors were making in the early seventies (by which time, I would argue, the Stones and other soul survivors had finally hit their stride in the long-player department), I was able to hear the music first, and acquire the context second. By so doing, I learnt to distrust a great deal of what I read from people who were 'there', and whose own experiences had failed to enhance the meaning of the music, preferring to obscure it all in a haze of nascent nostalgia.

Even that fine writer Ian MacDonald would prove guilty of this particular crime. In his *Revolution In The Head*, he baldly states, 'Anyone unlucky enough not to have been aged between 14 and 30 during 1966–67 will never know the excitement of those years in popular culture.' As someone who experienced his 'excitement' via Punk at the sharp-end, I find MacDonald's view rather condescending, not to say self-serving ('I was there, and you weren't – nah-nah-nah'). 'Excitement' is rather subjective, and a nostalgia for one's youth, whether it be MacDonald's hippy days or Legs McNeil's drunken nights down the Bowery, tells us nothing of the milieu, save that *they* had a good time. The creativity that spumed forth as the cage of propriety creaked open is what concerns me here (there and everywhere). Sociologists, leave by the door marked Savage Dogs.

As someone who moved through the whole of the sixties lost in the woods of childhood, the context I wanted – and that made me write this book – requires an appreciation of other musical landmarks from the era; specifically Brian Wilson's unrealised *Smile* and Syd Barrett's realised-just-in-time *Piper at the Gates of Dawn*. The best of the music made by The Beatles and their contemporaries between Dylan's Albert Hall apostasy in late May 1966 and the release of *Sgt. Pepper* a year later stands up against anything before or since. The worst, we must put down to the curse of living in interesting times.

This lil' tome is thus partly the story of the power of the record needle, and the damage sometimes done. It has its share of casualties. Syd Barrett, Brian Wilson, John Lennon survived but were never the same; while the two Brians, Epstein and Jones, and their pal, Jimi, did not survive, period. It is also about those who brought a new (and necessary) Ambition to pop, in the guise of two lads from Liverpool who originally just wanted to be bigger than Elvis. By June 1966, they were wondering what they might do for an encore. So may I introduce to you the act I've known for all these years . . .

Clinton Heylin, January 6th, 2007

PART ONE

MAY TO DECEMBER 1966

GET HIGH WITH A
LITTLE HELP

Whatever was blowing at the time moved The Beatles too. I'm not saying we weren't flags on the top of the ship. But the whole boat was moving. –

John Lennon, *Playboy*, 1980

Between 28 August, 1964 and 28 May, 1966, the itineraries of John Lennon, Paul McCartney and Bob Dylan – the trio of tunesmiths on whom so much of the future direction of Rock would hang – intersected just four times: in August '64 and '65 in Manhattan, when The Beatles were in that bustling borough on tour, and in May '65 and '66, when Dylan returned the favour by blitzing Britain with first an acoustic Martin, then a Fender-induced electrical storm.

Each visit afforded the songwriters the opportunity to compare notes, at a time when Dylan was accruing a trio of Rock albums without peer – *Bringing It All Back Home*, *Highway 61 Revisited* and the *Blonde on Blonde* double; while The Beatles were finally coming of age with the ever-redolent *Rubber Soul* and a quintet of singles – 'I Feel Fine', 'Ticket to Ride', 'Help', 'Day Tripper' and 'Paperback Writer' – that continued to best all-comers snapping at their hit-making heels.

That first 'Mr Tambourine Man meets the Mop Tops' soirée, at the Delmonico Hotel on a hot August night, arranged by Al Aronowitz, scenester to the stars, has become laden with Import over the years – as if Dylan was somehow passing a joint *and* the baton. In particular, FabFour aficionados have viewed the increasing sophistication in the songs of the period between, say, 'Eight Days A Week' and 'Eleanor Rigby' as somehow bound up with the 'seven levels' McCartney fleetingly found in the heady haze of that night's opiate-inspired enlightenment. If those 'seven levels' disappeared along with the smoke rings, The Beatles – so the story goes – were never the same again.

By the time the parties met again, at the end of April 1965, at least two Beatles were well on their way to matching Dylan's by-now-prodigious consumption of all things consciousness altering. According to at least one Beatles authority, John Lennon, fellow Beatle George Harrison and their respective spouses, Cynthia and Pattie, had recently added LSD to their personal list of mind-levitators. On this occasion – dated to 8 April, 1965 by Steve Turner – all four had been unwilling guinea pigs in a London dentist's idea of a freak-out:

> **George Harrison:** I didn't know about acid: it wasn't heaven and hell when I had it. It was quite legal and people were just beginning to talk about it. I had it shoved in my coffee anyway, so I didn't even know I was taking it. Once you had it, though, it was important that people you were close to took it, too. When John and I and Cynthia and Pattie took it that first time it was because the dentist dosed our drinks. He was trying to get a scene going and thought it was an aphrodisiac, but he didn't take it himself . . . But there was no way back after that. It showed you backwards and forwards and time stood still. It had nothing to do with getting high. It's so devastating because it cuts right through the physical body, the mind, the ego. It's shattering, as though someone suddenly wipes away all you were taught or brought up to believe as a child and says, 'That's not it.' You've gone so far, your thoughts have become so lofty, and you think that there's no way of getting back.

Lennon seems to have felt he could now share some of the sensibility that inspired Dylan's 'Mr Tambourine Man' (erroneously as it happens – Dylan had written the song some two months before his first documented acid-trip), a song which would top the charts on both sides of the pond before the summer was over. His own 'Help!' – a more ambiguous 'drug-song', apparently written in the immediate aftermath of that first dose of LSD – would replace The Byrds' bastardised rendition at the number one slot.

Back in spring, McCartney, the now confirmed convert to cannabis, felt less of a need to be around America's premier pop-

prophet than his band's two dosed disciples did. Lennon, in particular, was content to spend entire evenings at the Savoy 'very stoned',
listening to Dylan's speed-raps and playing guitar. And he was not
alone. As Dana Gillespie recalls, Dylan 'was the one person that
both the Stones and The Beatles had great admiration for; so when
he held court in one of the hotel rooms, everyone sat and listened'.

Largely absent from the American's appreciation society he
may have been, but McCartney was there the night Dylan introduced The Beatles to the original Beat poet, Allen Ginsberg –
on 11 May, 1965. It was Ginsberg at this juncture who was the
more interested party. As Barry Miles, who as his current keeper
accompanied Ginsberg, told Jonathon Green, 'He didn't know
them, but he wanted to know them.'

Barry Miles – known to one and all as simply Miles – had
recently organised Ginsberg's first London poetry reading at the
bookshop where he held down a day job of sorts. He had arrived
in London from Cheltenham Art School in 1963, securing himself
a job at Better Books on Charing Cross Road, at this time perhaps
the only bookshop in central London to stock the Beat poetry
almost exclusively produced by San Francisco's City Lights. At the
same time, he and friend John 'Hoppy' Hopkins had begun their
own esoteric (and sporadic) periodical of the arts, *Longhair Times*,
introducing the likes of Lawrence Ferlinghetti and Ginsberg to an
English readership. Not surprisingly, when Ginsberg came to London
that May, he called in at Better Books to introduce himself, and
got himself an invite to stay at the flat of Barry and Sue Miles.

It was Miles, rather than the author of 'Howl', who would
provide McCartney with a backstage pass to the London Art underground, introducing him to the avant-garde side of the city. To his
credit, McCartney was entirely open to the eclectic scene he was
now exposed to, thanks in no small measure to the seemingly beneficent smoke rings encircling *his* mind. As Miles says, 'Every night
he was out absorbing stuff – everything from night club singers to
the most avant-garde stuff.' For Miles and his circle of friends,
though, the sheer scale of McCartney's fame came as something of

a shock. To them, Ginsberg was a more notable figure than Dylan, John Cage more worthy than John Cale. Miles still remembers how he would often 'forget quite how outside of it we all were – our concerns were poetry and Art'. It didn't take long for him to find out just how famous this Scouse sponge was:

> **Miles:** I thought it would be very good for The Beatles to know about avant-garde music so I persuaded Paul to come along to a lecture by Luciano Berio at the Italian Institute. We got there. And almost immediately the press came bursting in. [DITL]

If McCartney was soon finding his way into the veritable nooks and crannies of London's alternative nightlife, the process accelerated rapidly after March 1966, when he moved out of the Asher residence, where girlfriend Jane Asher's parents continued to reside, and into his own abode in St John's Wood. His new Cavendish Avenue town house was little more than a mile away from Miles's West-End apartment, where he invariably ended up of an evening:

> **Paul McCartney:** We sat around [Miles's] flat many an evening; we'd ring each other: 'Are you doing anything?' 'No.' 'Great, come on over,' and we'd just hang out and he'd show me stuff from *Evergreen Review* and [other] stuff. Then, [via] people like Robert Fraser . . . I'd get into the art world . . . Miles was a great catalyst. [DITL]

The educational process inverted a lot of McCartney's acquired notions concerning sound and vision. As he put it in an interview the following year, 'I used to think that anyone doing anything weird was weird. I suddenly realised that anyone doing anything weird wasn't weird at all, and that it was the people saying they were weird that were weird.' Green eyes, though, were gazing at him from the foothills of Surrey, where his dearest friend and fellow Beatle, John, was living a life of suburban stultification; 'living out . . . by the golf club with Cynthia', as Paul later put it.

Nor was Lennon was making any secret of his desire to escape

Surrey suburbia. In March 1966, before Paul had even redecorated Cavendish Avenue, he was telling a reporter, 'I'm dying to move into town, but I'm waiting to see how Paul gets on when he goes into his town house. If he gets by all right, then I'll sell the place at Weybridge.' It would actually be another two years before he would abandon the wife and Weybridge, but he remained ever anxious to hear what his partner-in-song had been doing. When, in the first flush of fervour for all things avant, McCartney semi-seriously informed Lennon he had an idea for an album title, *Paul McCartney Goes Too Far*, Lennon's response was, 'Fantastic! Do it!'

So enthused was Lennon – while patently dissatisfied with his own life and work-to-date – that when he came to a Beatles recording session in early April 1966, with an unnamed, single-chord dirge he wanted to record, he allowed McCartney full rein to impose some of those avant-garde notions on the basic track of what George Martin labelled simply 'Mark One'. Ever self-conscious when he got 'wordy', Lennon was hoping to bury lines like 'lay down all thought, surrender to the void' and 'when ignorance and haste may mourn the dead' beneath a morass of effects. After a day recording a basic track, and applying the first transistorised vocal to what would become 'Tomorrow Never Knows', The Beatles returned the next afternoon with the idea of superimposing a plethora of tape loops over 'Mark One, Take Three'.

Barry Miles: If you went over to Paul's place in the evening, you'd sit around with a Revox on full echo and bang things, and it all sounded terrific if you'd smoked enough dope. Nobody [usually] bothered to play it back.

Geoff Emerick: The tape loop idea started because they all had Brennell [tape-]machines. Paul in particular used to make his own loops at home and walk into the studio with bags full of little reels, saying, 'Listen to this!'

On this occasion, Paul came up with a distorted guitar that sounded like a distressed seagull, a wine glass echofest and some sped-up instruments-to-hand. But the problem – at least in 1966 at EMI's Abbey Road studios, where four-track recording remained the norm – was that the FabFour could not afford to allocate more than one of those four precious tracks to such sounds, and so rather than superimpose each loop in turn, they were required to mix the various loops live to tape, with as many as five machines running at any given time, in a spontaneous sonic experiment.

Even after producing a basic track the boys were happy with, Lennon wanted the vocals to sound suitably subterranean, leaving it to producer George Martin and newly blooded engineer Geoff Emerick to get him to sound like 'the Dalai Lama singing from the highest mountain-tops,' by feeding his vocal 'through a revolving Leslie speaker inside a Hammond organ'. Whether this made his lyrics sound any more profound is a matter of debate, but the results were certainly startling in the context of a Beatles album (though not quite as startling as the studio recording of 'Venus In Furs' The Velvet Underground made the same month in New York).

After 7 April, work was suspended on 'Mark One' while The Beatles recorded half a dozen more orthodox pop ditties for their seventh pukka (i.e. British) long-player. Three weeks later, the full band attended what was ostensibly just a mixing session – itself a break from previous patterns of behaviour. Usually producer Martin had been left to get on with making a releasable mix. It was all part of a process which Martin semi-seriously portrayed, to Beatles biographer Hunter Davies, as a transition 'from being the gaffer [of] four Herberts from Liverpool, to what I am now, clinging on to the last vestiges of recording power'.

The penultimate of the nine mixes of 'Tomorrow Never Knows' completed that day – after a last-minute switch from a more effect-ridden mix – would be deposited on *Revolver* as the album-closer. Lennon and McCartney were especially delighted with the results and – as was common practice at the time – had acetates cut that evening to play at home, and to other, unknowing ears, garnering further feedback.

In an era when the term tape recorder meant reel-to-reel, which was neither standard home equipment nor simple to set up, the acetate was the preferred medium for a 'reference copy' of a recording. As Pink Floyd manager Peter Jenner says, 'You *had* to get acetates cut, 'cause you didn't have cassettes to listen to.' Though the life of an acetate – with its wafer-thin grooves – might be no more than a dozen plays before audible degradation interfered with one's listening pleasure, everyone could lay their hands on a record player; and every studio had acetate-cutting facilities. As such, McCartney left Abbey Road on the evening of 27 April with an acetate of 'Tomorrow Never Knows' – take 3, remix 8 – under his arm.

Six days later, McCartney turned up at the Mayfair Hotel, just off London's vibrant Piccadilly thoroughfare, with the same acetate, for a pre-arranged rendezvous with the man from Minnesota. Dylan, too, had a set of acetates he wanted to share with 'Macca' – ones he had been lugging around with him since the day The Beatles first cut 'Mark One'. Having travelled in the hold to Hawaii, Australia, Sweden and Denmark, they landed with the luggage in London on 2 May. Dylan had been convinced he had produced another masterpiece the very first time he had spun these white-labelled discs:

Jules Siegel: I was there when Albert [Grossman] brought [Dylan] the first dub of *Blonde on Blonde*. It was really funny. They didn't have a portable record player, so the hotel finally sent up a record player but it was missing the spindle, and he got really annoyed about this. Then Albert kinda pushed him aside and very, very carefully placed the LP in the exact centre of the turntable. And then we sat there and listened to it. [When] 'Sad Eyed Lady of the Lowlands' [came on], he said, 'Just listen to that! That's old-time religious carnival music.' He was just thrilled with his own work.

Dylan was right to be excited. Here was an album panoramic in its sweep, delivered by musicians who seemed genetically incapable of playing out of time or off key, and with a set of lyrics light-years removed from the pop sensibilities to which most chart acts still clung, The Beatles included. If – as is likely – he played McCartney the studio cut of 'Visions of Johanna' that evening, it would have convinced a lesser man than Paul to stop kidding about and join the Foreign Legion.

But a year and a half of sustained amphetamine use – now usually in the form of 'speedballs', comprising methamphetamine and cocaine, designed to counteract the devastating comedowns he was feeling from the heavy opiates that made up the other half of his daily cocktail of drugs – had made Dylan intolerant at best, and verbally vicious at worst, when it came to the efforts of his peers. When Phil Ochs had given him his honest opinion of Dylan's last single but one, the scabrous 'Can You Please Crawl Out Your Window?', Dylan had turfed him out of his long black limousine, and he was still refusing to speak to him when Ochs appeared at his rented villa, The Castle, in LA, a month later to apologise.

According to McCartney, when he took out the acetate of 'Tomorrow Never Knows' and put it on the turntable, Dylan's response was, '"Oh I get it, you don't want to be cute any more." And I was saying, "Yeah, that's it."' But the one eyewitness to the event not caught in the eye of the storm, part-time chanteuse and resident rock chick Marianne Faithfull, recalls Dylan's response being altogether more devastating:

> **Marianne Faithfull:** Paul got a very cool reception. I saw him come in … with an acetate of a track he'd been working on which was very far out for its time, with all kinds of distorted, electronic things on it. Paul was obviously terribly proud of it, he put it on the record player and stood back in anticipation, but Dylan just walked out of the room.

Such a response would probably have finished Lennon or Harrison, both of whom were more in the thrall of Dylan's paranoiac vision at the time. Even McCartney surely recognised that it was Dylan who'd been setting the agenda for the transition from pop to Rock in the past eighteen months, burning through pop culture like a roman candle doused with lighter fuel. But *he* was not about to be dissuaded from his chosen course by this luminescent peer. However, Dylan had one more jolt in store for Macca and his fellow Scousers, and it came at the end of the month, when the death-trip he seemed to be on was nearing its end.

The night before Dylan arrived in London, The Beatles had played their last-ever British concert (January 1969 rooftop rehearsals notwithstanding); at what to date had been an auspicious event in the Britpop calendar – the *NME* Pollwinners' Concert held at Wembley's Empire Pool. This time, though, the event was to prove a sour affair, even though it surely represents the greatest pop bill of all time. After the likes of The Small Faces, Spencer Davis Group and The Yardbirds warmed the crowd up before an intermission, The Who, The Rolling Stones and The Beatles concluded the evening's festivities.

However, unlike the previous year's *NME* concert – in which the likes of Them, The Animals and The Kinks got to share the stage with the Stones and The Beatles – the full concert was not filmed for subsequent TV broadcast; nor did the Stones and The Beatles appear on opposite halves of the bill, as in 1965, when the Stones closed the first half and The Beatles, the second. And, according to attendant *NME* reporter Keith Altham, at least one Beatle was less than amused. The ever-belligerent Lennon confronted *NME* owner Maurice Kinner 'backstage about going on after the Stones . . . A lot of swearing went on; and Maurice was very taciturn [afterwards], blood drained from his face, "That's the way it is." "Well, that's the last fucking time The Beatles'll ever work for you, Maurice!"'

And he was true to his word. Any pact between the top pop bands and the pop weeklies was fast approaching its expiry date;

evidenced by the fact that both the Stones and The Who went along with The Beatles' new black-out policy, refusing to allow their performance to be used on the ATV broadcast. The 1966 *NME* Pollwinners may also have provided a stark reminder to the FabFour that – for all their seemingly effortless command of the worldwide singles market – they could no longer hold their own live with the British bands who followed in their wake; not up there, on stage, where bands like The Who and The Yardbirds were becoming blast furnaces of auto-destruction.

Even before The Beatles made the fateful decision to surrender the stage to these powerhouse peers, the decision was being made for them. And a set featuring the likes of 'Nowhere Man', 'Day Tripper' and 'I'm Down' could hardly be said to reflect the state-of-mind of the self-same band who had just recorded 'Tomorrow Never Knows'. But nothing – not even the 'Maximum r&b'-era Who – could have prepared John, Paul and George for the apocalyptic aural assault they witnessed on 27 May, at the Royal Albert Hall, when Dylan and the Hawks played the final show of their six-week world tour.

It had been just ten months since Dylan had enveloped his folk audience in an electrical storm at the Newport Folk Festival, and in that single act of apostasy signalled the death of the (last) folk revival and the birth of Rock (before pop's progressives joined the party, in the guise of folk-rock). The reality of the situation, though, was only brought home to bewildered Brits in May 1966, when Dylan's speed-infused electric declamations rattled the fences folkies had been sitting on.

To put the fabled fury of the folkies in context, both the folk revival and Dylan's pop profile held somewhat greater sway in Britain than in his homeland. The British folk revival was as capital-centric as the pop scene, its bases being clubs like the Singers, the Troubadour and Bunjies, the very places Dylan himself had frequented on his first visit in the winter of 1962–63. By April 1965, though, when he made his third trip to the swingin' metrop-olis, Dylan was assuredly a pop star, worthy of national media coverage, with a number one album under his belt (*Freewheelin'* had just broken a two-year occupation of the top-spot by The Beatles and the Stones). And the (semi-electric) album issued in the wake of his first UK tour, *Bringing It All Back Home*, followed it to the top. Indeed, both Dylan albums went on to outsell The Beatles' latest long-player, *Help!*, according to the year-end charts.

And so, when Dylan returned to London from Paris, on 25 May, to play two sell-out shows at the Royal Albert Hall, he had been living the legend for more than a year, and his former folk status must have seemed like another lifetime. This was a show The Beatles weren't about to miss. They cleared their schedule for the twenty-seventh to catch Dylan's swan song this time around.

Lulling his former fans into a false sense of familiarity, Dylan began with just his trusty Martin and Hohner, and had soon bathed the hallowed hall in a magnetic field. To show that he hadn't lost his sense of humour, he even prefaced 'Visions of Johanna' by insisting, in the slurred diction of a man stoned out of his gourd, that this was not a '*drurg* song – it's just vulgar to think so'. In fact, no-one had suggested it was. How could they. It was still two months away from an official release – unlike 'Mr Tambourine Man', which remained perhaps his best-known song, thanks to The Byrds' abridged rendition, and was widely regarded as the first modern 'drug-song' to transgress the pop idiom. Here – on that last night of the '66 tour, as Dylan played the mouth-harp like a harp – was the birth of a particular kind of psychedelia-in-song. If the latter song had been penned by a man yet to experience the hallucinogenic high of acid, it was assuredly *sung* that night by a man disordering every sense with uppers and downers, distorting reality till the visions in his head were all that remained.

For The Beatles, in their box, starry-eyed and laughing, the acoustic set contained perhaps one uncomfortable moment: when Dylan introduced another new song, 'Fourth Time Around', which not only bore a remarkable melodic similarity to Lennon's

'Norwegian Wood', but had words which seemed to be parodying the one song of which the Scouse songwriter felt most proud.

It wasn't Lennon's first exposure to the song, or Dylan's withering wit, on that trip. As he told Jonathan Cott a couple of years later, 'He played it to me when he was in London. He said, "What do you think?" I said, "I don't like it."' If Dylan seemed bulletproof in those days, Lennon was acutely sensitive to criticism, and he was convinced – quite correctly – that Dylan was yanking his chain. And, as he later told *Playboy*, 'for a period I was very impressed with [Dylan]'. That period was circa '65–66, when he was looking for a way to escape the lyrical trap inherited pop forms had sprung for him.

When Dylan emerged after the intermission, though, The Beatles were as taken aback as the remaining RAH punters. Suffused with speed, Dylan was moving like a manic marionette on stage, hopped up on the joys of electricity (and the speedball he'd taken as his halftime refreshment). This was *not* pop music! Indeed, Dylan proceeded to taunt the audience by informing them that 'this is not English music you are listening to. You haven't really heard American music before'. When the folkies took umbrage and began to heckle, as they had at most pit stops along the way, The Beatles apparently lent over the balcony and bellowed, 'Shut up and let him sing!' There was no doubting which side *they* were on. But at least one Beatle was worried about the man:

> **George Harrison:** I felt a bit sad for him because he was a bit wasted at that time. He'd been on a world tour, and he looked like he'd been on a world tour.

Perhaps Harrison should have been equally worried about the man sitting next to him, with whom he had been sharing the joys of LSD for some time, and who was still as high as Mr Kite after spending much of the day in the company of Dylan, while documentary-maker Don Pennebaker filmed their otherworldly conversation in the back of a limo, driven by Tom Keylock (well known to Lennon from similar duties with the Stones). When a clearly drained-to-the-dregs Dylan admits he'll 'be glad when this is over, 'cause I'm getting very sick here', Lennon turns to Keylock and gives him 'permission to land'. Despite this individual insight into the toll it was taking on Dylan, Lennon was still looking to follow his pied piper into that Rimbaudian unknown.

Three weeks later, Lennon arrived at the final session for the seventh Beatles album – destined to be as much of a breakthrough as its predecessor – with his own unequivocal 'drug-song', 'She Said, She Said'. He had started on his own road of excess a couple of junctions after his erstwhile mentor in Advanced Rock Lyrics, but come late July he would be driving past the twisted wreckage of Dylan's Triumph Bonneville, on the route to Candlestick Park – itself the end of The Beatles as a live novelty act. It proved to be just the beginning of his own journey into an interior world where 'nothing is real'.

THE PENDULUM
SWINGS

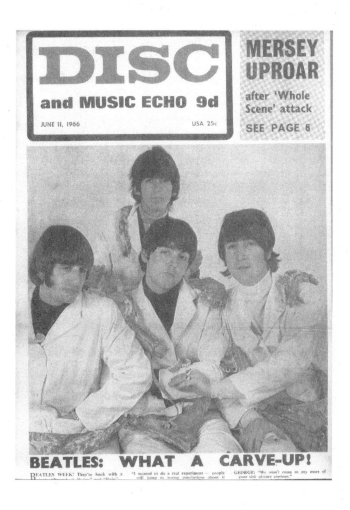

DISC
and MUSIC ECHO 9d

JUNE 11, 1966   USA 25c

MERSEY UPROAR
after 'Whole Scene' attack
SEE PAGE 6

BEATLES: WHAT A CARVE-UP!

BEATLES WEEK! They're back with a   "I wanted to do a real experiment — people   GEORGE: "We won't come to any more of
                                      will jump to wrong conclusions about it   your sick picture sessions."

In many ways, the summer of 1967 was the rest of the world catching up with those hip folk for whom the previous summer had been the actual moment the pop world turned upside down (much like punk, a decade later). The release in the UK, over a six-week period in the summer of '66, of three albums that still forty years later appear near the top of any serious poll of great Rock albums, certainly suggests some vital cultural streams were flowing into the same lysergic sea. These LPs – The Beach Boys' *Pet Sounds*, Dylan's *Blonde on Blonde* and The Beatles' *Revolver* – taken together, suggested not just that the era of The Album had well and truly arrived, but so had the use of mind-manifesting drugs as a spur to songwriting ('mind-manifesting' being Humphrey Osmond's definition of the term 'psychedelic', coined in a letter to novelist Aldous Huxley in 1956).

For Dylan, an accelerating drug use had already produced two albums of alchemical wizardry. And the opening track of the first of these, 'Subterranean Homesick Blues', contained his first overt drug reference: 'Johnny's in the basement/ Mixing up the medicine', i.e. separating the codeine from the cough syrup one could still buy across the counter. Though 'Mr Tambourine Man' was a year old by the time it appeared on the same album, it too suggested that something more than hashish had put the wind in the sails of Bobby's 'magic swirlin' ship'.

Back in August 1964, Dylan had referred to someone who hid 'lsd in his turban' in a private letter to Tami Dean. By the fall of 1965 he was brazen enough to tell journalist Nat Hentoff that 'opium and hash and pot . . . just bend your mind a little. I think everybody's mind should be bent once in a while'. If he later refused to see his use of drugs as a spur to creativity, insisting that they just kept him pumping the songs out, this did not stop him from adopting his own nightingale's code to slip drug references past any mass-media moralists.

When *Blonde on Blonde* appeared in early to mid-July 1966,[1] it included three tracks – 'Visions of Johanna', 'Stuck Inside of Mobile' and 'Sad Eyed Lady of the Lowlands' – whose unprecedented length and languorous lyrics seemed *designed* for endless replays in the bedsit equivalents of Victorian opium dens. Lines like 'It strangled up my mind/ Now people just get uglier/ And I have no sense of time' delighted those searching for implied drug use, who could interpret such lyrics on at least seven levels. Meanwhile, the opening track of *Blonde on Blonde*, 'Rainy Day Women #12 & 35' – with its memorable refrain, 'Everybody must get stoned' – spent much of the spring in the US charts, peaking at number two, without ever being yanked from the airwaves for its seditious message (unlike The Byrds' 'Eight Miles High').

If, by the time Dylan began work on *Blonde on Blonde* in earnest in late November 1965, he had developed more of a taste for methamphetamine than LSD, the West Coast's own wunderkind, Brian Wilson, had only recently taken his first dose of lysergic diethylamide-25. As he would coyly claim, in an article appearing the following November, 'About a year ago I had what I consider a very religious experience: I took a full dose of LSD, and later . . . I took a smaller dose. And I learned a lot of things, like patience, understanding. I can't teach you, or tell you, what I learned from taking it, but I consider it a very religious experience.' Ten years on, he would not consider the results quite so beneficent:

Brian Wilson: I did my dose of LSD. It shattered my mind . . . I came back, thank God, [but] in I don't know how many pieces. [1976]

In its immediate aftermath, LSD seems to have inspired him to replicate 'all these incredible sounds' that he told Capitol's Bill Wagner he heard when high. And so began a prodigiously produc-tive ten weeks, starting in late January 1966, during which Wilson almost single-handedly crafted a Beach Boys album unlike any leading up to it. Finding beauty in every grain of ferric tape, Wilson let the Beach Boys franchise tour the States while he put their name to a Brian Wilson solo album. Layering the sound in a way that was not open to The Beatles, who were still stuck in four-track land, Wilson used the eight tracks available in LA 'to the max.', with up to nineteen musicians at a time embellishing his new, God-like visions. Yet such innovation – and any atten-dant possibilities – didn't fill every LA engineer with joy; and some equally forward-thinking West-Coast bands met greater resistance:

Roger McGuinn: The eight-track was in [Columbia's LA] studio from the beginning, when we cut 'Mr Tambourine Man', but we didn't use it on that because the engineers were afraid of it – they had a hand-written sign taped on to it that said, 'Big Bastard'. They didn't want to play with it, and they were comfortable in their four-track world. I think Terry [Melcher] finally got them to wire up the eight-track and get it going.

The results of Wilson's winter of content – released in America that May, but held over until July in Britain – suggested it was high time every pop artist started considering the possibilities this new technology offered; and that the unadulterated live-recording-to-record might soon be a thing of the past. *Pet Sounds* had its flaws: the greeting-card lyrics; the incongruous 'Sloop John B' – a hit single recorded six months before the pukka *Pet Sounds* sessions, presumably included at Capitol's behest. But it set a standard for production to which everyone, The Beatles included, now felt a need to aspire.

As it happens, the belated release of the album in the UK – compounded by the 'rush-release' of *Revolver* – meant that the LP Wilson had, by his own admission, produced as a riposte to *Rubber Soul* afforded him barely a fortnight's repose before the bar was raised again. As Reg King, of Mod-movers The Action, told *Melody Maker* at the end of July – after the paper asked of *Pet Sounds*: 'The most progressive pop album ever, or as sickly as peanut butter?' – '*Pet Sounds* is the most thought-into, progressive LP that I've ever heard. That was until I heard The Beatles' LP *Revolver* just this week, which pips *Pet Sounds* to the post.'

Like *Rubber Soul*, *Revolver*'s impact lay with the fact that – aside from its songs' sheer immediacy – the lads had refrained from any single-size previews. Whereas *Pet Sounds* had had a series of singles ruthlessly ripped from Wilson's unified vision by Capitol – the sore thumb 'Sloop John B', the solo 'Caroline No', the sophomoric 'Wouldn't It Be Nice' and the transcendental 'God Only Knows' all appearing ahead of the (UK) album.

The Beatles extracted the 'Paperback Writer b/w Rain' double-hitter from early album sessions, providing themselves with a tenth consecutive number one without diluting the album. And while EMI *did* pull 'Eleanor Rigby b/w Yellow Submarine' from The Beatles' first psychedelic symphony, it was issued on the same day as *Revolver*, and, as the two least representative songs on the album, gave little sense of how far The Beatles had come in the past year. Following in Wilson's footsteps, the studio was fast becoming the FabFour's favourite playground. As Sean Mahoney wrote for the *Beatles Monthly* back in May, three months before *Revolver*:

Nowadays the recording studio is definitely home for The Beatles. It is their song factory. A place where they all like to be. Where they can do what they want and play their music without worrying about crowds, autographs, flashbulbs, or how they look. They sit, happy as bees in a flower-bed, surrounded by two grand pianos, an upright, an electric piano, two organs, three massive sets of amplifiers, a drum kit, many, many acoustic and solid guitars intermingled with dozens of marimbas, cymbals, drum sticks, tom-toms, even an Indian tamboura (very like a sitar) and a tabla (two little drums rather like tom-toms), to mention only about half of it. But what do they use it all for? . . . Once the outline arrangement has been finished, the 'frilling bit' starts. This is where all that extra equipment comes into use.

The increasingly complex arrangements and effects The Beatles were now applying to their still-solid songs placed ever greater demands on the Abbey Road employees. One of the defining, period-piece innovations, Artificial Double Tracking (ADT), came about, as Geoff Emerick explained to Mark Cunningham, 'as a result of John asking why he had to sing a part twice to double-track it. Ken [Townsend] realised that if we took the information off of the sync head of the multitrack machine as we were mixing, we could advance it before the replay head on to a quarter-inch machine and use varispeed to create a ghost image on top of the original sound. We would often move the distance between the two signals by altering the oscillators and that was what we called "flanging".'

Of course, ADT was not about to suffice for all the boys' new-fangled notions. Indeed, part of the problem for George Martin and his engineers was that every time they came up with a sonic solution to some seemingly intractable problem, The Beatles promptly attempted to apply said innovation to the next song, and the one after that. So when they took a break from The New Album to cut their first single of 1966, and Martin found a clever way to liven up the already effect-laden 'Rain', it was not the last time The Beatles wound up backwards:

George Martin: [It] needed something on the playout, to give it a lift; so I took one of John's phrases he had sung and turned it round, realising that musically it would fit – the line would fit the chords –

and that it might sound intriguing. I pasted it on, and it sounded good. That simple reversal, together with the drone of the tamboura, gave the song a kind of mystical feel that was very different from our other stuff to date. John flipped when he heard it, and so did Paul: they wanted everything recorded backwards after that! [MoSP]

Along with ADT, the backward phrase would become a favourite Beatle solution when required to spruce up anything ever-so-slight the following year. Such temptations, though, were generally held at bay in the two and a half months it took to complete *Revolver*, constrained by the demands for product from a nervous label and personal manager Epstein, and the ineluctable fear of losing fans along the way. Punters and press alike certainly seemed delighted with what *NME* reviewer Allan Evans typified as 'the discriminate use of electronics on *Revolver*.' Evans spoke for many when he wrote, 'John, Paul, George and Ringo are obviously enjoying the heady freedom of being able to translate their every whim on to record. But the freedom is not abused, and George's fascination for Indian music, and Paul's liking for classical effects, are put to good use.'

Equally ambitious were some of the words The Beatles were now utilising, barely eighteen months after turning their back on 'Baby's In Black'. If Brian Wilson had produced his beatific vision 'under the influence' of psychedelics, very little of Dylan's delight in dual meanings lurks within the lyrics on *Pet Sounds*, perhaps because Wilson had left most of its words to Tony Asher or Mike Love. The Beatles, though, wanted their new lyrics to be as multi-layered as the production. Lennon, in particular, hoped to show that time spent with Dylan (and his albums) had not been entirely wasted – even if he had been. 'I'm Only Sleeping' and 'She Said, She Said' – both largely Lennon's – delineated an incipient psychedelia his pop peers would refine accordingly.

Unfortunately, most American fans heard these two songs independent of each other, because they were separated at birth by the arcane demands of Capitol Records, the self-same label who had played around with *Pet Sounds* before its release. *Revolver* suffered a more brutal fate at the hands of these butchers, who continued to slice up every British album to make a leaner domestic version. The practice would still incense at least one Beatle a decade on:

> **George Harrison:** I liked when we got into *Rubber Soul, Revolver* . . . We put all the songs together into an album form – I'm talking about the English albums now, because in the States we found later that for every two albums we had, they'd made three because we put fourteen tracks on an album, and we'd also have singles that weren't included on albums in those days. They'd put the singles [on] – take off a bunch of tracks, change all the running order and then they'd make [these] new packages . . . just awful packages. [1977]

In the case of *Revolver*, The Beatles had been obliged to send Stateside early mixes of three songs – 'I'm Only Sleeping', 'Doctor Robert' and 'And Your Bird Can Sing' – to fill out a 'preview' album that also swept up remnants of *Rubber Soul*. The clue was in the title, *Yesterday & Today* (actually a lame pun on the *Rubber Soul* track 'Yesterday', which led off this shameless repackaging exercise, having already been a number one single in the US).

Whether The Beatles deliberately set out to sabotage this bogus album to make a point is still not clear; but when they sent along the artwork for the front cover, it was found to comprise a shot of the not-so-cuddly boys in butcher's aprons sitting among dismembered dolls and hunks of meat. As in stop butchering our albums, perchance? McCartney almost owned up to some such intent in a 1979 conversation with Paul Gambaccini: 'They wanted a repackage album, so we gave them butchers in white coats and babies . . . and meat and stuff.' Of course, they may simply have been reinforcing the contention that they didn't want to be cute anymore. After all, as Beatles publicist Tony Barrow points out in his recent memoir, photographer Bob 'Whitaker also took pictures of George hammering nails into John's head and, least tasteful of all, the four boys standing in front of a woman to whom they were linked by a string of sausages which [apparently] represented . . . an umbilical cord'.

The resultant furore proved that the Mayflower had not landed in vain, and resulted in the original album sleeve being pulled, hastily replaced with a more anodyne image. But it would be the last time Capitol would get to replace the chosen cover to any Beatles album, or would get to dismember a British Beatles LP. As it happens, *Yesterday & Today* would still be riding high in the charts when the truncated *Revolver* finally appeared in American shops in mid-to-late August, two or three weeks behind the UK, stripped of three of its best songs along with some of its cohesion and an essential integrity. Thus was the seamless progression from *Rubber Soul* to *Revolver* to *Pepper* muddied for many Americans.

The same week that the US *Revolver* was certified gold by the Recording Industry Association of America (before it even charted) The Beatles said their gigging goodbye to New York with two sell-out shows at Shea Stadium. The following week they played their final show at Candlestick Park in San Francisco. Both cities had developed vibrant underground scenes in the year since The Beatles last brought bedlam to their stadia. The Beatles' helter-skelter schedule, though, meant there was no real downtime in which to soak up the cities' new sounds, or interrogate the locals. And it would be another year before the fledgling Bay Area scene would opportunistically present itself to the world as the most progressive, psychedelic scene going.

In the spring and summer of 1966, the most drug-drenched lyrics in 'Pop' were to be found among the denizens of downtown Manhattan. It was here that the avant garde in music, in PopArt and in poetry first crossed the counter into pop culture. That very spring it produced two albums as seminal in their own, subversive way as *Pet Sounds* and *Blonde on Blonde*: the second Fugs album and the first Velvet Underground LP.

For the boys, in their Beatle bubble, New York's underground scene arrived via a London bookshop, on account; not from first-hand forays to the Lower East Side, where bands had been writing satirical polemics about societal ills ever since the 'folk revival' was taken off the life-support by Dylan. That one connection – Miles again – duly maintained this all-important contact between London's avant garde and the original pop underground.

As such, the first The Beatles knew of any downtown NY scene was when a record arrived, for Miles's attention, at Indica, the bookshop he and John Dunbar were in the midst of opening next to the Scotch of St James Club in March 1966. McCartney was helping to get the shop shipshape when Miles opened the package, sent by Ken Weaver, the ostensible drummer in a new NY combo, The Fugs. It was their first album on Folkways, *The Village Fugs*. Weaver presumably knew of Miles through his contributions to a brand-new underground journal, the *East Village Other*.

As Miles subsequently recalled, 'Paul wanted to hear it and, since Indica had no record player, everyone followed Paul into Mason's Yard to . . . the Scotch of St James'. What they got was the lyrical equivalent of a Lenny Bruce stand-up routine, the like of which they'd never heard. Nor had the manager of the St James, Joe Van Dykes, who did not appreciate the Fugs' liberal use of profanities.

The Fugs was the brainchild of two Jewish wordsmiths, Tuli Kupferberg and Ed Sanders, who were determined to do for rock & roll what their fellow Jew was doing for nightclub comedy: test the very boundaries of taste. Bereft of even the basics when it came to musical training, the pair drafted in Pete Stampfel and Steve Weber, aka the Holy Modal Rounders – whose own 'Hesitation Blues', issued in 1964, contained the first use of 'psychedelic' in a song lyric – to provide a rudimentary musical framework.

Pete Stampfel: When they started they sat down and decided to form a dirty rock & roll band. Knowing nothing about rock & roll whatsoever, they proceeded to write sixty songs . . . like 'Coca Cola Douche', exactly like punk ten years later. Just taken with an abrasive vision, despite the fact they had no technical knowledge or chops . . . [they] did it anyway, on pure balls.

McCartney loved the Fugs album, and its successor, issued on ESP later the same year. Both became perennial stock at Indica (named after *Cannabis indica*). In fact, as Miles says, 'We only sold about ten records at Indica, [but] that was one of them. We had standing orders with the Beatles, that anything interesting I should send them each one. It was for all four, [but] it was something McCartney set up. So they all got copies of [The Fugs], as well as Albert Ayler's latest and the first two Sun Ra albums on ESP. I had a similar arrangement with Jagger. This was just before you had all those import shops.' (It was on Lennon's first visit to Indica in March 1966 that Miles showed him a US copy of *The Psychedelic Experience*, a guide to LSD trips produced by Timothy Leary, from which he pinched the opening line of 'Tomorrow Never Knows': 'Turn off your mind, relax, and float downstream.')

The West Coast's answer to The Fugs was Frank Zappa's Mothers of Invention, whose *Freak Out* was also imported by Indica. It offered an altogether more musical experience, even if its creator had convinced himself that he was doing something a lot more outré than either The Fugs or their downtown contemporaries, The Velvet Underground. This double-album impressed McCartney enough for him to tell Miles that him and the boys 'were going to make their own *Freak Out*'.

Meanwhile, the Mothers were helping to put the kibosh on what would undoubtedly have been the most radical underground artifact of 1966, The Velvet Underground's debut album, an acetate of which had been cut as early as 25 April, 1966, for the benefit of the new head of A&R at Verve, Tom Wilson, who hoped to clean it up and put it out. As the man who had almost single-handedly invented the 'folk-rock' sound – producing Dylan's first electric album and 'Like A Rolling Stone' single, along with a hugely successful electric revamp of Simon & Garfunkel's 'Sound of Silence' (made without their knowledge) – Wilson had credentials galore, just not a lot of scruples.

Wilson had signed the Mothers to Verve back in November 1965, when he had yet to hear the demos the Velvets kept promising him, and had invested $25,000 of parent-company MGM's money recording and releasing their double-album debut, which appeared in selected stores in August after full-page adverts in comic books and teen magazines announced its appearance. Having blown the budget on his friend Frank, Wilson decided to re-record certain key songs from the VU repertoire in a 'proper' LA studio, while the New York band wowed the locals at The Trip during a fortnight-long residency in May 1966. Maybe not. The residency was curtailed by the cops after the third night, for threatening the moral fabric of La-La Land.

Even with new versions of vital Velveteen visions like 'Heroin', 'Venus In Furs' and 'Waiting For The Man', Verve delayed the album's release until the following year, when it appeared alongside the second Mothers offering, *Absolutely Free*. As such, for a period of eighteen months, the Velvets remained one of the most closely guarded secrets within the still-subterranean strata of Rock. And yet avant-garde London – and therefore, one must presume, at least one Beatle – not only knew *of* them, but had heard some of their most taboo tunes. One particularly persistent legend has even suggested that Beatles manager Brian Epstein planned to sign the Velvets to his management company, NEMS.

Once again, the tangled tale goes all the way back to Dylan's UK visit in the spring of 1965, and the retinue of New York scenesters trailing in his wake. Among those who arrived at London Airport on 26 April, 1965 with the pied piper of pop was Barbara Rubin, a friend of Dylan's (it is she who is massaging his head on the back of *Bringing It All Back Home*) and painter Andy Warhol. With Rubin was her friend Kate Heliczer, the wife of avant-garde filmmaker Pierot Heliczer. When Kate had left New York, her next-door neighbours, John Cale, Louis Reed and Tony Conrad, were just starting to put together their own folk-rock band (as Cale later described them in a letter to Kate, they were at this stage the Velvet Hermaphrodite Jug Band) to record a bunch of songs the young Reed had penned while making his weekly cheque writing bad knock-offs of the latest pop faves at Pickwick Records. Songs with titles like 'Heroin' and 'Venus In Furs' were not what the maker of albums like *Surfsiders Sing The Beach Boys Songbook* had in mind.

Kate thought nothing more of them until Cale turned up at her London home that summer with a tape of songs he, Reed and a young guitarist named Sterling Morrison had recorded at their Ludlow Street loft in July. He seemed quite convinced that she had the contacts to find them a record deal on the basis of this tape, a crude set of acoustic prototypes which barely hinted at the majesty to come. Despite all the protestations, he left her the reel and promised to keep in touch as she A&R'd the tape around London. Unfortunately, Kate contracted hepatitis shortly after Cale's visit, so it was left to the altogether pushier Rubin to spread the word (apparently getting as far as Marianne Faithfull).

As of 21 October, when Kate received a letter from Cale, she had got as far as playing it for folksinger Julie Felix, who expressed an interest in recording a couple of the songs. Though Cale apologises for 'the recording, [which] wasn't of professional level', he informs Kate that they continue to 'have no equipment to use', and that a second set of demos 'will take a long time'. At the same time, he asks Kate to press Bob (Whitaker, The Beatles' photographer) to 'take the tape to Epstein as is'. It would appear that Whitaker did what he was told, because the following year Rubin (now returned to NY) wrote to Kate to say that the Velvets had decided not to go with Epstein, electing instead to tie their mast to Warhol's clipper ship.

By then, the tape – or, more accurately, tapes – had set a number of London wheels in motion. By the time Cale sent an oft-promised second set of demos – presumably the same tape he tells Kate they are making 'for Tom Wilson' in a letter dated 2 December, 1965 – American artist Andy Warhol had caught their act at the apposite Cafe Bizarre and brought them into his own Factory enclave, promising to make them the perfect Pop-Rock adjunct to his own PopArt.

In the same December letter, Cale informed Kate that 'the songs "Heroin" and "Venus" have changed so dramatically for the better that we feel now we're into something and no-one can imitate it. VELVET SOUND.' Another letter, a week later, informs her that they now have a girl drummer who dresses like a man, but who is proving a stunning addition, and he promises to send the new tape soon. There the correspondence ends, until the following June, when Cale says he is 'now embarrassed by existence of the tapes' and asked for 'both [!] copies back'.

Though the tapes *were* returned, at least one copy must have been made, probably by John Hopkins, who was now spending evenings with Kate at 115 Queensway, and who would often put on the tape/s for friends like Miles to hear. Indeed, it was at a party at Hopkins' in the late summer of 1966, that London's newest pop manager, Peter Jenner, says he heard the tape and recognised a New York analogue to what his own band, The Pink Floyd, were starting to do in London:

> **Peter Jenner:** I was already managing a rock group, so it would have been after September – it all came out of a party at Hoppy's, and that [VU] tape was going around, and I remember phoning up, under the influence. Someone had Cale's number. Kate would have given it to me. I did think it was a very good tape . . . But the lyrics were not like pop lyrics.

Cale gave Jenner the same cold shoulder as Epstein, putting his faith in Warhol, and the Velvets stayed put, in a New York fast being cleaned out of resident rock geniuses. Dylan, who on his return from London in June had holed up at the Chelsea Hotel, proceeded to skid off his motorbike upstate on 30 July and was now sitting in traction, aka Woodstock, stunned to still be alive.

At the same time a young black guitarist who had spent the past two years learning his trade hiding in the shadows cast by the monumental egos of Richard Penniman, Sam Cooke and Lonnie Youngblood, began playing the Café A Go-Go, where he was seen by another English pop entrepreneur, ex-Animal Chas Chandler, who soon had him on the first plane to London, convinced that it would be a whole lot easier to make the man a pop legend there.

He was proven right. Jimi Hendrix landed in London on 24 September, by 1 October was jamming on stage with Eric Clapton's new band, Cream, and by 24 November was recording his debut 45, setting the whole of the West End a-flutter. As Monkee Michael Nesmith recalls, 'I was having dinner in London with John Lennon, Eric Clapton and a group of people. In the middle of dinner, John produced this portable tape player . . . and proceeded to play "Hey Joe" on his recorder, saying, "You guys gotta check this out."'

The Velvets thought they could buck the trend and still sell their deviant ditties to the heartlands, with a little help from Tom Wilson. They were wrong (though Epstein would keep his ear attuned, and when the VU LP finally appeared the following spring, would play it to all and sundry).

New York's 'Pop' underground was destined to stay that way. As Ellen Sander wrote retrospectively, 'It was anti-art Art made by anti-elite elitists.' On the Lower East Side, they refused to countenance the notion that it was possible to wrap radical, even transgressive ideas, musical and lyrical, in three-minute pop songs, and sell them to a wide, possibly uncomprehending, yet open-to-experience audience. Even the evidence of that summer's smartest sounds, those of The Beach Boys, The Beatles, The Byrds and Bobby D, failed to convince them otherwise (though the Velvets were much taken with 'Eight Miles High', which, like their own material, was deemed unsafe for American airwaves).

Meanwhile, back in Surrey, Spain and France, the four Beatles were finally taking a breather from any kinda group activity for three months in the aftermath of their live farewell. Though much needed, this sustained hiatus from recording handed the impetus to those Britpop bands who had been caught in their tailwind for the past two or three years. During this Indian summer in the Happening City, it seemed like the Stones, The Who, The Kinks and The Small Faces had all been stockpiling killer cuts with a view to claiming the Lancastrians' mantle.

For the Stones, it had been a long hard slog. In the past eighteen months they had issued 'The Last Time', 'Satisfaction', 'Get Off Of My Cloud' and '19th Nervous Breakdown', each one a classic encapsulation of teen angst. By May 1966 they were ready to make their first real departure from their r&b roots, 'Paint It Black', a salutary tale of the dangers of too many downers, which veered between the raucous and the raga. It was both an almost perfect parody of the sitar sound a certain Beatle found increasingly appealing and evidence of an early flirtation with different blocks of sounds juxtaposed. The latter process would hit overdrive with the successor to 'Paint it Black', 'Have You Seen Your Mother, Baby, Standing In The Shadow?', and its equally dense derrière, 'Who's Driving Your Plane?'. The Stones may to date have refrained from asking such pregnant questions of their audience, but they became increasingly sure of themselves after 'Paint It Black' returned them to the top of the pops.

For The Kinks's solitary songwriter, the transition to an original voice had been less sure-footed. As Keith Altham – then at *NME* – notes, '[The Kinks] started as the world's worst r&b group. They were dreadful. Ray Davies never had a rock & roller's voice, before he became an English Randy Newman. He was a misfit in rock & roll terms.' Even the surefire 'Set Me Free', Davies's first declaration of independence, was succeeded by the lame 'Dedicated Follower of Fashion', which, though a commercial success, was cast-iron proof that satire was not his strong point. Only with the two singles released in the second half of '66 did The Kinks become kultural kontenders. Though 'Sunny Afternoon' and 'Dead End Street' seemed like light and shade, both bespoke a new, peculiarly English sensibility. Yet it was the b-side to 'Sunny Afternoon' that clearly explicated why our Muswell misfit had hit upon this rich vein; the dawning realisation, 'I'm Not Like Everybody Else'.

If Davies was one supposed modernist looking to retreat into a mythical England far from the dead-end streets, his fellow Mod icon, Pete Townshend, was tapping into other, equally rich aspects of English culture. In seeking his own departure from teen angst he chanced upon reluctant transvestites and ostracised eccentrics. 'I'm A Boy' had no shortage of angst, but it was the anguish of a boy brought up as a girl. It was also, at least according to Townshend, originally part of a larger work, a pop opera he had been working on in the early months of 1966 (for which the following year's 'I Can See For Miles' may also have originally been intended).

Already Townshend was tearing at the constraints of the pop form. 'Happy Jack' was another such quirky work. Recorded two weeks before 'Strawberry Fields Forever', it was released just three weeks after the fact. As much a song of childhood as Lennon's, Townshend's focused on holidays on the Isle of Man and a half-remembered, harmless old man on the beach, around whom Townshend built an entire lifestory in three minutes and seven inches.

The Small Faces were another set of 'blocked' Mods looking to shed their r&b cloth for a more distinctive, richer sounding, lyrically ambiguous garb (still housed in a single sleeve). They got their sound in the pocket with the high-risk 'All Or Nothing', before veering off into the private world of 'My Mind's Eye', perhaps the first overtly psychedelic song to hit the English charts, in November 1966 (both 'Rain' and 'Who's Driving Your Plane' would have been potential candidates had they not been secreted on the b-side of their respective singles). 'My Mind's Eye' gave an idea of the pace with which the Faces would transcend their Mod roots the following year, mining an increasingly rich vein: English eccentricity viewed through psychedelia's prism.

And yet, The Beatles – ever anxious to retain their spot at the top of the totem pole – felt the real competition was coming from 6,000 miles away, from the sun-drenched shores of southern California, where The Beach Boys and The Byrds had an entirely different kind of psychedelic sound in mind, one where the good vibrations could still be felt eight miles high.

3

HEY, WHAT'S THAT SOUND?

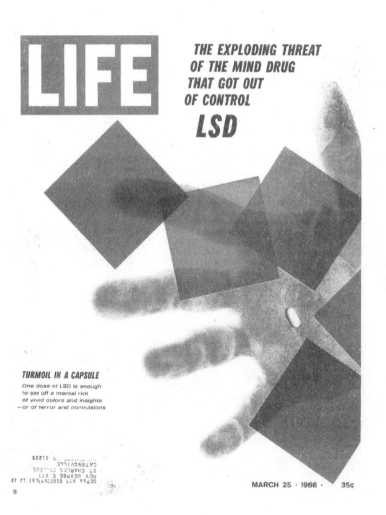

THE EXPLODING THREAT
OF THE MIND DRUG
THAT GOT OUT
OF CONTROL

LSD

TURMOIL IN A CAPSULE

One dose of LSD is enough
to set off a mental riot
of vivid colors and insights
—or of terror and convulsions

MARCH 25 · 1966 ·   35¢

What every American rock & roll band wants [is] to get back at The
Beatles. All Beatle fans, all wanting to make a dent in The Beatles
with their presence, which no band or musician has ever done.
There were The Beatles and the rest of pop music in descending
order. A great deal of the energy and sheer force of performance of
American rock bands is simply The Beatles, burning ass. –

Ellen Sander, *Trips*

As with Dylan – whom they openly endorsed in a famous March 1965 *Melody Maker* article, 'The Beatles Dig Dylan' – the FabFour had made no secret of their love of LA's top two bands, The Byrds and The Beach Boys. When it came to the former, Lennon and Harrison even turned out for their disastrous UK debut in late July 1965, a showcase at Blaise's which prompted some decidedly unkind reviews in an era when the pop weeklies rarely dished it out. As McGuinn recalls, promoter Mervyn Conn 'advertised us as "America's Answer to The Beatles", which incited the ire of the [British] press. We got murdered by the press, but the kids liked it.' So did The Beatles, and the bands became fast friends.

If that first trip to London established a firm bond between the bands, it also resulted in a song that served as the first indication that The Byrds were American pop's answer to no-one, not even Dylan. McGuinn later insisted 'Eight Miles High' was, at least ostensibly, about 'land[ing] here in London; [it] is a poetical way of saying that you're in cultural shock . . . When we were here, the British pop scene was really on top of it and, I think, was a little wary of being cut into by the Americans.' The song was also about departure, from the norms of both pop sounds and subject matter:

Roger McGuinn: It was a conscious decision [to change], based on being pigeon-holed as folk-rock. We were always fighting to get out of boxes, so we made a move into what people call psychedelia, but it was really jazz fusion. It was incorporating John Coltrane into the mix, and a little Ravi Shankar. But it was definitely a conscious effort to try and get out of folk-rock.

Because of the subsequent furore over its subject matter, it is easy to lose sight of how radical this compact classic *sounded* at the time. This was a long way from the chimes of twee-dom found on 'Mr Tambourine Man'. Though McGuinn stuck to his trusty Rickenbacker, he was determined to make it sound like a sitar placed in the hands of saxophonist John Coltrane. Only someone on drugs could believe he succeeds, but what he did construct was both unique and *within the idiom*. As McGuinn told biographer Johnny Rogan, it 'was our interpretation of those [Indian] instruments and musical styles, and that was what we [thought we] were doing. [But] we were translating it into a rock form.'

It was a lesson The Beatles' own lead guitarist would have done well to note. He certainly had the opportunity. When all four Beatles took some time out on their visit to LA in late August 1965 – prior to two fabled shows at the Hollywood Bowl – Crosby and McGuinn came to call and seized the opportunity to introduce Lennon and Harrison simultaneously to sitar music and lysergic acid (this time knowingly):

Roger McGuinn: I don't know where [Paul] was, but George and John and Crosby and I went to this big bathroom where they had this square shower, and we were sitting on the ledge of the shower, passing the guitar around. That's when we turned them on to Ravi Shankar and Eastern religion, too. They hadn't gotten into either of those things at that point . . . We had to kick Peter [Fonda] out. John was freaked out. David had invited Peter over, [and] John was so upset about what Peter had said on acid. Peter had frightened him, dealing with his mortality like that.

What actor Peter Fonda had said was, 'I know what it's like to be dead', a reference to a near-death experience as a child. And it was actually spoken in a spirit of reassurance to Harrison, whose second trip was proving no less disorienting than his first. As the Beatle later related, 'We were on the height of acid in a room full of starlets which some GAC man had wafted in for us. I'd gone so far from what I thought this life was about that it was a shock to land back in my body and realise I was still there.'

Lennon brooded about Fonda's aside for some months before demo-ing a series of fragments called 'He Said, He Said', its lyric solely comprising Fonda's cryptic comment. Out of this would come the song that would conclude the *Revolver* recording sessions and signal a new phase in Lennon's songwriting, in which he would become increasingly preoccupied by 'when [he] was a boy [and] everything was fine'.

For now, it meant he had crossed some divide, leaving his closest co-conspirator on the other side. As Lennon tellingly revealed, in his 1970 *Rolling Stone* interview, 'The second time we took [LSD] Paul felt very out of it, because we were all . . . slightly cruel, sort of, "We're taking it, and *you're* not."' The sense of separation experienced by an acidhead cannot be overestimated. It undoubtedly contributed to the birth of a sixties counter-culture that was as elitist as any previous art movement, even if its exclusivity was based upon drug consumption rather than wealth (though most had that, too). As per usual, Nik Cohn called it right in his valedictory to Pop, *Awopbopaloobop*:

> After acid, you walked around bulging with your new perceptions and you thought you'd been some place nobody else had ever seen. You knew all kinds of secret answers and you were smug, you couldn't help it. In this way, acid formed its own aristocracy and pop was part of it, pop was its mouthpiece. Not all of pop, of course. Just the underground.

The new pop aristocracy, as such, was founded on mutual experimentation. As Derek Taylor, publicist for The Beatles, Byrds and

Beach Boys (in that order) wrote in his memoir, *Fifty Years Adrift*, 'By the mid-Sixties, we had become convinced that wisdom resided in a group of which we, The Byrds, Dylan, The Beatles, Billy James . . . The Buffalo Springfield, . . . all folk singers, most Laurel Canyon residents, dope-smokers, radical comics and anyone who didn't have their own television show were secret-sign members.'

For those belonging to Taylor's Us (*not* Them) experimenting with hallucinogenic drugs was perceived in grandiose terms – as the eternal search for enlightenment. As McGuinn tells it, 'We all thought of [taking LSD] as a spiritual quest – it wasn't just to get high . . . It was about knowing God . . . [And] there is something to that – I think it does open you up to spiritual "sensitivity". People are probably born with it, but it gets covered over during their lifetime dealing with society, and LSD breaks through that barrier and lets you experience a raw, spiritual contact again.' It certainly had that effect on the two Beatles. Lennon told Hunter Davies, 'I was suddenly struck by great visions when I first took acid', while Harrison seemed to have chanced upon an all too real spiritual dimension:

> **George Harrison:** 1966 was the time when the whole world opened up and had a greater meaning. But that was a direct result of LSD . . . The first time I took it, it just blew everything away. I had such an overwhelming feeling of well-being, that there was a God, and I could see him in every blade of grass . . . There was no way back to what I was before. [But] it wasn't all good, because it left a lot of questions as well. We still had to continue being 'fab' . . . with that *added* perspective. It wasn't easy! [1987]

Of all The Beatles, it would be Harrison who most keenly felt this sense of separation from all he had been, and those he had known. Which did not win him many friends. As NEMS employee Tony King told Steve Turner, 'When I first met George in 1963, he was Mr Fun, Mr Stay Out All Night. Then all of a sudden, he found LSD and Indian religion and he became *very* serious.' It was as if he had been placed in Douglas Adam's Total Perspective Vortex (itself probably a cipher for the acid experience). Talking openly about LSD at the end of 1967, Harrison admitted, 'It's really only after acid that it pushes home to you that you're only little.'

For McCartney, at this point, his fellow Beatles' trips into their own psyche represented a genuine cause for concern. As he later told Jonathon Green, 'I resisted [taking LSD] . . . because I could see what it was doing to them. And what it was doing to them basically was making them sit around very dopey, and making them hear noises I couldn't hear, from miles away.' Nor were the post-acid Byrds an inspiring example of shiny happy people. Gene Clark, in particular, was increasingly prone to staring out of the window for two hours at a time. And among London's avant garde, Paul started to encounter many a double-barrelled socialite to whom he might nod a hello 'but they were generally tripping or a little bit too out of it, actually, for my liking.' For someone who prided himself on being open to every experience, it must have started to resemble a psychedelic version of *Invasion of the Bodysnatchers*.

The Beatles, to date, had been a unity of four. McGuinn recalls how, when he first met Harrison, 'before we took acid together, [I asked] what he thought about Eastern religion – [indeed] religion in general – and he said, "We don't know about that yet." He answered for all The Beatles! . . . It was almost like The Beatles were one mind, and I envied that . . . because The Byrds were every man for himself.' Though it would be some time before it became every man for himself within England's answer to The Byrds, the process began that day in August 1965.

At this time, most upper-echelon pop bands continued to enjoy a camaraderie which bridged both sides of the Atlantic. As Hollie Graham Nash insists, 'I never felt a sense of competition so much as discovery. I didn't feel we were trying to outdo [The Beatles], or pull more people than them.' When The Hollies found themselves with a day off in LA in February 1967, they phoned up Elmer Valentine, owner of the Whisky a Go Go, suggested putting a free show together, and invited all the local bands. A day's notice sufficed

for the likes of The Mamas & the Papas, Jim Morrison of The
Doors, David Crosby and assorted members of The Beach Boys and
The Monkees to join in the fun. Such was the ease with which
London and LA meshed at this crossroad in cultural time.

If the rapport Nash, still a Hollie, established with one Byrd
would ultimately lead to the Anglo-American supergroup Crosby,
Stills & Nash, the relationship between The Beatles and The Byrds
was one astutely maintained by publicist Derek Taylor. He had left
Brian Epstein to his irrational outbursts and settled in LA in February
1965, in time to take flight with The Byrds. Comfortable with his
new role, lending 'a presence to that city's publicity outpourings'
– as Ellen Sander put it – Taylor served as a conduit for musical
in-jokes between Beatle and Byrd, as when Harrison instructed him
to 'tell Jim [McGuinn's real name] and David "If I Needed Someone"
is the riff of "Bells of Rhymney" with the drumming of "She Don't
Care About Time".'

Harrison had been afforded a sneak preview of the latter when
he visited an early September 1965 LA Byrds recording session.
Afterwards, he asked, 'Hey, can I have a dub of this before I leave?
If I know anything about record companies, it won't be released
until Christmas.' Six weeks later, The Beatles were recording 'If I
Needed Someone' at the *Rubber Soul* sessions. Not that the exchange
of ideas was entirely one-way:

> **Roger McGuinn:** There was a constant stream of new material going
> back and forth [between London and LA]. We'd get to hear it before
> it came out, and when we got together we'd play our new stuff. That
> camaraderie's gone. We didn't [feel we had] anything to worry about
> – I think we all benefited from each other's ideas.

As and when The Byrds set about putting their notion of raga-rock
into practice, in December 1965, an acetate of the scheduled single
was despatched to London, only for The Byrds' label to baulk at
its release; though not because 'Why?' and 'Eight Miles High' constituted a dramaturgy of drug-infused inspiration spread over two

seven-inch sides. When it came to content, Columbia was not so much understanding as oblivious:

> **Roger McGuinn:** I don't recall anybody saying, 'You need a hit.' I think we had a built-in feeling that we needed hits because that's how the business worked. It was a singles[-orientated] business at that time. If you had a hit record, you could continue doing albums. But I don't remember anyone from the record company ever telling us what we needed to do to get a hit. They really didn't put a lot of constraints on us – look at what we did!

Unfortunately, the label was not so flexible when it came to established industry practice. Having recorded both cuts in a single day at RCA's LA studios, with Jim Dickson at the console – and hit upon the next new sound – The Byrds found that an asinine adherence to union rules on Columbia's part meant that they were unable to release these recordings in the winter of 1966, when 'Turn Turn Turn' was still descending from its number one berth Stateside (instead of which the label rush-released the retro 'It Won't Be Wrong', which did not so much fly as plummet).

> **Roger McGuinn:** [Columbia] had an agreement with their union that all their releases had to have been recorded in Columbia studios . . . We loved the 'Eight Miles High' we got with Dave Hasinger over at RCA. We brought it to them and said, 'Here's the single,' and they said, 'No, you're gonna have to do it again.'

And so new sessions were set aside at the end of January 1966, where The Byrds would *re-record* both sides of a single they still hoped would break the folk-rock mould before it set them in concrete. If the original 'Eight Miles High' had been issued – irrespective of whether the re-recorded version is the equal of its prototype (now on the remastered *5D* CD) – it would have appeared ahead of the issue of *Life* magazine that would alert a Middle America looking for the next witch-hunt to the dangers of LSD.

The edition in question appeared on the stand in mid-March, and though the ten-page feature itself was surprisingly level-headed and informed, the front cover was not so balanced:

THE EXPLODING THREAT OF THE MIND DRUG THAT GOT OUT OF CONTROL

— TURMOIL IN A CAPSULE —

One dose of LSD is enough to set off a mental riot of vivid colours and insights – or of terror and convulsions.

With photos of individuals 'freaking out' after taking the drug, and a stark warning that 'LSD is especially risky for anyone with an unstable personality', the *Life* cover story was followed a matter of weeks later by a report from a Senate Committee on Juvenile Delinquency that seemed to suggest drug use per se explained away complex societal ills. Evidently, the spirit of McCarthy still rode through the US Senate. When 'Eight Miles High' appeared in May, and began to pick up radio play, it became a target for what McGuinn typifies as 'the quote-unquote Establishment . . . over-reacting to the LSD "threat"'. And though, as David Crosby duly admitted, 'we [could] justifiably say that it wasn't a drug-song, because it was written about the trip to London . . . of course it was a drug-song. We were stoned when we wrote it.'

Nor did The Byrds' counter-culture supporters do a great deal to sustain the notion that it was all a big misunderstanding, and 'Eight Miles High' was a paean to test pilots. LA journalist Paul Jay Robbins had recently hand-painted a design for some new flyers for the band, which said 'Listen to them Sing as you Dance.' Oh, and the letters LSD were painted in psychedelic colors. Whatever did he mean?

If 'Eight Miles High' stalled at fourteen in the US charts, it never made it off the runway in the UK, where the band had still to recover from the bad press their promoter had brought down upon their heads. Stuttering to twenty-four in the hit parade, it effectively signalled the end of The Byrds as a commercial force – especially as the intended follow-up, 'I Know You Rider', recorded in July 1966, singularly failed to appear. By then, it was clear that if the West Coast was going to continue to offer a credible competitor to The Beatles, it would have to be the reliable hit-machine that was The Beach Boys. They, too, had now requisitioned the services of that arch conduit Derek Taylor, who quickly found their sole songwriter to be an even greater headache than the manager he had left behind:

> **Derek Taylor:** Brian . . . hired me to help *Pet Sounds* take them to what he called 'a new plateau'. Brian Wilson shared more than just a first name with [Beatle manager] Epstein; he was just as impossible to please, just as edgy and, unlike Epstein, he nurtured grudges and didn't write letters of remorse and regret. We slugged it out through *Pet Sounds*, 'Good Vibrations', 'Heroes & Villains', a British tour; and with all that talent and paranoia around, it was marvellous that we accomplished so much that was coherent. [FYA]

Taylor's first contribution to the cause was to market The Beach Boys around songwriter Brian, now rebranded as the band's resident genius, solely responsible for the breakthrough that was *Pet Sounds*. As he would later inform Nick Kent, 'I started off . . . the "Brian Wilson Is A Genius" thing . . . I seem to recall it all came about because Brian told me that he thought he was better than most other people believed him to be. So I . . . went around town proposing the contention to people like Van Dyke and Danny Hutton and they all said, "Oh yes, definitely." . . . Then I started putting it around, making almost a campaign out of it.' There was no 'almost' about it. Taylor himself, still providing copy for the likes of *Disc* in the UK and *TeenSet* in the US, painted a portrait that swelled an already oversize ego:

> He alone in the industry – at the pinnacle of the pop pyramid – is full creator of a record from the first tentative constructions of a theme to the final master disc. Brian is a writer – words and music – performer and singer, arranger, engineer, producer, with complete control over packaging and design.

The fact that Wilson had no real control over Capitol's release schedules or their ubiquitous exercises in repackaging, and was generally only responsible for the *tunes*, was glossed over in a glissando of praise for the prismatic production techniques found on *Pet Sounds*.

When Wilson came up with his next breakthrough, a song called 'Good Vibrations', during the sessions for *Pet Sounds*, he quickly had the title, the tune and a rough idea of the lyric to which he planned to set the song. When work began in the studio on 18 February, 1966, though, all he had were a series of rag-bag phrases: 'She's working on my brain'; 'I only looked in her eyes/ And I picked up something I just can't explain'; and 'It's weird how she comes in so strong/ And I wonder what she's pickin' up from me'. Not exactly 'Norwegian Wood', let alone 'Like A Rolling Stone'. Yet clearly a song about a girl who affects the singer just like a certain drug.

As Wilson told Tom Nolan, one of the local journalists Taylor had targeted in his 'build up Brian' campaign, 'It's a song about a guy who picks up good vibrations from a girl. Of course, it's still sticking pretty close to that same boy–girl thing you know, but with a difference.' That difference came down to one triple-letter acronym. Good vibrations, or good vibes, was drug-slang, coined by an LA scenester only one step removed from Wilson's world. Taylor already knew the term:

> **Derek Taylor:** It was around The Byrds and their followers that I first heard of 'vibrations', 'vibes', as in 'good' and 'bad'. A young writer called Paul Jay Robbins sent a contribution to my publicity campaign. It was an essay, in which he explained at considerable length the meaning of the new phrase, 'where it's at'. [FYA]

Wilson turned his lyrical sketch over to Tony Asher, who had penned most of the *Pet Sounds* lyrics, but Asher was no longer on the same wavelength, i.e. had not 'turned on'. It was probably this – rather than any notion of what might come next – which ensured that the song would be held over until the completion of that landmark album (Wilson did not return to the song until 9 April, six days after *Pet Sounds* was put to bed).

Finally, fellow Beach Boy Mike Love – who was determined to 'stick pretty close to that same boy–girl thing' – came up with a usable set of lyrics, retaining just one vestige of the hallucinogenic quality Wilson originally had in mind ('I look in her eyes/ She goes with me to a blossom world'). At least it gave Wilson something on which to begin building what he later called 'a pocket symphony – changes, changes, changes, building harmonies here, drop this voice out, this comes in, bring this echo in, put the theremin here, bring the cello up a little louder here ... The biggest production of our lives!'

Thanks to the breathing-space afforded by the release of 'Sloop John B', the completion of *Pet Sounds* and the scheduling of a *Best of The Beach Boys*, Wilson was given free rein to play with his 'pocket symphony' to his heart's content. And Taylor was determined to make a virtue of the obsessive-compulsive way Wilson worked on this one three-minute song; encouraging Tom Nolan at the *L.A. Times*, Jules Siegel at the *Saturday Evening Post* and a *TeenSet* reporter (probably Taylor himself, with his pop critic hat on) all to portray Wilson's pernickety approach as a thirst for perfection.

Siegel didn't need a lot of persuading. Fresh from a penetrative profile of Dylan's speed-infused vision for the *Post*, presciently published the week of his motorcycle accident, Siegel was delighted to find that 'Brian was the opposite of Dylan, an unbelievably likeable person and a good guy. He was accessible, open, unpretentious, sincere – and he was into fun and games. I listened to some of the music he was doing for *Smile* at that point, and I was just blown away.' Having been recently convinced to check out *Pet Sounds* by his friend the novelist Thomas Pynchon, Siegel realised that Wilson was indeed reaching for that next plateau. However, he also recognised that 'it would take more than "Good Vibrations" and *Pet Sounds* to erase three and a half years of "Little Deuce Coupe".'

One overweening problem was the company Wilson kept. Unlike LA contemporaries like The Byrds, Buffalo Springfield and The Doors, Wilson saw his immediate circle as a barrier to keep the world out, rather than a way to bring new ideas in. When Jules Siegel brought Pynchon up to Brian's house, there was no great intellectual exchange. Instead, as Siegel explains, 'We went up to the Babylonian mansion – that was when he had an Arabian tent made out of brocade in a side-room off the living-room – and I explained that [Pynchon] was the hippest of hippest writers, and we went in the tent to get stoned.' Getting stoned was fast becoming a way of life for Wilson. No-one 'straight' was allowed into the inner sanctum, making his relations with Capitol – who were picking up the tab for his studio indulgences – strained to say the least.

If he betrayed none of the fascination with artists from other disciplines evident in his English peers, Wilson had also lost some of his previous generosity of spirit. McGuinn recalls how, in 1964, after recording a demo 'single for Elektra records, as the Beefeaters, we played it for Brian Wilson and he said, "Well, it's almost there. You need to work on your sound a little bit." [Back then] he was a big star, and we were on the street.' By 1966, though, he felt a keen rivalry with other pop proponents, and none greater than with The Beatles, which was fast becoming a source of some worry to a man who knew both parties well:

> **Derek Taylor:** Brian had become very, very competitive, so much so that it was no longer that healthy sort of competitive spirit thing. It was a mad possessive battle against the Stones and particularly The Beatles. [1975]

This fierce rivalry existed largely in his head, yet it meant that Epstein's boys didn't get to hear *Pet Sounds* until an advance pressing was brought over to London in May, and played to them at a listening session at the Waldorf. When during the same summer Wilson talked to a reporter from *Go* magazine, he articulated his musical aims in terms of toppling England's favourite sons:

Brian Wilson: I suddenly realised that The Beach Boys weren't giving the young people what they wanted. While Lennon and McCartney were exciting everyone with their new sounds, we were static. [1966]

The *Go* article was one more volley in Taylor's carefully orchestrated campaign to pre-sell not only 'Good Vibrations' but the album Wilson had been working on since the week after he completed *Pet Sounds*, originally called *Dumb Angel*, but now known as *Smile*. And 'Good Vibrations' was its starting point. Tom Nolan at the *L.A. Times* obligingly played his part, placing Wilson at the 'frenzied frontier of pop music' in his profile, which was published as 'Good Vibrations' finally appeared in the shops in late November 1966:

Perhaps the most impressive sign of his devotion to the music comes when it is 4:30 and he has yet to approve a final take; in three minutes all those studio musicians will go on overtime . . . But Brian Wilson ignores all those people, the musicians, the engineer, everybody watching him, because it just isn't right . . . [After another take] the engineer looks at Brian's wife, Marilyn . . . and says, 'He should be satisfied with this one, don't you think?' And she says, 'No, when he gets home he won't be satisfied. He's never satisfied.' She shakes her head.

Yet the appearance of 'Good Vibrations' seemed like another Validation Writ Large for the man's methodology. Most reviewers couldn't help but follow the *NME*'s lead: 'A technically perfect and impeccably performed disc (I should think so, with forty attempts needed to make it!)' *NME* also predicted it would be 'a big one! Probably a Number One'. On both sides of the Atlantic, as it happens. And yet, according to David Anderle – who had recently taken over Brian's business affairs, hoping to form a dedicated record label for his teeming output – after some ninety hours of studio-time, forty takes and at least eight sessions entirely dedicated to this singular song, it nearly didn't come out:

David Anderle: Right around the time of the fourth, 'final' 'Good Vibrations' – I heard it, and it knocked me out . . . And then, the next time I came up, it was different. And the next time I came up, it was different again. And then I came up one evening, and Brian said . . . that he had decided to totally scrap 'Good Vibrations'. [1967]

Wiser counsel prevailed, but it was a worrying presentiment of the doubts to come. In all likelihood Wilson felt that the song's lyrics were too much of a throwback to the old Beach Boys formula – cars and girls. By August 1966, he had met former child prodigy Van Dyke Parks, the kind of lyricist he felt was needed if he was going to stop standing still and start challenging those increasingly erudite Englanders.

However, for all his musical genius, Wilson had no reliable antenna when it came to employing a wordsmith in the post-Dylan pop world. Van Dyke certainly had a way with words, which cascaded out of him verbally and lyrically. He even had a schtick to explain what he was trying to do: 'I was interested in the thoughtfulness of cadence that had preceded rock & roll.' But very little that he wrote made any more sense than the preceding sentence, comprising little more than columns of non sequiturs from a man who once swallowed a thesaurus. When he wrote the lyrical counterpoint to the hymnal 'Surf's Up' in October 1966, he gave the guileless Wilson and the not-so-naive Siegel the same portentous explanation as to its meaning:

[Surf's Up is about] a man at a concert. All around him there's the audience, playing their roles, dressed up in fancy clothes, looking through opera glasses, but so far away from the drama, from life . . . The music begins to take over . . . Empires, ideas, lives, institutions – everything has to fall . . . He's off in his vision, on a trip. Reality is gone; he's creating it like a dream . . . And then hope . . . Go back to the kids, to the beach, to childhood.

The key phrase here is 'he's off . . . on a trip'. Parks and Wilson might have thought a song about someone at a classical recital 'tripping out' was a subject that would bring a smile to most record-buying folk, but The Beach Boys' constituency hardly corresponded to Dylan's. Even Wilson was starting to worry that the words might be getting in the way of what he was trying to say. As he confided to Siegel at the time, he hoped that 'if they don't get the words, they'll get the music; because that's where it's really at, in the music. You can get hung up in words, you know. Maybe they work – I don't know.'

Unfortunately for Parks, the return of the touring element of The Beach Boys from a wildly successful visit to the UK in mid-November, eleven days after Brian had made his first studio pass at 'Surf's Up', brought him face to face with Mike Love, who was less than pleased by the little lovefest he encountered on his return. As Parks later remarked, Mike Love decided 'that I had written some words that were indecipherable and unnecessary'. Surely not. Love was also perturbed to find, in David Anderle's words, 'this bunch of people [around Brian], who all of a sudden were saying a lot of things – Michael Vosse, and myself, and Paul Robbins somewhat, Van Dyke, very strongly, Jules [Siegel], a lot of people [he] hadn't seen before'.

Meanwhile, at the label there was a general assumption that Wilson would do another *Pet Sounds*, and pull months of work together into one cohesive whole in a couple of weeks, delivering the eagerly awaited *Smile* to Capitol by the end of the year, thus trumping the semi-retired FabFour. *TeenSet* allowed their roving reporter to suggest as much in the December '66 issue, perhaps more in hope than expectation: 'Thanksgiving has just passed and an awesome recording schedule faces [The Beach Boys]. The new album *Smile* and the new single 'Heroes & Villains' must be completed by Christmas. Day and night and long weekend sessions are planned.'

Nor was there any let up in the *Smile* sessions. Fourteen sessions occupied the four weeks after Thanksgiving, as Wilson continued to apply yet more overdubs to the twelve songs – 'Good Vibrations' excepted – scheduled for *Smile*. He now allowed his fellow Beach

Boys to add vocal parts to 'Child is the Father of Man', 'Heroes and Villains', 'Wonderful', 'Surf's Up' and 'Do You Like Worms?' Meanwhile, he recorded an entirely new basic track for 'Heroes & Villains', a song he had already expended three whole sessions on, but felt inclined to assign eleven more; all part of what Siegel would later depict as 'an obsessive cycle of creation and destruction'.

The other Beach Boys remained just as in the dark as Brian's immediate confidants when it came to the organising method their resident genius intended to apply in order to gather up all these songs and snippets, many slight, but a couple fully the equal of 'Good Vibrations'. In fact, Wilson still had no firm sequence set in his mind, as a track-listing written out for the record label that December demonstrates. Though it contained all of the elements (sic), it listed the three most realised cuts – 'Good Vibrations', 'Heroes & Villains' and 'Surf's Up' – one after the other, while the supposedly central suite of songs, 'The Elements', came neither at the beginning nor the end (as it would in 2004).

For all of Capitol's optimism that they would have an album to market in the winter of 1967 on the back of the unprecedented success of 'Good Vibrations' – which even prompted them to place an ad for the still-unfinished album in the March *TeenSet* – the promised seven-inch successor to 'Good Vibrations', 'Heroes & Villains', showed no sign of appearing on the label manager's desk, despite five sessions devoted to this one song between 13 and 28 December.

Frustration was setting in for both camps – the band's and Brian's. Everyone concerned began to fear that all the momentum accrued from a year of immense commercial gains – *Pet Sounds'* disappointing showing in the States notwithstanding – was about to disappear into the LA fog. Outsiders were now carefully vetted and rarely allowed to witness Wilson at work. But in those rare instances when it was in his interest to allow strangers in, they were utterly baffled by the process. When CBS-TV asked to film the man at work for an ambitious documentary on pop, to be narrated by the celebrated composer Leonard Bernstein, their producer Oppenheim found the whole *Smile* smorgasbord on the verge of collapsing around Brian's one good ear:

> **David Oppenheim:** A film crew and I went to Columbia Records' studios with Brian and his friends, and they were doing tiny little pieces that made no sense in and of themselves . . . The sessions didn't make a scene that was at all interesting . . . It was terribly spread out . . . I had heard the stories before we got there about how crazy he was. [And] Van Dyke seemed . . . intelligent, [but] off-the-wall and smashed.

Despairing of getting anything usable, Oppenheim persuaded Wilson to let the film crew return with him to his 'Babylonian mansion', where they would film him alone at the piano, singing 'Surf's Up'. The performance he gave was riveting, and the lyrics, obscure as they remained, didn't hinder Wilson from delivering a tour de force of such power that the one writer still close to the man broke the general code of silence, making one last attempt to cajole him into releasing this very recording 'as is', unadulterated:

> **Jules Siegel:** I was there when he did 'Surf's Up' for the CBS cameras. I was in the car with him – we smoked a joint before he went and did that; and afterwards, I said to him, 'Why don't you just stop fucking around with this stuff, and just release that as a single now, like *now!* Don't wait for the album to do it.' But he was afraid to do it.

In that single moment – irony of ironies – Wilson achieved all he had set out to on the day he first heard *Rubber Soul*, back in 1965. That performance, as broadcast the following March, would also do more to imbue *Smile* with weight and import than any of the subsequent trawls of the Capitol vaults, by bootleggers and label alike. The week before he made this recording, Brian had learnt that 'Good Vibrations' had finally hit the number one spot on the

Billboard charts, their first US number one since 'Help Me Rhonda', and a replay of its British success.

On the same December day, Wilson was informed that The Beach Boys had knocked The Beatles off their perch in the Best International Group section of the annual *NME* poll, occupying a position The Beatles had held since 1963. At the end of the year, The Beach Boys duly appeared as the Best-Selling Artist in England's *Record Mirror*, with The Beatles languishing in ninth position behind the likes of Ken Dodd, Cliff Richard and Dave Dee, Dozy, Beaky, Mick & Tich.

As it happens, the FabFour's lowly position reflected not any great descent in popularity, but rather in output, with just two singles (rather than the previous three or four) issued during the twelve-month period. The Beach Boys, on the other hand, were riding the crest of a wave of singles, first from *Pet Sounds* and then the record-breaking 'Good Vibrations'. On all sides there was general excitation that, as and when it was completed, *Smile* would replicate *Pet Sounds'* commercial and critical acclaim in The Beatles' once impregnable fiefdom. It was time The Beatles returned to the fray, preferably with their pop sensibilities intact.

4

LIVING IS EASY

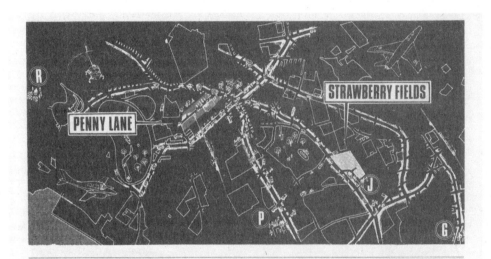

'PENNY LANE' 'STRAWBERRY FIELDS FOREVER' THE BEATLES

PARLOPHONE OUT FRIDAY FEBRUARY 17 1967

Everything we've done so far has been rubbish as I see it today. Other people may like what we've done, but we're not kidding ourselves. –

George Harrison, *Daily Mirror*, 11/11/66

Brian Wilson was not the only 'would-be genius' to spend several months of '66 working on a single song that would codify all he had achieved to date. Unlike Wilson, though, John Lennon didn't initially feel that the studio was the place to sketch out ideas. Instead, he spent from 18 September to 23 November using first a portable five-inch Uher reel-to-reel, and then the trusty Brennel tape-machine in his Kenwood home studio, to get from a single verse (the second) of something called 'It's Not Too Bad' to a recognisable prototype for 'Strawberry Fields Forever'.

Lennon had probably got it in his mind to write something 'about' his childhood since at least October 1965, when he penned the memorable 'In My Life', a song he later admitted was 'sparked by a remark a journalist and writer in England made after *In His Own Write* came out.' The comment was along the lines of, 'Why don't you put some of the way you write in [your] book, as it were, in the songs? Why don't you put something about your childhood into the songs?'

The Liverpudlian had only recently considered the possibility of writing from personal experience. In future, 'Help' (April 1965) would become the song he'd cite as the first of his really written 'from experience and not projecting myself into a situation and writing a nice story about it. I always found that phony, but I'd find occasion to do it because I'd have to produce so much work.'

The more personal the subject matter, the less inclined Lennon now seemed to co-opt McCartney into the writing process. When it came to 'Strawberry Fields', he seems to have always intended to produce a working demo before he showed it to the others. In this sense, he was breaking from his Fab past at precisely the moment he was re-examining the fraught childhood of a disaffected soul. With 'Strawberry Fields' Lennon was evidently looking to pinpoint that acute sense of separation he had rekindled on recent acid-trips to a specific time and place – post-war Liverpool and the local orphanage (in its original guise, he even sang the key line as 'let me take you back'; not 'let me take you down').

> **John Lennon:** 'Strawberry Fields' is my attempt at expressing that [feeling]. The second line goes, 'No-one I think is in my tree.'[1] Well, what I was trying to say in that line is 'Nobody seems to be as hip as me, therefore I must be crazy or a genius.' It's that same problem I had when I was five: 'There is something wrong with me, because I seem to see things other people don't see.' . . . I was always seeing things in a hallucinatory way that always saw beyond the mask. And it's scary when you're a child, because there is nobody to relate to. Neither my auntie, nor my friends, nor anybody could *ever* see it! . . . [So] I belonged to an exclusive club that sees the world in those terms. Surrealism to me is reality. Psychedelic vision is reality to me, and always was. [1980]

The exclusive club to which Lennon is referring includes the likes of William Blake, Bob Dylan, Patti Smith and George Ivan Morrison, all of whom when adults referred to a similar disloca-tion from the world first experienced through the eyes of a child. Though Strawberry Field was a real place, a Victorian manor with spacious grounds in the area of Liverpool in which Lennon grew up, Strawberry *Fields* was a more abstract vista.

As Lennon told Jonathan Cott in 1968, when Cott was hard at work on his doctoral thesis on Victorian children's literature, 'Strawberry Field was a place near us that happened to be a Salvation Army home. But Strawberry Fields – I mean, I [still] have visions of Strawberry Fields . . . Strawberry Fields is anywhere you want to go.' In this sense, McCartney is right to suggest it 'was a secret garden, like in *The Lion, The Witch & the Wardrobe*, and [John] thought of it like that, it was a little hide-away for him where he could . . . live in his dreams a little', and as such not the kind of physical locale he would recreate on his own 'Penny Lane'.

Lennon clearly hoped that 'Strawberry Fields Forever' would be more than just another song for the canon. One might not discern it from some startlingly original Lennon compositions on the album EMI released six weeks earlier, but when he began sketching out this song he was finding it hard to motivate himself to keep writing. As he admitted to Cott, 'I was going through a big scene about writing again – I seem to go through it now and then, and it took me a long time to write [the song]. I was writing all bits . . . I wanted the lyrics to be like conversation.'

On one level, Lennon's decision to play a bit part in Dick Lester's cinematic version of *How I Won The War*, which meant six weeks in Spain far from the madding crowd, was a way to shut himself off from the responsibilities of a Beatle. But composing the song also provided a therapeutic purpose all its own: 'It took me six weeks to write the song. I was writing it all the time I was making the film. As anybody knows about film work, there's a lot of hanging around.'

In fact, Lennon was still someway off a ready-to-record song when he returned to Weybridge in early November. Essentially, the song as it stood when he began overdubbing guitar parts and demo-ing vocals in the tiny attic studio of his Surrey home was strong on atmosphere, but weak on structure. Lennon's attempt at writing lyrics 'like conversation' had ended up like a monologue. Nor was 'Living is easy with eyes closed/ Misunderstanding all you see' – something of an impossibility – the best way to start a song that meandered to its heartfelt resolution: the wish to sit in strawberry fields forever.

Nonetheless, this was the way the song remained until the four Beatles, engineer Geoff Emerick and producer George Martin convened at Abbey Road Studio Two at seven p.m. on 24 November, 1966, planning to start work on *Revolver*'s successor. At some point they knew they would also have to decide on a suitable single to satiate growing demand from fans not used to waiting six months between Beatles' records.

As was becoming the norm, the entire session was devoted to working on one new song – John's. Although Ian MacDonald in *Revolution In The Head* suggests 'that the first three days of recording amounted to a sustained false start', the song was quickly realised. At the evening's close, as Martin has observed, everyone thought 'we [had] arrived at a take that . . . would be the final one. [And] that first take is brilliant, especially John's vocal: clear, pure and riveting'.

This 'take one' (later issued on *Anthology 2*, but with some rather effective harmony vocals from the Beatle boys, in *Pet Sounds* mode, mixed out) was still very much the song Lennon had expended such effort crafting. But for all its exquisite vocalising, and the way the track gorgeously builds to its crescendo couplet by couplet – something none of the later incarnations do – this was an album track, and a short one at that (just two and a half minutes), at a time when the shackles of the three-minute song were being broken by every hopped-up hippy combo.

When The Beatles left the studio early in the morning, everyone seemed happy at the start made to Rubber Revolver Revisited. Lennon, though, spent the weekend reviewing the acetate he'd taken with him, and when he returned to West Hampstead the following Monday evening he had changed his mind, abandoning yet another working practice, the one of leaving well alone. Though he hadn't said anything at the time, Martin hadn't been so sure about the arrangement:

George Martin: The first time we recorded the song, it turned out much heavier than expected. So I wasn't very surprised when he said he'd like me to do it again. [But] that was the first time we'd ever remade a Beatles song. [1987]

Later on, Lennon would come to view the recutting of this little gem, which in its rough diamond state still shone clear, as a mistake; and, as so often with this quixotic individual, he began to convince himself that he had been cajoled into remaking it by his partner-in-song:

John Lennon: [Paul] subconsciously tried to destroy songs, meaning that we'd play experimental games with my great pieces, like 'Strawberry Fields' – which I always felt was badly recorded . . . Usually we'd spend hours doing little detailed cleaning-ups of Paul's songs; [but] when it came to mine, especially if it was a great song like 'Strawberry Fields' . . . somehow this atmosphere of looseness and casualness and experimentation would creep in. [1980]

In fact, the 28 November session – at which everyone expected to move on to Paul's latest ditty – ended up devoted entirely to the (first) remake of 'Strawberry Fields Forever'. And when it came to embellishing an existing song with interesting sounds, it was to Martin that both main songwriters still deferred. Even if they no longer ran songs by him, they were happy to leave a lot of the technical decisions – the 'means' – to their producer:

George Martin: In the early days they used to write a song and then come along and play it to me . . . It's very different today. Often they come to the studio and haven't even written a song. Maybe there's an idea, a basis to work on, the bare bones . . . It's true to say they must depend on me a lot. They know many things – but they don't know detail. [1967]

Increasingly, Martin's brief was to figure out how to realise what were often little more than abstract ideas when they came to John or Paul (or George). And having heard some of the sounds coming out of American eight-track studios, the lads considered it perfectly reasonable to demand the impossible. As Miles asserts, 'You needed someone like [Martin] if you're working in basically a museum of ancient recording equipment.' For now, they were grateful for every suggestion – though that would change by the following summer, as Martin began to grant interviews in his own right, taking credit for many of the solutions found for *Sgt. Pepper*. When reviewers took note, at least one Beatle was not amused:

> **Paul McCartney:** One of the reviews . . . about *Sgt. Pepper* . . . said, 'This is George Martin's finest album.' We got shook. I mean, we don't mind him helping us – . . . it's a great help – but it's not his album, folks! [1974]

The 28 November, 1966 session – and a further one the following day – saw Martin in his element, as The Beatles threw the kitchen sink of sound effects previously spread over all sixteen (sic) *Revolver* cuts at Lennon's one little song of yearning. The results made for a spectacular soundscape, but they also took the focus away from *the song*, a move The Beatles had previously been wary of making; but one that would become a *modus operandi* on the album they imagined they had begun. The acerbic Richard Meltzer, reviewing 'Strawberry Fields' on its release in America's first rock-zine, *Crawdaddy*, couldn't help but satirise the results:

> Maybe the entire vocal (which does contain strange enunciation, with peculiar marginal speed variations) had been recorded, played backwards, learned as backwards, recorded as performed backwards, and played backwards again to sound, ultimately, "forwards".

In fact Meltzer, with a little help from his ears, came surprisingly close to the truth. The version The Beatles completed on the 29th, take seven, was subjected to three mono mixes and was again cut to acetate. The vocal in A Major – already subjected to ADT – would be adjusted to B Natural before its release, to 'sync.' with an alternate vocal introduced a third of the way through the song; while the backing vocals, piano and bass overdubbed on to the track had all been recorded at various speeds.

But despite astutely transposing the chorus, so that it now operated as the song's introduction, there still remained an essential problem with the song – it had no real ending. After Lennon's triple incantation of the song title, successive attempts from The Beatles to vamp through a fade-out merely confirmed that the instrumental workout was not one of their strong points. As Martin justly observed in his monograph on the making of *Sgt. Pepper*, 'Sometimes they would jam for hours in the studio, and we would be expected to tape it all, recognising the moment of great genius when it came through. The only trouble was, it never did come through.'

The 'final' version of 'Strawberry Fields' on the 28th (take four) was their most sustained attempt to drive the thing on, but it still stuttered to a close. There was more going on than on take one, where McCartney had mellotroned his way towards the fade, but even after the following day's session – which yielded three more 'takes' – there was a sense that they still hadn't seen the last of Lennon's latest little lyric.

It was time they cracked on with other material, even though it appeared that McCartney had devoted even less time in the past five months to writing songs than his erstwhile collaborator. The song he played to the others on 6 December was actually a reworking of an old, pre-EMI parody of vaudeville (at a time when they still thought they needed 'variety' in their sets, hence the likes of 'Besame Mucho' and 'Sheik of Araby'). It is usually suggested that McCartney was 'inspired' to return to 'When I'm 64' because his own father had reached that landmark the previous July. But there is a more relevant autobiographical element underlying the song, which essentially asks, Are you the right one for me? Not surprisingly, his relationship with girlfriend Jane Asher had become more strained since he had acquired his own pad and, even as she moved in with him, he had begun to question their future together:

Paul McCartney: During that period with Jane Asher I learned a lot and she introduced me to a lot of things, but I think inevitably when I moved to Cavendish Avenue, I realised that she and I weren't really going to be the thing we'd always thought we might be. [MYFN]

Though one misguided American scholar sought to suggest Paul was satirising 'a marriage of unsurpassed stultification, to what appears to be a mail-order bride', the lyrics have no such spin. If it is a satire, it is a gentle one, from someone who *almost* longs to return to the normal, suburban existence he knew as a child. Pondering whether the life his parents (or even grandparents) enjoyed might not have its own charms, McCartney is asking himself (in song) whether he can imagine still being with his current partner forty years down the line. As such, on one level 'When I'm 64' was as concerned with the search for meaning as 'Strawberry Fields', with which it now almost became a companion piece.

The band must have been aware that there was a great deal of concern about the gap that the break in group activities was leaving in the release schedules of EMI and Capitol. And according to McCartney, in *Many Years From Now*, the next Beatles single was originally going to be 'Strawberry Fields Forever b/w When I'm 64'. Which makes sense. One, it would provide the band with some breathing space as any album was clearly some way off; two, it followed the pattern for *Revolver*, when 'Paperback Writer' and 'Rain', both recorded early on, were quickly marked out for use as a single; and three, it would explain why in both cases the songs were mixed (and in 'Strawberry Fields' case *remixed* at least four times) on completion of a 'final' version (this practice was not unknown, but on *Revolver* – and in general – the majority of Beatles songs were mixed only when an album began to come together).

A suggestion in a number of histories, recently reinforced by Tony Barrow's memoir, has been that 'all four Beatles were considerably angered when these first two album tracks were snatched from under their noses'. This smacks of hindsight's magical properties bending the truth, to refract light away from the single's relative failure and the inclusion of filler tracks on *Pepper*. In the past any pressure to produce had merely aided the songwriting process. And in their own country, it was the norm to consider singles as separate entities, The Beatles ever striving to make each artifact provide real value for money.

Miles: They really were concerned that 6/8d was a lot of money, and the idea of a throwaway b-side was something they always hated, growing up working-class kids themselves. [So] Beatles records were always going to have *two* great sides!

There was another factor to consider: the last single took *both* cuts from their latest LP. Another two-sided preview of the next long-player would not sit well with British fans. Already the powers-that-be were hastily releasing a single-album greatest hits (*A Collection of Oldies But Goldies*) for a Christmas market otherwise bereft of Beatles product. For The Beatles, then, there was no argument. The next single would be a return to the rich vein of non-album singles which had preceded 'Eleanor Rigby'.

By now, there was another imperative at work with the band that was once a unity of four. As Philip Norman suggests, in his wretched Beatles biography, *Shout!*, 'The double A-side formula was less a boast than a political necessity, since one side was wholly John's and the other entirely Paul's; the weight of creativity packed into each only emphasised what a gulf lay between them.' This reads as one of many of Norman's oversimplifications. Yet there is a grain of truth underlying that tabloid slant, even if the rivalry between John and Paul was still a beneficent force on the band – having already pushed McCartney to produce the likes of 'Paperback Writer', 'We Can Work It Out' and 'Eight Days A Week'.

George Martin: Their collaboration as songwriters was never Rodgers and Hart, it was always more Gilbert & Sullivan. If John did something, Paul would wish he'd thought of it and go away and try to do something better and vice versa. [1987]

In this instance, McCartney decided that 'When I'm 64' was not a strong enough ballast to underpin 'Strawberry Fields Forever'. Or, as he later informed *Uncut*, when Lennon 'wrote "Strawberry Fields", it was like he'd upped the ante, so I had to come up with something as good as "Penny Lane"'. By the time McCartney appeared at an Abbey Road session with 'Penny Lane' – on 29 December – 'Strawberry Fields Forever' itself had become an altogether grander concoction, after Lennon – still unhappy – had asked Martin if he could bring 'in some outside musicians to supplement The Beatles' playing'.

Sessions on 8 and 9 December saw The Beatles themselves adding backward cymbals, timpani, bongos, guitar-breaks, further percussion and a swordmandel; to which Martin added four trumpets, three cellos, two new Lennon vocals (and a partridge in a pear tree) the following week. The result was a tribute to the quintet's almost unerring instincts for keeping the listener engaged, and solved most of the structural issues the song had originally thrown up (though the amount of 'bouncing' from four-track to four-track, with all its attendant audio degradation, hardly aided anyone hoping to distinguish cello from swordmandel).

But Lennon was convinced that they had lost some quintessence of inspiration in souping up the song's instrumentation and formalising its structure. In an effort to amalgamate the best of both approaches, he asked Martin to edit together the first third of take seven, from 29 November, with the semi-orchestral take twenty-six, from 15 December – even though they were a semitone apart. In a pre-digital age it was sheer good fortune that Martin found, when he sped up the November take and reduced the speed of the December recording, the edit was almost (if not quite) seamless.

Lennon was quite correct – 'something had been lost'. But all things considered, the single version of 'Strawberry Fields Forever' *was* that great leap he was looking to make after the song-centric *Revolver*. There was a downside, a doubt that dare not speak its name: were The Beatles travelling too fast for their fan-base? It was a concern McCartney voiced in conversation with Miles for *International Times* – a new bi-weekly English equivalent to *East Village Other* – just a couple of days after 'Strawberry Fields Forever' was finally completed to everyone's satisfaction:

Paul McCartney: I'm trying to take people with me, of course. I don't want to be shouting to people, 'Listen, listen, I've found it! Listen, this is where it's at!' and everybody going 'Oh fuck off, you fucking crank.' [1967]

Miles had been inspired to found *IT* the previous October by John Wilcock, a maverick magazine publisher who after co-founding New York's *Village Voice*, had gone west to set up the *L.A. Free Press*, before returning east to provide the Village with another voice. For the first time in an English paper, McCartney felt comfortable discussing musical and intellectual ideas in everyday language. In particular, he made it clear that the traditional way of recording no longer offered enough of a challenge for him personally:

Paul McCartney: What is still magic for other people, for me it's a bit, 'Well OK, I see why he's done that, and how he's done that, and I'll learn from it', but I tend to just take it and file it [away], instead of being knocked out about it . . . With any kind of thing, my aim seems to be to distort it . . . To take a note and wreck it and see in that note what else there is in it, that a simple act like distorting it has caused. [1967]

Delighted by the direction Lennon's 'Strawberry Fields' indicated, McCartney demonstrated a desire to go further himself, something that was occasionally in evidence during the sessions for what had become the new Beatles single. Even while recording a twenty-second Christmas greeting for pirate station Radio London, in early December, he was suggesting they fed playback tape-echo into the studio, prompting Martin to ask, 'Do you want to make a production out of it!?' Lennon steps in, masking his ignorance with a typical piece of Goonish word-play, suggesting that they 'can double-splange the [tapes]!'

It was at the 5 January session, on the day McCartney finally nailed the vocal for 'Penny Lane', that he went 'too far', using EMI studio-time to record his own *Freak Out*, as previously promised, for a 'happening' at the Roundhouse later in the month. At close to fourteen minutes, the so-called 'Carnival of Light' has been described thus by Mark Lewisohn in his survey of Beatles recording sessions:

> The longest interrupted Beatles recording to date, [it used] the combination of a basic track and numerous overdubs. Track one of the tape was full of distorted, hypnotic drum and organ sounds; track two had a distorted lead guitar; track three had the sounds of a church organ, various effects (the gargling with water was one) and voices; track four featured various indescribable sound effects with heaps of tape echo and manic tambourine . . . On track three . . . John and Paul [were also] screaming dementedly and bawling aloud random phrases.

Though intended to provide a soundtrack to a one-off event, 'Carnival of Light' was apparently under serious consideration for the *Anthology* collection, until Harrison exercised his veto. Miles, one of the few to have heard the great 'experiment', suggests it 'is really dreadful. It doesn't bear being released. It's just masses of echo. It sounds like they put it through twice. It was the same thing that everybody was doing at home.'

Indeed it was. The Hollies' Graham Nash recalls how he would 'have four tape recorders, one in each corner of the room, all connected, and I'd put a tape on one and send it to the next one, and the distance between the record head and the erase head was such that it created quite an experience'. Meanwhile, Pete Townshend was using two Vortexion CBLs 'to bounce in stereo', allowing the demos he made for The Who to become ever more ornate. At the same time, he was dabbling with early electronic suites, parts of which would later crop up on his *Scoop* series. A couple of months after McCartney spoke about distortion, Townshend also talked to our *IT* editor about the relationship he envisaged between 'electronic music' and pop:

Pete Townshend: There is a place for electronic music, and there is probably a place for it in pop. I think that someone should take it up, but I don't think that it should be a course of development for *any* group to take. We're going to take a very blatantly commercial move which will be very, very big . . . And it will probably upset a few people that thought we were making progressive moves. [But] what is more important is that record sales were going down. [1967]

In fact, The Who continued going from strength to strength (the failure of 'Magic Bus' to chart was still some months away). But both The Who's songman and The Beatles' trio of songwriters couldn't help but notice the most spectacular commercial failure of 1966. On 23 September, The Rolling Stones had issued their successor to the chart-topping 'Paint It Black', 'Have You Seen Your Mother, Baby, Standing in the Shadow b/w Who's Driving Your Plane'. It was their noisiest record to date, an unprecedented barrage of sound. To these Dartford renegades it seemed the ideal way to assert themselves while The Beatles were at play. It also generated some of the best reviews of their career, NME's Derek Johnson enthusing about a new 'complexity of startling sounds', and Penny Valentine at *Disc* calling it 'The most certain Number One they've ever had.'

Yet the single was a bathetic bellyflop, peaking at number five and spending just six weeks on the charts (in the States, it fared even worse, peaking at eight). A chagrined Ms Valentine ran a piece in *Disc*, asking, 'What Went Wrong?' It was a fair question for a band who hadn't had a single outside the top three in the past three years. Eric Clapton, whose own band, Cream, had just seen their debut single ('Wrapping Paper') not even tickle the charts, 'didn't think this was a good enough record to reach No. 1. It wasn't as well-constructed or as commercial as records they've made.' The Hollies' Bobby Elliott was equally unimpressed: 'The record was just basically above the fans' heads. It was too hippy.'

Keith Richards would later suggest that they had issued the wrong mix; and certainly Mike Leander's brass arrangement was buried deep in the grooves. However, it is a song that has grown in stature over the years (along with its equally punch-drunk b-side). Indeed, Sex Pistols bassist Glen Matlock suggests it provided the basis for what his own iconoclastic band were trying to do a decade later:

> **Glen Matlock:** That's where the Pistols' construction of songs came from . . . On [manager] Malcolm [McLaren]'s jukebox there was 'Have You Seen Your Mother' and it's just the sound of it, everything's in the red . . . When it was recorded, it was all valves, there's one riff, and everybody in the whole band . . . plays everything together always, all the time, it's just like this incessant row, but it's a glorious racket.

'Strawberry Fields' was less of a racket, but its instrumentation still seemed too dense for a Dansette. Perhaps fearful of alienating fans unduly, McCartney was again cast in the role of the great popu-lariser, as he came up with a more prosaic depiction of the Liverpool of their youth for the flip-side; which he set to another of his eminently hummable melodies. 'Penny Lane' really was another side to a lost Liverpool. As McCartney told Alan Aldridge the following year, 'It's part fact, part nostalgia for a place which is a great place – blue suburban skies as we remember it.'

It also set Macca thinking, why not an album along these lines, comprising only northern songs? The only problem was that – come 17 January, when 'Penny Lane' was completed – the still fab four were all but back to square one when it came to *Revolver*'s successor. At least they had a single that was the equal of anything they had produced before; and anything they expected to come from their immediate peers. His fellow Beatles, though, were about to be taken unawares by the latest London had to offer in the way of claimants to their pop crown.

5

INTO OVERDRIVE

The next move seems to be things like electronics, because it's a complete[ly] new field and there's a lot of good new sounds to be listened to in it. But if the music itself is just going to jump about five miles ahead, then everyone's going to be left standing with this gap . . . that they've got to cross. –

Paul McCartney, *IT* #6

I f McCartney was staking out an early interest in 'electronics' in his December conversation with Miles, he had already been acting as Macca the magpie, flitting around a burgeoning London scene where experimentation and extemporisation were the order of the day. As the gap between electronics and Rock grew smaller and smaller, he may well have grown less and less sure that his band could still take the lead when it came to pop's future direction, his boundless self-confidence notwithstanding.

> **Miles:** In my discussions with him, McCartney had always been convinced that there would be a new synthesis of electronic music and studio techniques and rock & roll. [But] he didn't see The Beatles as being quite the vehicle for that.

Actually, the decision all four had made back in the summer to stop touring threatened to render any ongoing leadership a moot point. The Beatles weren't the only ones who had retired from the road. So had a recuperating Dylan and a recalcitrant Brian Wilson. By the end of 1966 a seemingly spent Stones were about to follow suit.[1] And yet, Rock was becoming increasingly a live medium, as the equipment improved exponentially in the second half of the sixties; the package tours that promoters loved and bands hated were fast becoming an anachronism; and songs were stretching out in a way that no-one who'd cut their teeth at Hamburg's Star Club would have recognised. The change from pop to Rock was acted out in the bright lights of the clubs of London, New York and LA.

The one band from 'the Britbeat era' readily equipped for such a transition were still challenging all-comers on all-night bills. Bursts of feedback and Sten-gun drumming was The Who's preferred method when it came to announcing themselves. If few came away unbowed, the boys from the Bush would meet their match at year's end when five lads from Birmingham rocked the Roundhouse; succeeded by a set of Cambridge students dispensing their own deafening soundtrack to the first psychedelic light show this side of the pond.

By December 1966 the live circuit was fully in the throes of 'the big change'. Clubs dedicated to one kind of pop band, with late hours and long sets, were challenging more tried and tested establishments. The result, on more than one occasion, was a night like the one June Bolan described to Jonathon Green: 'You'd do three gigs [in] a night: a club called the Rikki-Tik in Windsor and another Rikki-Tik . . . in Hounslow, and then your third gig for the night, at two in the morning, would be UFO in Tottenham Court Road.' The band in question were The Pink Floyd; who at the start of 1967 were trying that most difficult of highwire acts, maintaining their hard-won underground status whilst wowing pop fans. The Floyd, as Miles says, 'were the very stuff that [Paul and I] had been talking about'.

Back in the winter of '66, it had been a new venture at a familiar Soho site that had started this particular cart rolling. On a lazy Sunday afternoon in January at the Marquee, something psychedelic was stirring. And one of those London–NY underground connections was responsible for these first ripples. Steven Stollman had arrived in London from New York at the end of 1965, operating in an A&R role for brother Bernard's ESP label, the same jazz label who had recently signed The Fugs to what Fug frontman, Tuli Kupferberg, has called 'a strange, shackling contract . . . [with] one of the lower [royalty] percentages in the history of western civilization'. Knowing little of the London scene, Stollman devised a plan whereby the local underground would come to him:

> **Miles:** It was [Steve's] idea that – rather than seek out all these [underground bands] in a city he didn't know – he would start an underground club and they would all show up, and he would be able to sign them up [to ESP] . . . [And] The Pink Floyd Sound [turned up] – it was written on their amp, and someone projected a movie on to them, which had been shot by a paraplegic from a wheelchair just rushing round London. They quite liked the effect. They went down really well . . . They still played [r&b] . . . They'd start up, do these very quick intros and then there'd be a very long, psychedelic noodling period and then they'd somehow get back to the chords. Then it'd be some other r&b classic. It was quite bizarre . . . I think it was the same evening that AMM were playing. Syd took very close notice of what [guitarist] Keith Rowe was doing, and pretty much took his guitar-style.

Unfortunately for his brother's label, Steve was not really sure what he was supposed to be looking for. Though the Floyd apparently played at all of the Sunday Spontaneous Happenings (including the first one, billed as a Giant Mystery Happening, on 30 January) – which he'd clearly modelled on similar 'happenings' in New York, though these involved renting the Marquee for the afternoon – they were not signed to ESP. Perhaps this was because the two-song demo ('Lucy Leave' and 'King Bee') they either gave to ESP, or at the very least played to Stollman, contained precious few of the psychedelic undertones they were beginning to develop in concert.[2]

If Floyd were at one end of the spectrum, AMM were certainly nearer the other. Esoteric enough to make even the pre-Velvets Theatre of Eternal Music sound accessible, they were fronted by avant-guitarist Keith Rowe, whose most celebrated ruse was to run ball-bearings up and down the neck of his guitar. The sound he produced was surreal enough for Syd Barrett, the Floyd's frontman, to adopt it sparingly himself. Like McCartney, Barrett was content to operate in the uncharted territory that still lay between 'noise' and pop. In sleepy London Town that winter/spring all kinds of weird and wonderful bills remained possible.

> **Keith Rowe:** It wasn't yet clear how it would turn out, therefore one had concerts in London which had the AMM and you had Rock groups which were trying to make career moves and becoming famous, like . . . Cream, Pink Floyd, [John Mayall's] Bluesbreakers; and AMM would . . . be playing the same gigs.

For the Floyd, Stollman's Spontaneous Happenings gave the band much-needed impetus while providing an environment where they could extemporise. Formed in Cambridge in 1965 as a five-piece, they had ventured out infrequently until the departure of second guitarist Bob Klose, at year's end, removed one bulwark to the blues, giving Barrett more room for exploration of psyche and psychedelia.

Throughout the winter and spring, Floyd enjoyed the opportunity of playing a fortnightly slot at the world-famous Marquee, Stollman keeping up his experiment until early June, and school's out.[3] At what was either the final Spontaneous Happening or an undocumented private show, a London School of Economics lecturer who lived next door to guitar-God Eric Clapton, decided to take a break from marking exams and trundle 'along to this mad gig at the Marquee, which was being run by people like Steve Stollman and Hoppy', for an afternoon of atonality. What Peter Jenner saw signalled the end of his academic career, as another young, bright, energised entrepreneur enamoured with the potential of pop threw in an existing hand to risk all on an up-and-coming band:

> **Peter Jenner:** I was very suspicious of English blues bands – in a way that was probably why I was attracted by the Floyd because, although they were playing the normal hackneyed old blues songs, what they were doing in between was . . . something different . . . They were playing these very weird breaks; so weird I couldn't even

work out which instrument the sound was coming from. It was all very bizarre and just what I was looking for – a far out, electronic, freaky, pop group.

Jenner's timing was a little awry. Not only was this (perhaps) the last of Stollman's afternoon affairs, but the band informed him they were taking a break for the summer; and to contact them when they returned from their annual 'hols'. Jenner was undeterred. When he resumed contact in early September he immediately steered them in a more rewarding direction. As Pete Frame wrote in his famous *Zigzag* profile, 'The Floyd ... [now] dropped most of their r&b repertoire in favour of the more electronic/freaky stuff ... at Jenner's insistence ... [He] thought the electronic stuff sounded better than the American imitations which he'd never really been keen on. Also, thinking that there was nothing difficult in composing new numbers, he impressed on them that they should write more original material, of a "weird" nature.' He found Barrett a willing ally and, though they had their doubts, the rest of the band went along with the plan:

> **Roger Waters:** We'd already started to do the things that we continued to do. [But] even though we were still amateur, we stopped playing blues and started thrashing about making stranger noises and doing different things. [1970]

On 30 September, 1966, the Floyd (still billed as The Pink Floyd Sound) resumed their explorations at the All Saints Hall in Notting Hill Gate where they were part of a 'Celebration Dance', presumably for the London Free School, which had recently made its base there. After the dance, Jenner convinced the school board, i.e. John 'Hoppy' Hopkins, to make this a regular arrangement. Their return two weeks later inaugurated a weekly residency which would run to the end of November. By then, Floyd were the very vanguard of British psychedelia. In the interim, they made their first, fifteen-minute recording of 'Interstellar Overdrive', the paradigm of their psychedelic explorations, which would provide the soundtrack to a short, underground film, *San Francisco* (though it is unclear whether this recording was originally intended for such a purpose).

Meanwhile, the Floyd had caught an early Cream live perform- ance (or three), presumably at Jenner's instigation. Seeing their blunderbuss approach to the blues probably convinced the Cambridge combo that they would be on a road to nowhere if they attempted something similar. They also learnt something else, the virtues of volume, from the loudest band around (when they played Manchester University at this time, Cream were so loud they cracked the ceiling). For drummer Nick Mason, it was a necessary palliative, prompting him to pick up the sticks again, and forsake his studies: 'Listening to Cream, and The Who . . . was what turned me on to being in a band again.' Floyd's bassist was equally bowled over:

> **Roger Waters:** Cream had been such a turn-on when I saw them . . . The curtains parted and there was a big bank of Marshall gear and it was [an] all-enveloping, loud, powerful bluesy experience. [1987]

The formation of Cream also marked a turning point for the purist strain of English r&b, which up until now had seen itself as more jazz than pop. Here was a band who, though dedicated to playing heavier, louder and longer than anyone previously, applied a psyche- delic slant to their studio sound, courtesy of the songs Jack Bruce was writing with poet Pete Brown. The pedigree of all three musi- cians, who had been dues-paying in the Graham Bond Organisation, John Mayall's Bluesbreakers and Manfred Mann [!], ensured there was a great deal of interest in the outfit from the off, the 11 June issue of *Melody Maker* announcing the fact that Bruce, Ginger Baker and Eric Clapton had joined forces.

Cream's live debut, though, did not come until the end of July, when they headlined the closing night of the Windsor Jazz & Blues Festival. The festival, an annual event at the time, was a perfect place to introduce the original powerhouse trio, who played a barn-storming set to an appreciative crowd. Yet as long as they continued to target blues aficionados, they were never going to be the bridge from pop to something more progressive.

If anyone stole the show at Windsor, it had been a band slotted in as a last-minute substitution on Saturday evening's bill. The headliners, The Who, felt so challenged by these Brummie inter-lopers, who called themselves The Move, that they had managers Lambert and Stamp throw smoke bombs on the stage, while 'Pete smashed his guitar and pushed amplifiers over, Keith scattered his kit, and Roger threw microphones and kicked in the footlights'. Or maybe it was just your average Who finale. Either way, the crowd soon joined in, high on England's World Cup soccer victory that afternoon. By then, The Move had already made converts in the crowd:

Will Birch: I'd seen The Who and The Action plenty of times. They were probably the best two white groups. But The Move were just completely something else. July 30, 1966 was the day England won the World Cup, but the greatest thing for me that day was seeing The Move for the first time at the Windsor Jazz & Blues Festival. The Sunday night was Cream, Georgie Fame and The Action; but the Saturday night, the headliner was The Who and second on the bill was The Yardbirds. But they didn't play; and The Move were announced as the replacement. I'd read about The Move in The Raver column in *Melody Maker*. They were like a hip Cliff Richard & the Shadows – singer, three guitars and drums. Looking back now, I can see that they were five quite straight blokes. They were just growing their hair out. Summer of '66 was the greatest time – it was betwixt Mod and what became Flower Power. It was satin shirts, crushed velvet. It was also the period of the military jacket – you'd go up to Portobello [Road] and went home and [your] Dad, who was in the war, went mad, 'You can't do that!' These five guys came out and they all looked about nineteen, skinny and moody-looking, particu-larly [Ace] Kefford and [Trevor] Burton, [who] looked the fucking

business. And their repertoire was absolutely astonishing – this was
the period where soul imports had a lot of cachet. No-one else was
playing this stuff! They had the look, they had the repertoire, and
they had the moves down – four-part harmony across the front-line.
They would take it in turns to do the lead vocal and they'd segue
the first four numbers together, so there was no time to think. And
in the middle of the set they did an extended raga instrumental with
Roy Wood on guitar. He sat down cross-legged and he went into this
eight-minute raga thing.

Birch, later of the Kursaal Flyers and The Records, felt he had
witnessed the band who could take Britbeat to a higher plane. The
following Thursday he went to see them again, at their weekly residency at the Marquee. In such a compact environment, he couldn't
help but be bowled over again by what he calls 'this constant movement all the time [from the] four frontmen. Ace Kefford used to
do this trick with the bass where he'd play it [upright], and he'd
switch it over and play it upside down'.

Also there that night was Harvard-educated Elektra A&R
man Joe Boyd, who seems to have taken over where Stollman
had left off. In fact, Joe Boyd had already taken AMM into the
studio, having caught them at one of Stollman's last gigs, and
agreed to make a cheap and cheerful record, with no expectation that it would sell. And so it proved, *AMMusic* becoming an
almost instant collector's item. Boyd, though, was absolutely
convinced that The Move would make it big, and like Birch
believed he had stumbled on probably the most inventive live
band in England:

Joe Boyd: In August '66 I started going down every Thursday night
to the Marquee to see The Move . . . They were Brummies who were
getting psychedelic-ed on beer and doing a very good job of it as
well. What they were doing was in fact something that was never
properly recorded but was very much in the same line as The Pink
Floyd, and in a way rather more advanced. It was cod-psychedelic,

but very, very good. Long extended solos, feedback, all that stuff, and they were doing it right at the beginning, when [few] people were doing it. [DITL]

When Boyd took two key components in Elektra's leading electric blues band – Paul Butterfield and Mike Bloomfield – down to the Marquee, they were equally astonished by what they saw. The Paul Butterfield Blues Band were already stretching out 'East/West' to epic proportions, but The Move were doing something quite different, yet equally elastic, placing everything in pop to date in one ultra-eclectic sonic blender. Their favourite current influence, as Roy Wood's eight-minute raga-rock instrumental at Windsor perhaps indicated, was the 5D-era Byrds, which they effortlessly combined with a penchant for Beach Boys harmonies and long, feedback-strewn solos, à la The Who.

Indeed, when Joe Boyd finally convinced the band to play London's home of psychedelia, the UFO Club (pronounced U-Fo), the following June, their second set consisted of a single song, an album-length rendition of 'Eight Miles High'. Wood and co. were attempting to concoct, not entirely consciously, this heady brew from what they *imagined* to be West-Coast psychedelia aligned with a strong, *British* strain of pop. In this sense, at this time, they had the city to themselves.

But The Pink Floyd's Syd Barrett had also been immersing himself in West Coast progressive pop. His favourite two albums that summer were The Byrds' 5D and Love's lyrical debut long-player – though he also told *Melody Maker* the following April that he had 'drawn quite a bit' from The Fugs and The Mothers of Invention. This blend came out tasting very different from The Move's.

Peter Jenner: We thought we were doing what they were doing in New York and California. But in fact very few of us had been to America; people didn't just hop on planes then. Import records were expensive and hard to find, and there was no Rock press really, so

> the information was incredibly filtered and vague. There were just
> sort of rumours about things like The Velvet Underground and The
> Jefferson Airplane.

Both would-be songwriters also spent much of that glorious summer
writing a set of original songs, as their managers encouraged each
to find a sound of their own. In Roy Wood's case, he had been
scribbling out song ideas for some time prior to Tony Secunda
taking the band under his wing and out of Birmingham, having
grown thoroughly 'fed up with being a human jukebox to get work'.
Unfortunately, though Secunda had a vision of sorts, he was not
thinking of The Move as anything other than pop, which in the
end would prove his (and their) undoing.

For Barrett, it was a summer of crystalline inspiration. By the
time of Floyd's second show at the London Free School on 14
October, the night before their Roundhouse debut, their set was
almost entirely Barrett originals, with 'Louie Louie' and Bo Diddley's
'I Can Tell' the only obligatory throwbacks. Even these, NME
reviewer Nick Jones suggested, could be dispensed with, as 'psychedelic versions of "Louie Louie" won't come off. But if they can
incorporate their electronic prowess with some melodic and lyrical
songs . . . they could well score in the near future'.

In fact, those 'melodic, lyrical' songs were already in place, in
a set almost equally divided between rambling excuses to extemporise, assigned titles like 'Gimme A Break', 'Stoned Alone',
'Interstellar Overdrive' and 'Flapdoodle Dealing'; and an entirely
new type of pop song, Syd displaying an almost fey English whimsy
with 'The Gnome', 'Matilda Mother' and 'Let's Roll Another One'
(later sanitised into 'Candy & A Currant Bun'). All they required
was a better setting.

At their manager's behest Floyd even had a name for this schizophrenic amalgam of pop styles, adopting the *mot juste* 'psychedelia'
as an ideal description for what they were trying to do. It came
just in time for them to become the favoured sons of an energised
underground: in the form of, first, the *International Times*, formed

the same month they began their Free School residency; and then, in December, as the UFO club's house band.

Actually the new-born *International Times* seemed uncertain at the outset whether Floyd were the real thing. It described a Floyd gig in issue one as both a 'pop dance' and 'psychedelia'; as 'psychedelic pop' in issue two; as a 'sound + light workshop' in number three. Finally, they were just 'the fabulous psychedelic Pink Floyd' in issue four. The following issue the paper got as far as reviewing the band, Norman Evans describing 'their work [as] largely improvisation ... lead guitarist Syd Barrett shoulder[ing] most of the burden providing continuity and attack in the improvised parts ... [with] a huge range of sounds ... from throttled shrieks to mellow feedback roars'.

Thankfully, 'Psychedelia' was new enough to resist any clear definition, at least in a pop context. Like folk-rock, the previous summer's phenomenon, it was entirely open to interpretation. No-one was even sure what qualified as West Coast psychedelia, though the term had become ubiquitous there. Indeed, by October it was common enough for Brian Wilson to predict that, 'Psychedelic music will cover the face of the world and colour the whole popular-music scene. Anybody happening is psychedelic.' So, not the most rigid of definitions!

The same week Wilson's pronouncement appeared in *Go!* there was a two-page spread in *Melody Maker*, entitled 'Psychedelic: The New In-Word', in which Graham Nash helpfully explained that psychedelia was 'trying to create an LSD session without the use of drugs', thus paraphrasing Frank Zappa's own definition of a freak out: '[Trying to] get the same effect as from taking acid, but without any of the bad stuff.' When *Melody Maker* proceeded to categorise The Monkees, Left Banke and The Association as exemplars of psychedelic pop, it was clear that the term, and its parameters, was very much up for grabs.

Even if no-one was admitting it, the connection between The Byrds, The Fugs and the Floyd was a simple one – and it came in tablet form. Both artists and audiences were out of their minds most of the time, hence the rambling improvisations from the former and benign acceptance by the latter. But even the fledgling Floyd knew to be wary of making the connection overt in the same month that lysergic acid diethylamide was made illegal for the first time.

When Floyd's agent, Andrew King, was questioned by the *Sunday Times* after the fabled *IT* launch bash at the Roundhouse, he batted the word right back at the journalist, 'We don't call ourselves psychedelic. But we don't deny it. We don't confirm it either. People who want to make up slogans can do it.' Likewise, when a university paper wanted a soundbite from the band before a show the following February they got, 'Our music, like drug taking, is a total experience. But we make no claim to be a reconstruction of one's feelings under acid.' By April 1967, they were already distancing themselves from all things psychedelic, even creating a spoof ad which invited people to a 'Freak Out-Schmeak Out', where they could 'turn up, shell out, get lost'. Somewhat prophetically, they also billed their brand of music as 'schizophrenic psychedelic pop'.

Barrett had already begun to acquire a messianic fervour about what (he thought) they were doing. Whatever they proclaimed to the press, the new Pink Floyd sound, and the songs he was now penning, were entirely reflections from an acid-induced aesthetic. As Jenner later commented, 'Syd got very enthusiastic about acid, and got into the religious aspect of it.' His partner, King, suggests that he held a quite specific belief 'in some sort of gnostic, poetic revolution that was [now] blowing through his body, and through the world'. For now, though, Syd was still more likely to indulge in a little reefer madness than risk too many acid dreams:

Peter Jenner: [The scene] wasn't too psychedelic [in 1966]. Smoking dope [yes], but not much acid. We'd read about it, but there wasn't much around. And the only people [in Floyd] who smoked, in any considerable sense, were me and Syd. Roger Waters was convinced at that time that I was a drug dealer. [DITL]

If the Floyd belonged to a disconnected pop underground before-
hand, everything changed with the *IT* bash at the Roundhouse,
the night after their second Free School show. On 15 October,
according to the posters pasted up around north London, there
would be the party to end all parties, an 'All Night Rave', revellers
being asked to 'bring your own poison, bring flowers and gass (*sic*)
filled balloons'. Floyd were second on the bill to another band
formed a stoned throw from London, The Soft Machine.

Another band of young musicians with a desire to extemporise within a pop context, The Soft Machine were a weird and
(fleetingly) wonderful amalgam of jazz aficionados from Canterbury,
a pot-smoking poet/muso and a wannabe songwriter whose songs
were off-kilter enough to be quirky, but melodic enough to be pop.
The poet and the popster, Daevid Allen and Kevin Ayers, were
old friends by the time Ayers had turned up in Majorca the previous
year to rescue Allen from the hospitable clutches of muse-poet
Robert Graves:

> **Daevid Allen:** Kevin Ayers turned up [in Deya] with a bunch of Beatles
> records and 'Still I'm Sad' by The Yardbirds. We did an acid-trip and
> I thought, 'Bugger it, maybe I can make a living out of what I was
> doing before and call it pop.'

As soon as The Soft Machine ventured beyond their Canterbury
cabal the following spring, they found themselves caught in the
same weird time-warp as contemporaries like Floyd and The Move,
expected to entertain the masses with their pop sensibilities and
even the odd cover of some pop or soul staple while changing the
parameters of the form. Only with the launch of *IT* and, shortly
afterwards, its sister club, UFO, would The Soft Machine find the
audience they had sought all along:

> **Robert Wyatt [drummer]:** Our management had immediately put us
> on the road on a circuit where you had to play for dance audiences.
> We weren't very good at that . . . [At UFO] the audiences weren't

demanding in the same way. They were sitting about, most of them were asleep as far as I could see. The very things that were our faults on the regular circuit – that of all the bands playing 'Midnight Hour' or 'Knock On Wood' on any particular evening we would play it worst, if we played it at all – became bonuses [there]. [DITL]

That 'accepting' audience had first made its presence known at Chalk Farm of a mid-October evening, hoping that the promised 'All Night Rave' would offer sex, drugs and, as an afterthought, maybe some rock & roll. They were sadly disappointed when it came to sex, LSD was too precious a commodity for anyone to indulge in a mass kool-aid acid test, and as for rock & roll, neither The Soft Machine nor The Pink Floyd seemed greatly inclined to rock out.

Because both bands loved to improvise, they were at least as likely to lose their way as unlock the doors of perception. Floyd keyboardist Rick Wright was speaking for both parties the following month when he suggested, 'We play far more like a jazz group than anything else because . . . to produce the right sound we have to think musically together. Most of our act is spontaneous and un-rehearsed. It just comes when we are on stage. It does sometimes get to a point where it is a wow. That is when it works, which is not always.'

Though the Roundhouse show was a hit-and-miss affair for both bands, it was an event of immense significance, a coming-out party for the London underground. And because they had the better songs, the greater stage-presence and a psuitably psychedelic light show, the Floyd couldn't help but be noticed by anyone who stopped looking for stars in the audience long enough to notice the one onstage. Barrett was now assuredly the star of the show, something Cream's new lyricist, Pete Brown, readily recognised: 'Whether it was drug-driven or not . . . Syd always seemed on a high level of inspiration, which was beyond what the rhythm section could do, to be brutally honest.'

Also taking it all in that night, dressed as a sheik (of Araby?), was Paul McCartney, there in the company of Marianne Faithfull (who may or may not have been dressed as a nun). He seems to have been quite taken with the Floyd, and with The Soft Machine too; and through the early months of 1967, whilst he crafted his own response to the ever-shifting parameters of pop, would be seen regularly down the 'U-Fo', watching both bands go from strength to length.

> **Miles:** I remember at UFO once, [Paul] and I sat down for a whole set on the floor, and it was an interminable Soft Machine set, but he was very keen on hearing what was going on – particularly the organ stuff. They were very innovative, actually.

The *IT* launch attracted an enormous amount of media coverage – despite the Floyd's light show fusing the entire electrical supply at one juncture, highlighting the precarious nature of a venture organised on a shoestring and a prayer – in part because the likes of McCartney, Faithfull and Italian film director Antonioni (in London to film *Blow-Up*) wanted to be seen on the scene. As *IT* co-founder Jim Haynes has said, 'It launched the paper, and launched the Roundhouse as a space.'

Whether it was the most significant show in town that month, seen solely from a pop perspective, is debatable. Many would put it second to a show at the London Polytechnic on the first, when Cream became a four-piece for one night only. And what a four-piece! As Jack Bruce recalls, 'I was having a drink in the pub opposite, and Jimi [Hendrix] came up to me. He obviously knew we were playing that night. We'd all heard of him through Linda Keith, who was one of Eric's girlfriends. She'd seen Jimi in New York and had told Chas Chandler about him. Anyway, he came up to me and asked if he could sit in.' And, as Clapton readily admits, 'He just stole the show!'

In the insular world of London's pop peerage, the news of Hendrix's prowess spread quickly, and he had not even begun playing with the English rhythm section Chandler had found for him. By the end of November, The Jimi Hendrix Experience was ready to play for The Beatles, the Stones, The Hollies and The Who, as part of an invited audience at the Bag o' Nails. That night he also described his kind of sound for *Record Mirror*'s Peter Jones: 'If it must have a tag, I'd like it to be called "Free Feeling". It's a mixture of rock, freak-out, blues, and rave music.' He clearly shared the same sense of ambition as Cream and The Who, whom he now knew, as well as the Floyd and The Move, whom he didn't.

In the limited time he'd been given to make his mark, Hendrix could hardly be expected to keep tabs on everyone looking to mix rock, 'freak-out' and 'rave'. The following November he would find himself on the road with Syd Barrett's Pink Floyd and The Move, but for now he was expected to wow France and Germany. Meanwhile, The Move were setting Soho alight – almost literally. As their swansong to the Marquee they debuted their new single, a new light show, and a belated tribute to Guy Fawkes:

> **Will Birch:** The last time I saw them was in November '66. You were just starting to hear about mixed media . . . When we got there, they had a projector in the middle of the room and they were showing Biff! Bang! Pow! [like the *Batman* TV show] at the back of the stage, with liquid lights. Their set was pretty much the same, but at the end of the [second] set they let off rockets. The roadies were putting these rockets in bottles, leaning up against these AC-30s. [Then] they trashed the gear. When we exited the Marquee there were three fire engines in Wardour Street. It was so fucking exciting . . . [but] they got banned from the club.

The explosive gesture was intended to announce their transition from club act to pop stars, knowing their debut single 'Night of Fear' was in the can, awaiting its December Deram release. But it also removed the one reliable gig from their London itinerary. They need not have worried. Within the month, they were on the bill for a New Year's Eve extravaganza at London's newest Rock venue, the capacious Roundhouse. The show itself was billed as 'Psychedelicamania', and The Move again found themselves

warming up the crowd for The Who. This time they were determined to make any upstaging that little bit harder, and after another
incendiary set, they proceeded to demolish a Cadillac as part of
their finale. The Townshend who spoke to IT a couple of months
later about the performer-as-exhibitionist surely appreciated the
gesture:

> **Pete Townshend:** It's THE exhibitionist's delight, to do something really
> big in front of people. OK, they know you're going to go out there
> and sing and play, so that becomes nothing . . . Then you want more.
> You want people to tear their hair out when you appear; and when
> they don't, you feel you've got to extend your end a bit, you've really
> got to make them spew up. [1967]

However, PT was less impressed by the Roundhouse sound system,
which 'crapped out' again (and again), along with the lighting rig,
during The Who's set, leading to a particularly adrenalin-fuelled
auto-destruction finale from the fuming foursome. Then it was time
for the Floyd, who were again in their element, but were also
exhausted from hurtling down the A11 immediately after playing
another New Year's Eve party, at the Cambridge Technical College,
earlier in the evening. They compensated by playing at a deafening
volume, led by a Barrett who seemed dangerously close to the edge.
For Townshend, it was his first sight of Syd and he was both amazed
and appalled:

> **Pete Townshend:** I thought what Syd was doing was very interesting
> . . . although you could never quite hear what he was up to, because
> he used two or three different echo units in a row . . . But if Syd was
> innovative at anything, it was at getting completely and totally out of
> it. He was the first person I had seen who was totally 'gone' on stage.

Evidently, when Barrett saw the show advertised as a 'Double Giant
Freak-Out Ball', he had taken the organisers at their word. When
they promised 'psychedelic psounds from The Mothers of Invention,

the Fugs . . . [and] the Radiophonic Workshop', he wanted to ensure that the audience knew who was *really* 'happening man!', even those who had largely come to 'watch the pretty lights'. Floyd had come a long way from that first Spontaneous Happening, even if they were still unsure about the best way to capture their sound (and fury) on tape. That challenge remained, not just for them, for all the bands who had made their mark in the London clubs that year, but had yet to do it on black vinyl, where it mattered most.

STILL SINGLE-MINDED

HAVE YOU SEEN YOUR MOTHER, BABY, STANDING IN THE SHADOW?

The Beatles, man, they were where it was all at. When they dropped out altogether, things changed, because . . . they were the group who really kept the scene going. They were holding it up. As soon as The Beatles begin to relax their grip, the bottom starts falling out. –

Jimi Hendrix, *Melody Maker*, 28/1/67

There are just a few groups that are progressing the way we've tried to, [but] all the rest are going to be left behind. The Cream, us, The Who are all moving in one direction. So's Jimi Hendrix. –

Roy Wood to Alan Freeman, spring 1967

The inferno of English pop, fired up in 1962 and rising steadily through 1966, reached meltdown in the winter of 1967 – specifically the first week of January, when the charts had perhaps the highest density of pop staples and greatest diversity of musical styles it would ever know. 'Good Vibrations' was finally on its way out of the Top Twenty, after seven weeks in the Top Ten (two at number one); as were The Four Tops, whose smoulderin' smooch-along 'Reach Out I'll Be There' almost got there. The former's place would be taken the following week by The Monkees, at the top of their game, and still generating headlines like 'Monkees Top Beatle Record!' (*KYA Beat* 28/1/67) in the US press. Their moment in the sun would culminate in the impossibly catchy 'I'm A Believer', number one for four weeks through late January/early February.

But it was the British brands of pop which seemed unable to stop effortlessly churning out memorable single after memorable single. Even when there was a shortfall of releases, or quality, from a previous worthy – like the Stones – there always seemed to be someone ready to claim their berth. That first week of '67, The Who, The Kinks and The Small Faces all sat snugly in the Top Ten with their latest contributions to the Britpop canon of classics. Coming up on the inside track were The Troggs, whose own brand of primitivism had given them three 'top-two' singles the previous year. They now went into power-ballad mode for their fourth 45, 'Any Way That You Want Me'. And in an era that easily accommodated one-off classic 45s, The Easybeats expressed the mindset of every young workaday wannabe with 'Friday On My Mind'.

Yet it was outside the rarefied air of the Top Twenty that real change was afoot. That very week saw three bands of stature make their debuts in the lower regions of chartdom. All would have some say in pop (and Rock)'s future course. The singles were as follows: 'I Feel Free' (Cream), 'Night of Fear' (The Move) and 'Hey Joe' (The Jimi Hendrix Experience), entering at 25, 32 and 41 respectively.

All three had something else in common. Each had recorded their first single at their manager's behest, who used this evidence of a pop sensibility to secure a record deal *after the fact* (in Cream's case, that single was 'Wrapping Paper', which almost did the deed). It was a technique pioneered by the Stones' Svengali, Andrew Loog Oldham (at Phil Spector's prompting); before being adopted by the likes of Chas Chandler, Tony Secunda and Robert Stigwood on behalf of Jimi Hendrix, The Move and Cream.

And in the month these three brightly lit beacons all charted, Peter Jenner's Pink Floyd, who would emulate them next time around, recorded 'Arnold Layne' at Sound Techniques in Chelsea with American producer Joe Boyd, using it to convince EMI to take a punt on the pink ones. Meanwhile, The Beatles put the finishing touches to their first non-album single in six long months. 'Strawberry Fields Forever b/w Penny Lane' had taken almost as long to record as 'Good Vibrations', the Beach Boys single it was intended to supersede at the top.

A general aura of experimentation was abroad, and British labels proved surprisingly amenable to band managers who told them what might sell. Largely, this was because the labels didn't have a clue themselves – events were moving too fast for their small bear brains. But most had the wit to recognise this deficiency, and a very real fear of being 'the next Dick Rowe', head of A&R at Decca.[1] As Joe Boyd observes in his own memoir of these times, '*No-one* wanted to be Dick Rowe . . . who turned down The Beatles. If a band was halfway decent, they quickly got signed.'

This was particularly the case if they had a well-dressed, fast-talking, speed-driven manager to plead their case – and provide proof on acetate. For The Move, this was Tony Secunda, who even told the band to tweak the lyrics of their debut 45, 'Night of Fear'. According to Ace Kefford, songwriter Roy Wood had 'written, "Just about to flip your mind . . ." for me to sing, but [Secunda], who'd heard about the drug scene in America, got me to sing "trip your mind"'.

Secunda's strategy was simple – create controversy, generate a stir, stir some more. Main Move singer Carl Wayne gave the game away when interviewed by NME the week after 'Night of Fear' charted; telling the journo, 'I'm instructed to say it is all about LSD, but to tell you the truth, I haven't a bloody clue what it's all about.'

It certainly wasn't about acid, or at least not from any first-hand experience on Wood's part. Rather, as Kefford subsequently suggested, 'All his songs seemed to be about going mad, [or] being a bit bonkers.' Wood's songs 'about going mad' included the punchy b-side 'Disturbance', which the songwriter wanted to be the a-side as he felt it 'was probably more representative of the band', but found his wishes blithely ignored by the all-seeing Secunda. Though Wood was probably right, the force was with them and 'Night of Fear b/w Disturbance' peaked at number two.

If The Move for now all agreed that they were a pop band, Cream were considerably more conflicted. Their first single, 'Wrapping Paper', bore more resemblance to the last record Jack Bruce had played on,

Manfred Mann's 'Pretty Flamingo', than anything the trio were playing at paint-stripping volume in rinky-dink clubs throughout the last five months of '66. For Bruce (and co-author, Pete Brown) integrity came second to interesting:

> **Jack Bruce:** When we started out . . . the big challenge . . . was to write singles and to use that form. I mean, two minutes and fifty seconds to get in everything you wanted to say, to make it musically interesting and also commercial. The people that showed the way were The Beatles. We all wanted to emulate that.

> **Pete Brown:** For some reason, we got it into our heads . . . that we had to write pop songs in order to be a success. We sat and wrote down all these ideas that were *like* pop songs. But they were one step removed from the reality of pop songs, in the sense that they were really naive, but also very hip . . . ['Wrapping Paper'] is about two people who can only meet in a picture on the wall in an old house by the sea . . . The last pop thing we wrote was 'I Feel Free', which was a kind of happy accident as far as the lyrics were concerned.

But such was the dichotomy between their single output – where Bruce-as-songwriter held sway – and their live act, where Baker and Clapton generally got their way, that although they evidently *could* play 'Wrapping Paper' and 'I Feel Free', as live radio-session recordings demonstrate, none of the (three) early extant tapes of Cream gigs feature either song. Instead, the blues run the show. In fact, by the time they recorded 'I Feel Free' in October 1966, it was already evident that Bruce and lyricist Pete Brown, winning the battle when it came to putting out 'musically interesting' singles, were losing the actual war to a belligerent Baker.

After 'I Feel Free', Cream would only fleetingly return to such economy of expression in their subsequent studio work, preferring to put an increasing distance between their performing selves and such expressions of brevity and wit. At least 'I Feel Free' was a masterfully infectious requiem to a time when Cream still thought they 'had to write pop songs in order to be a success'.

It was a notion that another powerhouse trio, The Jimi Hendrix Experience – being new to the ways of this planet – went to greater pains to investigate. Under Chas Chandler's astute tutorship, and beginning with the quasi-traditional 'Hey Joe', recorded on the day The Beatles *commenced* the long-haul across 'Strawberry Fields', the Experience easily laid down both album cuts and a series of potential singles, culminating in early February 1967 with Hendrix unveiling two potential a-sides at a single session, 'Purple Haze' and 'The Wind Cries Mary'. Both exercises in esoteric economy were issued in the first five months of '67, each breaching the Top Ten.

If 'Hey Joe' had already been recorded by the likes of Love, The Leaves and The Byrds, it was Hendrix who imbued it with a sufficient sense of drama to kiss the sky; thus announcing his presence to those for whom the Bag o' Nails, Blaises and the Flamingo were not regular pit-stops on the nightclub circuit. However, it was 'Purple Haze', issued less than three months later, which bore the true stamp of originality – as well as the unmistakable watermark of an acid experience (or two). Or as *NME*'s reviewer put it, 'Climbing to freakish heights, it contains all the stunning Hendrix characteristics . . . but [it's] difficult to assess its commerciality'. The Soft Machine's guitarist shared the weekly's concern:

> **Daevid Allen:** I heard 'Purple Haze' for the first time down [the Speakeasy]. It sounded like classical music to me . . . I couldn't see it being in the charts. I mean, how would the charts accommodate something like this?

Neither Allen nor *NME* need have been so concerned. 'Purple Haze' reached number three, proving it wasn't just the labels that were becoming open to new experiences, and that the limitations of a seven-inch single did not hinder free expression. Rather the reverse.

Though Cream quickly dropped out of the reckoning, no follow-up single even being recorded until May, the Experience found itself competing second time around with The Move, whose 'I Can Hear The Grass Grow' appeared just a fortnight after Hendrix's 'Haze'; and The Pink Floyd, whose 'Arnold Layne' rolled off presses the week before. 'Twas another bumper crop.

If the sound of 'Purple Haze' stretched the boundaries of pop, both the sound *and* subject matter of 'Arnold Layne' might have raised eyebrows a year earlier. The NME broke it gently to their readers, suggesting that the song was 'about a guy who got himself put inside because he got screwed up while learning of the birds and the bees'. Syd the scribe was not so coy, informing *Melody Maker*, 'Arnold Layne just happens to dig dressing up in women's clothing. A lot of people do – so let's face up to reality.' Cream's lyricist was stunned by Syd's new song:

> **Pete Brown:** 'Arnold Layne' was probably the first-ever pop hit that dealt in an English accent with English cultural obsessions and English fetishes. There had never been anything quite like it; everybody had been behaving like Americans.

Actually, there had been some precedent for songs about cross-dressing, including at least two Top Ten 45s the previous year. Both Townshend's 'I'm A Boy' and Ray Davies's 'Dedicated Follower of Fashion' had flirted with this particular fetish, even if neither character had resorted to nicking knickers off washing-lines, like Arnold (allegedly). Though the Pink Floyd song ends with Arnold in the dock, the Floyd claimed that the 'real' Arnold – or the Cambridge culprit on whom he was based – was never caught. Perhaps the song reflected one of Barrett's own nightmares, concerning itself with possible consequences of his own surreptitious activities, cleverly disguised as a piece of Anglo-whimsy.

Surprisingly, no-one ever seems to have suggested that the song might be autobiographical, despite Barrett's staunch defence of those who 'dig dressing up in women's clothing' at the time, his well-documented use of mascara, his effete androgyny (evident in *every* photo of the time) and Peter Jenner's comment about how Syd regularly 'had this permanent, which cost twenty quid at the time, and he looked like a beautiful woman'. If, as is now commonly accepted, Syd was schizophrenic, his identity issues could well have been tied up with gender.

Whatever the case, the single met with surprising favour from both a meritocratic pop audience and the notoriously elitist London underground, even if the latter hardly thought it representative of 'real' psychedelia. As John Hopkins wrote in his *IT* article, 'The Pink Floyd vs. Psychedelia', '[Pink Floyd]'s [first] record is worth hearing, if only to see how a group playing mainly instrumentals and relying on a light show for in-person attraction can make a single with sales potential.'

When 'Arnold Layne' came out in March, Kevin Ayers, song-writer in Floyd's sister UFO band, The Soft Machine, had just put out his own piece of Anglo-whimsy, 'Love Makes Sweet Music'. He clearly remembers thinking, 'Fuck, that's so good,' making his own effort passé by comparison. The Cambridge quartet, and producer Joe Boyd, had succeeded in condensing one of their extended concert work-outs and still retaining its quintessence:

> **Joe Boyd:** There was a feeling in the industry in general, and in Britain in particular ... that long, extended tracks were kind of an indulgence and that they disqualified you from getting played on the radio. The Pink Floyd used to do a version of 'Arnold Layne' that went on for ten minutes, but when we recorded it, we did a three-minute version.

Floyd's manager made it clear that the single-length structure achieved on 'Arnold Layne' was a deliberate ploy aimed at commercial success. In conversation on Canadian radio the month before Arnold's 'outing', Jenner admitted, 'If you had the sort of sound they're making in the clubs coming over the radio while you were doing the washing up, you'd probably scream! I suspect that the records will have to be much more audio, written for a different situation . . . Listening to a gramophone in your home or on the radio is very different from going into a club or watching a stage show. They . . . require a different approach.'

In this way Floyd were emulating – independently – their 'real' rivals at this juncture, The Move, whose 'I Can Hear The Grass Grow' was another single which came with knicker elastic – accommodating any size it might take on stage, in 45 form it stayed a svelte seven inches of psych-pop. If The Move and the Floyd were currently contesting the very soul of psych-pop, parts of the Floyd were already getting a little high and mighty:

> **Carl Wayne:** When we worked at BBC Manchester, The Floyd went on and played all this freaky stuff, and had oil lights and all those weirdo things they were into. The Move came on and set the place on fire, so they closed the studios. The producer, after the problem had been sorted out, said, 'Well lads, I want you all to go on together and finish the show.' Roger Waters said, 'We won't go on with them! They don't play music!'

Whatever higher plane Waters thought Floyd existed on, both Wood and Barrett were immersing themselves in a world straight out of Victorian children's literature, shot through a psychedelic lens. In Wood's case, the innocence was quite real. As Move frontman Carl Wayne told *Shindig*, 'Roy never took drugs . . . What he did, though, was write songs that people thought were related to drugs. [If you] think about them, they were fairy stories for kids . . . [Yet] they looked for meaning, thinking it was deep.' In fact, the idea behind 'I Can Hear The Grass Grow' dated back to Wood's own school days:

> **Roy Wood:** Towards the end of my school life, I had an idea for writing a book which was of fairy stories for adults and it had quite a lot of weird stuff that I was going to put in. Obviously in those days I hadn't a clue about how to go about getting it published or even who to contact. So I ended up using a lot of that material in the

songs . . . I didn't particularly write ['I Can Hear The Grass Grow']
with psychedelia in mind. I thought more of some sorta mad person.

For Barrett – just like the Lennon of 'Strawberry Fields' – it seemed
like some childhood trauma underlined his inner explorations.
Indeed, Jenner believes 'it all became disturbed when Syd's father
died. That was the last time Syd probably felt really happy, and so
he was always looking back to childhood.' If so, he shared a kinship
with Lennon, and not just because 'he utilised fairytale technique,
surrealistic juxtaposition of psychedelic detail and plain fact, childhood experience and adult confusion', as Kris DiLorenzo puts it in
his 1978 essay on Barrett.

The fact that 'Strawberry Fields' appeared in the shops a matter
of weeks before the psych-pop singles of the Floyd and The Move
has led some foolhardy folk to suggest direct inspiration. Ian
MacDonald expressed the opinion that 'Strawberry Fields' 'effectively inaugurated the English pop-pastoral mood explored in the
late Sixties by groups like Pink Floyd, Traffic, Family and Fairport
Convention . . . for the true subject of English psychedelia was
neither love nor drugs, but nostalgia for the innocent vision of
the child'. MacDonald overstates the case, bestowing undue credit
on The Beatles, as he seeks to eulogise *their* contribution to *his*
golden age – the sixties. Both Barrett and Wood had already hit
upon their 'pop-pastoral' vision, independent of Lennon, and probably *previous* to him (just as Ray Davies's more 'adult', yet equally
pastoral, concerns began to dominate his songwriting from early
1966).

What should not be doubted was the cumulative effect of all
these records on pop itself – even if 'Strawberry Fields Forever b/w
Penny Lane' was failing to fully ignite the charts. Released in mid-
February, The Beatles' double a-side met a mixed response from
the English music papers, NME's Derek Johnson reflecting a
consensus of sorts that this 'most unusual and way-out single' may
not enhance their commercial standing, for all its obvious innovation 'in lyrical content and scoring'. When it stalled at number

two, breaking a run of twelve consecutive number ones – held at bay by the wretched 'Release Me' – the pop papers became prophets of doom. Perhaps, as Nik Cohn suggests, the shift in pop's audience was such that even The Beatles were unable to bridge the divide:

> While the monster ballad was taking over, pop itself was splitting into two distinct approaches . . . On one side, there were the straight noise-machines, angled at a mass teen public and at sub-teens, ages six to twelve . . . On the other side, there were specialists: soul bands, blues bands, folk singers, freaks and just people who wanted to make good music. In the middle of this, there was a small avant garde, musical experimenters. Most of them, they took their bearings from The Beatles and they were hip to everything that came out of America . . . Between them, they formed something approaching an Underground . . . trying to make pop expand and progress.

The trick, for those bands who remained single-minded, was to strike the right balance between pop and progress. Not so easy. At the underground end of the spectrum, The Soft Machine's 'Love Makes Sweet Music', released at the end of February, was one such curio, on which, as guitarist Allen admits, 'you could hear all the peer pressures of the time'. What it was not was a hit. At the other end of the rainbow, The Hollies followed up the irrepressible pop confection of 'Carrie Anne', a top-three single that June, with their most progressive incantation to date, 'King Midas In Reverse'. It barely scraped into the Top Twenty.

Graham Nash: Pop was very different from the psychedelia and folk of the era – [all] three [were] very distinctive forms of music. And [yet] everybody [was] trying to use little bits of everybody else's stuff – 'King Midas In Reverse' was a pretty psychedelic record [for us].

If there was one band who were certainly trying on every hat – psychedelia, English whimsy, wall of sound, raga-rock – it was the

Stones, whose sureness of touch disappeared in the aftermath of 'Have You Seen Your Mother, Baby?' As 1967 dawned, they were ready to try a less frenetic, not so Chess-derived sound. Meanwhile, the subject matter of their songs was starting to seem decidedly out of time. The b-side to their January single, 'Ruby Tuesday', was another 'Lady Jane', given a name-change, and as such familiar fare to every fan out there. Ditto 'Back Street Girl', 'She Smiled Sweetly', 'Cool Calm & Collected' and 'Miss Amanda Jones' on the album *Between the Buttons*, scheduled to appear the week after 'Let's Spend The Night Together b/w Ruby Tuesday'. The sharp sureness had gone from their material, just as The Beatles' break from recording activities appeared to have left the way clear.

If the Stones were content to portray women the same ol' way, their own lives were increasingly shrouded in paranoid recrimination. 'Yesterday's Papers', 'My Obsession', and 'Connection' represented the band lashing out, but at moving targets. When the nightmare Jagger tried to send up on the final song of their fifth album – 'Something Happened To Me Yesterday' – became a reality just three weeks after the LP's appearance, as police raided Richards' Redlands home and took away 'various substances of a suspicious nature', the Stones found themselves out for the count, commercially and creatively. Their (temporary) has-been status was confirmed by the chart returns for both single and album, neither of which had restored the band to the top spot; each stalling at number three and spending little time descending the charts.

Between the Buttons, in particular, represented a galling failure, as neither The Beatles nor Dylan were holding the Stones back this time, just a neo-Nazi musical and a bunch of Monkees. The looming court-action for 'possession' against Jagger, Richards and Jones served to make the band withdraw into itself. After the briefest of spring tours across Europe, they decided to follow The Beatles' lead (for a change), curtailing live performances for the foreseeable. It was a mistake; one that left Jones in particular at a dangerous loose end.

Those looking to insulate themselves from the wider pop constituency in their fashionable London clubs – where they could convince themselves that the world was ready to hear their latest drug-fuelled vision in the key of H – wouldn't have had to venture very far from the West End to find a very different kind of audience; one who not only knew what they wanted to hear, but knew how to express themselves when they didn't get no satisfaction. By removing themselves from the one environment guaranteed to reveal a certain honest immediacy, The Beatles and the Stones were perhaps taking the greatest risk of all. Not that the likes of Pink Floyd and Soft Machine wouldn't have happily traded places at the time. As Roger Waters pointed out when a BBC interviewer started complaining about the volume they played at:

Roger Waters: The main scene with pop music . . . is that you play gigs round ballrooms and dance halls . . . [but] dance halls generally speaking are not very good places to actually listen to the music – [for] most people [who] come along . . . the music . . . [is] just a sort of background noise that they can jig about to. [1967]

Rick Wright's view of provincial audiences was even more condescending: 'In England, they come to pick up scrubbers.' Floyd's solution was simple – but brutal. As Wright told Go! at the time, 'You can't come into a place where we're playing and order a drink and have a chat. You have to concentrate on what we're trying to say.' All four Floyd members made damn sure they played loud enough to make concentration on anything else impractical. The Soft Machine came up against the same barrier of incomprehension but had less audio armoury:

Daevid Allen: In England the expectation was that you would be a pop band and perform chart material. We were pelted with stuff by Move fans at the Cambridge Corn Exchange. There was certainly an uneasy truce a lot of the time.

It was Dylan at the Albert Hall all over again; but this time it was psychedelia that was under threat, and the boppers who were getting verbal with the bands. It seemed like every innovation in sixties rock – at least when it was introduced live – was given not so much the Games For May as the *Rites of Spring* treatment. The one solution, in the short term, was to find a place where pop was the pariah. The UFO Club was just such a place, opening its Tottenham Court Road doors for its first weekly all-nighter on 23 December, 1966, and closing them for the last time on 28 July, 1967. For the first five months, it welcomed only 'underground' bands – no 'Move fans' allowed. That is, until Joe Boyd insisted – and reminded the staff that the club was largely his idea:

> **Joe Boyd:** The majority of the UFO crowd just wanted to get high and laid and listen to great music. They believed in the social and political goals of the movement , but weren't prepared to dig a trench on the front-line to achieve them . . . [But] nothing so symbolised my apostasy in radical eyes as booking The Move . . . I was determined to introduce our audience to my favourite faux psychedelics, [but] when the staff heard about it, they were horrified. [WB]

The Move's May gig at UFO, on the first anniversary of Dylan's Albert Hall aural assault, marked one more parting of the ways. Their appearance, a month after the rather more faux psychedelia of one-hit wonders The Smoke ('My Friend Jack'), suggested the infidels were no longer at the outskirts of town. They had reached the inner sanctum. Whatever the musicians might say, for UFO devotees there was no such thing as a psychedelic band who didn't take psychedelics.

And yet, in Miles's opinion, 'The Move played arguably one of the best sets in their lives . . . [but] still people didn't much like it. They thought the group's overnight conversion to hippiedom was hypocritical, nor did they much like the mohair fans they'd brought with them.' The fact that those private darlings of the underground, The Pink Floyd – who had played on almost every UFO bill between

23 December and 21 April – had spent the previous weekend recording a second single and the final cut to a debut album – both of which were intended to project them into the realms of pop stardom – was lost on these faux Diggers.

Irrespective of any personal feelings, by that May weekend the seemingly beneficent, but befuddled, UFO dream was over. Appearing in a handful of shops in the West End a week ahead of its official release was a certain album with a fold-out sleeve and a set of lyrics on the rear sleeve into which one could read almost anything. The link between psychedelics and pop was official. The Beatles were back from the crusades. Time to reclaim the citadel.

PART TWO

JANUARY TO DECEMBER 1967

IN THE LIFE OF ...

KYA BEAT

San Francisco, California   January 28, 1967

TOM JONES AWARDED GOLD RECORD; FIRST IN HISTORY OF DISC LABEL

Tom Jones became the first British artist in the history of Decca Records to receive a Gold Record for British sales when his "Green Green Grass Of Home" passed the million mark last week.

While Gold Records are admittedly hard to come by in the States, they are almost impossible to win in England. In fact, the popular Mr. Jones was the only British artist to win a Gold Record (for English sales) during 1966!

Following Tom's South American tour, he flies to New York where he is tentatively set for an appearance on the "Ed Sullivan Show" before winging back to England to headline the bill on "London Palladium."

Monkees Top Beatle Record!

The Monkees are one up on the Beatles. The four Monkees have broken the existing Beatle record by selling over three million copies of their first album, "The Monkees," — more than any previous Beatle album has sold!

"Last Train To Clarksville" has sold well over the one million mark and "I'm A Believer" has already passed the two and half million point. Meanwhile, advance orders on the Monkees' second album, "More Of The Monkees," indicate that it will, in all probability, out-sell their first LP.

Controversy

Ever since the Monkees first graced the nation's airwaves, they've been the object of heated controversy with one side claiming the Monkees are nothing but Beatle imitators while the other side stoutly proclaims the Monkees are not imitators but an original, talented group.

Perhaps the only objective way to decipher who is the world's top group is through the number of discs sold and the number of attendance records set. Judging popularity on that basis, the Beatles are still the number one group. However, in the span of only four months, the Monkees have already topped the Beatles in the number of albums sold—leaving only single records and personal appearances to go before they officially take-over the Beatle crown.

With two and half million copies of "I'm A Believer" sold in the U.S. alone, the Monkees are not even near the all-time Beatle record of five million copies of "I Want To Hold Your Hand."

Monkee personal appearances have necessarily limited due to the filming of their television show. However, they have managed to break away for short tours—their last grossing $159,753 in only four concerts. They still have quite a way to go before they top the Beatle records of selling-out such places as Shea Stadium in New York and the Hollywood Bowl.

The Monkees have managed, though, to cause the same sort of wild hysteria which goes hand-in-hand with a Beatle concert. Their first personal appearance, in Hawaii, saw the Monkees playing before a packed audience while wave upon wave of anxious Monkee fans hurled themselves bodily at the stage.

Mob Scene

"Fifty cops were fighting them off with clubs," said Davy Jones, recalling the mob scene in Hawaii. "I don't want any part of that. But I suppose they have to do it. If the girls got to us they would tear us apart."

Up until December 31, the Monkees belonged exclusively to the U.S. but now their television show is being aired over the BBC and "I'm A Believer" sold over 400,000 in the first week of British release.

(Turn To Page 3)

THE CAPTAIN CROCODILE SHOW

... MONKEES READ fairy tales and sell over three million albums!

MITCH RYDER LEAVES WHEELS—FORMS SHOW

... MITCH RYDER

Mitch Ryder, who has been termed "the white man's James Brown," is now set to give Brown a run for his money by forming the Mitch Ryder Show, which will include a ten-piece orchestra to back Mitch.

"It seems more like a Broadway production," said Alan Strok, Ryder's manager. "The total investment will be in the area of $30,000 with some of the best talent around guiding us because we decided that since we are taking this giant step, we should do it right.

"Jamie Rodgers of 'Golden Boy' is directing choreography and Husch Davis is doing the arrangements. Special lighting and electronic systems have been designed and Mitch's costumes by Charles Lisenby will cost $3,000."

The Detroit Wheels will no longer travel with Mitch but are still signed to New Voice Records and will continue to release discs.

Bob Dylan For Films

Bob Dylan, who has not been seen since his accident, has reportedly left Columbia Records for MGM.

The MGM deal supposedly gives Dylan full control of the production of his records and also gives the leader of folk a chance to enter movies via the label's father, Metro-Goldwyn-Mayer.

The new deal certainly puts an end to the recent round of "Dylan is really dead" rumors which have been floating around since his "disappearance."

Inside the BEAT

The KYA BEAT is published bi-weekly by BEAT Publications, Inc., editorial and advertising offices at 6290 Sunset Blvd., Suite 504, Hollywood, California 90028. U.S. bureaus in Hollywood, San Francisco, New York, Chicago and Nashville, overseas correspondents in London, Liverpool and Manchester, England. Subscription $5 per year. Subscription price: U.S. and possessions, $5 per year, Canada and foreign rates, $9 per year. Second class postage prepaid at Los Angeles, California.

HERMAN, HOLLIES SPECIAL

Herman's Hermits and the Hollies were joined by a CBS-TV crew during their concerts in Green Bay, Wis.; Charlotte, N.C.; Fort Worth and El Paso, Texas; Albuquerque, N.M.; Indianapolis and Chicago.

During the concerts and airport mob scenes, the television crew shot valuable footage which will form the basis of an hour-long television special to be shown on April 11 over CBS.

After a bit we got a bit bored with twelve bars all the time, so we
tried to get into something else. Then came Dylan, The Who and
the Beach Boys . . . We're all trying to do vaguely the same kind of
thing. We are all trying to make it into something we know it is . . .
Most people still think it's all just pop – [as if] it's a bit below every
other kind of music, which of course it isn't. –

Paul McCartney, *IT* #6

There are things past drums and guitars which we must do. In the
last two years we've been in a good vantage point inasmuch as
people are used to buying our records . . . We can do things that
please us without conforming to the standard pop idea. We are not
only involved in pop music but all music, and there are many things
to be investigated. –

George Harrison, 1967

With hindsight, it seems surprising just how long it took The Beatles to start exercising their undoubted economic clout to ensure things got done *their* way. Though they had been unquestionably the biggest band in the world since 1964, as late as spring 1966 they were allowing themselves to be dictated to by their label in ways that directly impinged on their art – witness the *Yesterday & Today* debacle.

Back in March, before beginning work on *Revolver*, Lennon had informed *NME*, 'The next LP is going to be very different. We wanted to have it so that there was no space between the tracks – just continuous. But they wouldn't wear it.' Amazingly, Lennon did not insist – at least, not until the following album. Evidently, deep down the band still felt like Scouse 'scallies' in the Big Smoke; not quite sure that they belonged there. Harrison admitted as much to Hunter Davies, who would be working away at his authorised biography of the band throughout 1967:

> **George Harrison:** We were held back in our development by having to . . . stick to the basic instruments. For a long time we didn't know what else you could do. We were just lads down from the North being allowed to make music in the big EMI studios. It was all done very quickly, in one go on one track. [1967]

The Beatles weren't alone in being made to feel permanently at odds with the denizens of EMI, yet still graciously allowed to make obscene profits in exchange for a criminally small royalty (around 2% on domestic sales, half that on overseas sales). The Hollies may not have been The Beatles, but they were still earning the label a tidy sum. Yet Graham Nash had found that Abbey Road studios was run largely for the benefit of the engineers and producers, not those bands who justified the whole EMI edifice:

> **Graham Nash:** EMI was very much like the BBC. When we were first recording with them, they were still wearing white overcoats, and you couldn't put your hands on the board. They'd slap your wrist if you touched it! . . . I thought that the echo machines turned off at ten-thirty. It was only years later I realised it was the pubs that closed at ten-thirty, and the engineers wanted to be out of there by ten, to make sure they got the last pint.

Despite having a fourteenth consecutive Top Twenty hit with 'Carrie Anne', in early 1967 little had changed for The Hollies. Also working at Abbey Road throughout the winter on their *Evolution* LP, they rarely crossed paths with their old Lancastrian friends. Nash recalls how if he and his fellow Mancunians were recording, it was usually in the afternoon, and 'it'd be over by six. The Beatles were just waking up. So we were at a different end of the day.' The Hollies were still shackled to the pop treadmill. But their Liverpudlian peers had begun to break their bonds.

When the FabFour began *demanding* the right to record through the night, it was the first indication that they were no longer prepared to toe the corporate line. On one level, their 'request' had an entirely practical dimension – teenyboppers weren't likely to be hanging around the Abbey Road gates at midnight. But the change also reflected the increasingly nocturnal lifestyles of the band members. The all-night sessions certainly took their toll on one co-worker:

George Martin: The Beatles and I have different ways of life. They're night people and they don't like working in the mornings. Usually we start recording at seven in the evening and work through till three . . . That was the most arduous part of the LP for me. [1967]

Martin had already cut loose from the EMI bonds, back in 1965, having failed to convince the powers-that-be he was entitled to 'points' on the product he produced. Unable to renegotiate his contract, he simply set himself up as an independent producer, forming AIR (Associated Independent Recording), taking John Burgess and Ron Richards – producers of Manfred Mann and The Hollies respectively – with him. In one fell swoop, EMI lost its three most experienced pop producers, and so would have to negotiate for their services with other interested parties.

However, The Beatles were never going to countenance another change in studio personnel – they were already losing their long-standing engineer, Norman Smith, to the A&R division – and it was made clear that Martin would remain The Beatles' producer. And yet their own relationship with Martin couldn't help but change as they came to realise it was not only possible, but desirable, to forsake making records 'in one go, on one track'. *Rubber Soul* and *Revolver* demarcate the great transition. As Miles observes, 'Those two albums were when they got away from George Martin, and became a creative entity unto themselves.' Just about everyone in their immediate circle felt the force of change:

> **Tony Barrow:** By 1966, their relationships with both Martin and Brian
> Epstein had altered. They no longer bothered to say 'please' or 'thank
> you', but expected everything from the trivial to the impossible to be
> done for them automatically.

If EMI remained under any illusion that their progenies were
still the callow lads they signed back in 1962, it was dispelled
at the turn of the year, when Epstein renegotiated a new world-
wide contract with the label which raised royalty rates five-fold;
almost the last useful thing he ever did for them. His own management contract was up in August, but he would be dead by then,
ostensibly from drugs, but in truth from a broken heart. His boys
were moving on, and he was being left behind. As he exasper-
atedly exclaimed to Barrow that spring, 'There are many ways
in which The Beatles are no longer co-operating with me.' By
finding themselves, they were slowly but inexorably casting this
lost soul adrift.

Yet Lennon and McCartney still courted Epstein's opinion when
they decided to make their next album a thematic collection of
northern songs. Barrow states that he 'was present on several occasions when John and/or Paul talked about the concept with Brian
Epstein'. At this stage, according to Barrow, 'They had a vague
idea of getting back to basics by writing a set of songs about their
own past, The Beatles' beginnings and their hometown haunts.
The music would be progressive, but the lyrics could be nostalgically retrospective.' For McCartney, having a theme – any theme –
would make the album stand out from what came before:

> **Paul McCartney:** We realised for the first time that someday someone
> would actually be holding a thing that they'd call 'The Beatles' new
> LP' and that normally it would just be a collection of songs with a
> nice picture on the cover, nothing more. So the idea was to do a
> complete thing that you could make what you liked of; just a little
> magic presentation. [1967]

At the time that they were involved in these discussions, it wasn't certain whether 'Strawberry Fields' and/or 'Penny Lane' would be part of the larger exercise. Irrespective of the outcome, Martin felt that 'Strawberry Fields' 'set the agenda for the whole album'. However, Barrow believes that as soon as the decision to 'pull' those tracks was made, the whole idea of 'northernness' also died a death:

> Although both John and Paul resented having the two first titles plucked from their proposed new set of hometown/nostagia album songs, they fully recognised that the market demanded a new single and these were the two strongest Lennon & McCartney songs available. They decided to agree to the use of this pair on a single in preference to dashing off two new songs and recording them in a rush. But this did put paid to the whole 'nostalgia' concept, and in the event *Sgt. Pepper* had little or no clearly defined theme to it . . . beyond the 'Billy Shears' idea.

Actually, both McCartney and Lennon had been working away at songs which reflected their very different ideas of northernness. Lennon later informed *Rolling Stone* that 'the North is where the money was made in the eighteen hundreds; that was where all the brass and the heavy people were, and . . . where all the despised people were'. Not surprisingly, the two songs he sketched out at this point ('A Day in the Life' and 'Good Morning') contrasted the life of the average, 'northern' working-class stiff with the spoilt southerner who doesn't know he's got it made, and in whom Lennon now caught his own fearful reflection.

In the song he wrote over Christmas, and presented to McCartney for his input the second week in January – originally called 'In The Life Of' – Lennon focused on Tara Browne, a London socialite and heir to the Guinness fortune, who jumped a red light in South Kensington on 18 December, and careened into a van, thus displaying the same sense of finality and futility as Paul Simon's 'Richard Cory'.

If Simon's 'Cory' 'put a bullet in his head', Lennon memorably suggested Browne 'blew his mind out in a car', evidently believing this acquaintance around town was high at the time of the 'accident'. According to McCartney, when Lennon brought the rough outline of the song to his bachelor pad on Cavendish Avenue, he 'brought the newspaper [cutting] with him ... We went upstairs to the music room and started to work on [the song]. He had the first verse, he had the [bit about the] war and a little bit of the second verse.' Like 'Strawberry Fields', it was not the finished article. And this time he was prepared to let his partner help him finish the song, so that they could start recording the new album in earnest the following day:

> **John Lennon:** In a lot of [songs] you'll get so far. You've lumbered yourself with a set of images and it's an effort to keep it up ... I had the 'I read the news today' bit, and it turned Paul on, because now and then we really turn each other on with a bit of song, and he just said 'yeah' – bang, bang, like that. It just sort of happened beautifully, and we arranged it and rehearsed it, which we don't often do, the afternoon before [the session] ... I needed a middle-eight for it, but that would have been forcing it, all the rest had come out smooth, flowing, no trouble, and to write a middle-eight would have been to write a middle-eight, but ... Paul already had one there. [1968]

McCartney not only came up with a whole 'dream' section to the fatalistic fable, he offered the most contentious line in the whole mind-manifesting song, 'I'd love to turn you on'. With this audio equivalent of the cross-cut, he set up the middle-eight, transplanted from a song of his own that was as 'nostalgically retrospective' as 'Penny Lane'. Again McCartney idealised his northern upbringing, in a way that allowed it to act as a counterpoint to the mundane daily existence into which Lennon's present-day anti-hero is trapped. Like 'Strawberry Fields', it was largely about that special place where one could (day)dream:

Paul McCartney: It was just me remembering what it was like to run up the road to catch a bus to school, having a smoke and going into class . . . It was a reflection of my schooldays. I would have a Woodbine and somebody would speak and I would go into a [day] dream. [1967]

If Lennon was still coming up with dazzling song ideas, those like 'Strawberry Fields' – which he worked on till he was satisfied – would remain the exception. As Martin told Hunter Davies in 1967, 'John is very lazy, unlike Paul. Without Paul he would often give up . . . John's concept of music is very interesting. I was once playing Ravel . . . to him. He said he couldn't grasp it because the melodic lines were too long . . . [and that] he looked upon writing music as doing little bits, which you then join up.'

Even when Lennon was seemingly more inspired, McCartney remained the more assured songwriter. As Davies wrote in his original edition, whenever McCartney appeared with new songs and began 'singing them to others, he was not looking for suggestions, the way John might do'. Indeed, in many ways, the songwriters' relationship paralleled their contemporary cultural revolutionaries, Monty Python pair Graham Chapman and John Cleese, of whom fellow Python, Terry Gilliam, once observed, '[Cleese] was so frustrated writing with Graham – yet Graham would make those leaps that nobody [else he] has worked with has done. Graham was just on another planet at times.'

So it was with Lennon, who was slightly surprised when he had to coax McCartney into contributing to 'A Day In The Life': 'I think he thought it's already a good song. Sometimes we wouldn't let each other interfere with a song, because you tend to . . . experiment a bit [too much]'. But once they slotted in Paul's contribution the duo had a song fully the equal of the two songs already given away in the cause of chart success. It was an auspicious (re)start to the album.

Before the next session, though, McCartney had an appointment to record a spoken-word endorsement of the 'new' underground – and its exemplar, Pink Floyd, who had been filmed performing part of 'Interstellar Overdrive' at the UFO – for a half-hour Granada TV documentary, *Scene Special*. McCartney, as ever, was keen to reinforce his own connection to the counter-culture:

> They're talking about things that are a bit new and . . . things that people don't really know too much about yet. And so people tend to put them down a bit – and say, weirdo, psychedelic – but it's really just what's going on around . . . So the next time you see a strange word like psychedelic, or drugs, or freak-out music, don't immediately take it as *that*!

When he turned up at Abbey Road at half-seven the following evening (the nineteenth), McCartney was already thinking about how to fix the hole in their new song with something resembling a 'freak out'. But for now all four Beatles worked on what they had, which was Lennon's two sections and McCartney's interlude, leaving the song's problematic segue to a later date:

> **Ringo Starr:** [Recording] it was very simple. We worked on the first section, which was John's, and then Paul said he had something. So we recorded that section. But we had this huge blank space between the two, so we counted out the bars, and thought we'd fill it in later. By then, we were comfortable in the studio, and with what we were trying to do. It was just part of how we worked . . . We weren't sitting around going, 'Oh my God, look what we're doing.' We were just going, 'Let's do that.' [1987]

One happy coincidence came when Mal Evans added an alarm clock to signal the last bar of the bridge – 'just to make sure that everyone knew when to restart,' as Martin later put it. They duly discovered that 'the alarm going off fitted perfectly with the lyrics that started Paul's middle section': 'Woke up, got out of bed . . .' But that pleasant surprise would have to wait until the following day's session, when McCartney overdubbed his vocal to the ongoing work-in-progress.

Gone, for sure, were the days when The Beatles recorded and mixed a whole track, let alone half an album, in a single day. Now they were using Abbey Road as a rehearsal studio with recording facilities (facilities that remained under-used because of EMI's fabled parsimony, and a failure on The Beatles' part to say, 'Look [at] what we're doing'). The process itself had become increasingly drawn-out:

George Harrison: Now that we only play in the studios . . . we haven't got a clue what we're going to do. We have to start from scratch, thrashing it out in the studio, doing it the hard way. If Paul has written a song, he comes into the studio with it in his head. It's very hard for him to give it to us and for us to get it. When we suggest something, it might not be what he wants, because he hasn't got it in his head. So it takes a long time. [HD]

If The Beatles remained high on ideas as they began 'thrashing it out in the studio', the engineers – already hanging on well past their bedtime – found this new working method less than ideal. As Peter Vince subsequently informed Mark Lewisohn, 'Although they'd use the studio as a rehearsal room you couldn't just clear off because they might be trying something out – just piano or bass or drums – and they'd want to come up and listen to the thing before carrying on. So you couldn't just disappear or nod off . . . The nights were so long when you had nothing to do . . . What people don't realise is the boredom factor. *Sgt. Pepper* took four months to record, and for probably more than half that time all the engineers were doing was sitting around, waiting for them to get their ideas together.'

Even after a second late-night session working on the baroque 'A Day In The Life', the song still only had a guide vocal for the middle-eight, a 'huge blank space' for a bridge and no surefire way of ending it. As it is, the boys ended up adding some plinkety-plonk piano and what sounds like a whistle (a factory whistle?), before McCartney suggested indulging in a little electronic experiment as an alternative to the instrumental jam he perhaps suspected was not their forte.

Lennon was as interested as McCartney in seeing how far they could go. As he'd informed a reporter the previous March, 'Paul and I are very keen on this electronic music. You make it clinking a couple of glasses together or with bleeps from the radio, then you loop the tape to repeat the noises at intervals.' They had already 'loop[ed] the tape to repeat the noises at intervals', on the very first track recorded for *Revolver*, and were looking for a similar way to shake up the sound, to provide a springboard for the sessions ahead. But when McCartney played a recording of the new song to their manager, Epstein saw dollar signs disappearing before his eyes:

> **Miles:** Brian Epstein was definitely worried that they were going way over people's heads – particularly [with] 'Day in the Life' . . . As far as he was concerned, The Beatles were live performances and screaming girls. He thought they were just gonna disappear up their own arsehole if they keep on making this weird shit . . . I was even there for the tailend of one conversation. He was quite upset by the direction they were going in, and Paul was assuring him, 'It'll be alright. Everyone's gonna love it.'

What was probably also concerning Epstein was how slowly work was progressing. After two whole months of studio-work, they had recorded just three usable tracks, two of which were now consigned to Single-land. And while 'A Day In The Life' may have been the skeleton key to the Sergeant's locker, it still needed work. Being stuck with four-track technology was partly to blame, slowing the boys down at every turn. Each time they wanted to overdub a new instrument or a different vocal or guitar track, they would either have to mix down the existing tracks and 'bounce' the recording from one machine to another, or cram the chosen take on to at most three tracks, leaving room for any bright ideas to come.

Either way, on a technical level, the results were horrendous.

The former method added wads of hiss, the latter stacked instruments like a pancake platter, making any subsequent remix of the particular musical mélange an exercise in futility. Once stereo became the norm (as it would by the end of the decade) – coinciding with many listening to Rock music on headphones, like a classical recital – the hiss 'bouncing' brought about became wholly unacceptable.[1]

The constraints of four-track did have an up side: you were obliged to work 'in the moment', even when you were mixing. As Joe Boyd points out in his sixties memoir, *White Bicycle*, 'In '67, mixes were like recording takes; you had to get it in one pass or go back to the top and start again.' The result was that everyone involved in the process – engineer, producer, musicians – had to be at the top of their game, anticipating problems further down the road; because in order to find out if something *didn't* work, one had to try it in a 'live' situation. It was a breeding-ground for fertile ideas, sorting out the men from the boys:

> **George Harrison:** Nowadays you can overdub individually with each person having his own channel to record on. Then we'd have to think of all the instrumental overdubs, say, a guitar coming in on the second verse and a piano in the middle and then a tambourine. And we'd routine all of that, get the sound and the balance and the mix and do it as one performance . . . We had old microphones and pretty antiquated machines, but we'd find new meanings in old equipment . . . It was exciting to try and come up with new ideas. [1987]

This put constant pressure on the engineers and producer, especially as The Beatles had stopped taking no for an answer. As Geoff Emerick told Mark Cunningham, 'The Beatles were screaming out for change. They didn't want the piano to sound like a piano anymore, or a guitar to sound like a guitar.' McCartney wasn't even prepared to let an orchestra sound like an orchestra. On 3 February, when he and Ringo redubbed the rhythm-track to 'A Day In The Life', and Paul completed his vocal part without a single expletive,[2] he was primed to suggest something to the others that condensed a year of immersion in avant-garde sounds into just sixteen bars of the latest Lennon–McCartney song:

> **George Martin:** Paul had been listening to a lot of avant-garde music by the likes of John Cage, Stockhausen, and Luciano Berio. He had told John he would like to include an instrumental passage with this avant-garde feel. He had the idea to create a spiralling ascent of sound, suggesting we start the passage with all instruments on their lowest note and climbing to the highest in their own time. [MoSP]

McCartney had been itching to execute something similar for some months, delighted as much by Martin's quizzical look as the light in Lennon's eyes. He had already made a habit of putting on some particularly atonal Albert Ayler LP, like *Spirits* or *Bells*, thus filling 'the room with Albert's honks and squeals', and gauging Martin's reaction. Though Martin went along with McCartney's notion of an orchestra playing not as one but as many, he did rein in at least one aspect of the idea – the sheer scale of Macca's vision. When he asked for ninety musicians, Martin negotiated it down to forty. And yet, as Lewisohn notes in his account of the 10 February session, Paul still ended up with 'more' musicians than originally requested 'because the orchestra was recorded four times, on all four tracks of a tape, and this was then mixed down to one. So he had the equivalent of *160 musicians*.'

While McCartney had to rely on Martin's grasp of logistics, he also needed the approval of Lennon, whose song he was using for the grand experiment. Thankfully, he loved the idea; and would probably have liked Paul to go still further. McCartney, though, had an innate self-discipline that continued to act as the kind of check many contemporaries would have done well to emulate. Miles recollects one occasion when McCartney accompanied him to a performance of Cornelius Cardew and AMM at the Royal College of Art in 1966, and though he 'understood their serious purpose, [he] told the organiser Victor

Schonfeld, "It went on too long."'" It was not a mistake *he* was about to make:

> **Miles:** [Paul] always wanted to bring the fans along. As far as he was concerned, he just took all this stuff on board and used it whenever it was appropriate for The Beatles' music. The Beatles' stuff, as far as he was concerned, was a separate category. You could feed in all these ideas from John Cage, and Cornelius Cardew and Albert Ayler, but it had to be digested first; whereas I think John was a bit of a spewing-it-all-out undigested kinda guy. Yoko would tell him about something, and he's in the studio next day doing his own version of it.

Lennon, who had first met the Japanese artist the previous November, at an exhibition of hers at the Indica Gallery, exercised no such restraint. As *Pepper* progressed, it almost became a running joke with the engineers how each Lennon song would end up treated with every effect imaginable, as if he could thus mask every bad idea and enhance each good one.

One song he demoed in his home studio that winter he was still working on two years later – which was when he owned up to its existence to *NME*, 'I had a song I wrote around *Pepper* time . . . [which] is still in the can – called "You Know My Name & Cut The Number"[sic]. That's the only words to it. It just goes on all the way like that, and we did these mad backings. But I never did finish it.' The fact that this throwaway puzzle should end up as the last Beatles song released during the band's existence (as b-side to 'Let It Be') suggests he stopped drawing a line between work and play once Yoko got under his skin.

In fact, by the end of January '67, Lennon seemed to have (temporarily) shot his bolt songwise. 'Strawberry Fields' and 'A Day In The Life' were as ambitious as pop got, but they left Lennon with little in reserve. The month after their 'completion' he seemed bereft of ideas. The two songs he produced for *Pepper* in those weeks – 'Good Morning, Good Morning' and 'Being For The Benefit of Mr Kite' – both received the full palette of special effects, but Lennon knew he could do a lot better.

In the case of 'Good Morning, Good Morning', Lennon never changed his tune; from 1968, when he told Cott, 'I just knocked it off to do a song', to one of his final interviews in December 1980, with *Newsweek*, in which he called it 'a dumb song' that has 'absolutely nothing to say . . . but "it's okay. Good morning, good morning, good morning", as the dumb song goes. Quack, quack, quack. It wasn't [just] a matter of nothing to say – it was a matter of no clarity and no desire to do it.'

Yet 'Good Morning, Good Morning' had begun life as almost a sister-song to 'A Day In The Life', infused with an even greater dose of self-loathing recast as contempt for ordinary life. Lennon even claimed 'it was [me] writing about my past, so it does get the kids because it was me at school, my whole bit', which suggests *he* thought it might have some relationship to the album's supposed theme. But when it came time to record the song on 8 February (spreading into March), Lennon's disgust with the life he was portraying seems to have been transferred to the song itself; and the very technique he had been playing with on 'You Know My Name' – taking one repetitive phrase set to a simple riff and burying it beneath a veritable library of sound effects – ended up interring what little the song did have to say.

'Being for the Benefit of Mr Kite' was another song ostensibly connected to the dual notions of northernness and nostalgia, portraying as it did the kind of entertainment enjoyed in Victorian times in towns like Rochdale – the kind of place 'where all the despised people were'. Again, in conversation with Hunter Davies, Lennon managed to give the impression that he invested little time and energy in this period piece:

John Lennon: 'Mr Kite' was a straight lift . . . I wasn't very proud of that. There was no real work. I was just going through the motions because we needed a new song for *Sgt. Pepper* at that moment . . . People want to know what the inner meaning of 'Mr Kite' was. There

wasn't any. I just did it. I shoved a lot of words together, then shoved
some noise on. I didn't dig that song when I wrote it. I didn't believe
in it when we were recording it. [HD]

There were certainly some elements in the lyrics which would
qualify as 'a straight lift'. Among the boasts made on the 1843
poster Lennon found while filming the 'Strawberry Fields' promo
video, and which formed the basis for the song, were statements
like: 'Mr Henderson will, for the first time in Rochdale, introduce
his extraordinary TRAMPOLINE LEAPS and SOMERSETS! Over
Men & Horses, through Hoops, over Garters, and lastly, through
a Hogshead of REAL FIRE! In this branch of the profession, Mr
H. challenges THE WORLD.'

Lennon seems to have always intended to give the song an
olde worlde sound, in keeping with the peculiar cadences of the
poster-cum-lyric. He fully expected George Martin to rise to the
occasion again, hitting just the right note. As such, after they laid
down the basic track on 17 February, he can be heard at take's end
saying, 'And after this we'll have the Massed Alberts, won't we,
George?' This was one of Lennon's little in-jokes,[3] which worked
as a verbal Post-it note to Martin, to remind him 'it was time to
add on "the clever stuff", the brass'. Unfortunately for John, there
was a little more to this than met the I. As a track-by-track review
of *Sgt. Pepper* in the June '67 *Beatles Monthly*, ostensibly penned
by Mal Evans and Neil Aspinall, observed:

John wanted to use an authentic sound of an old steam organ but
there isn't one anywhere in the world which can be played by hand
– all existing models work on punched cards, like a pianola works
from a long roll which has holes punched in it. Instead George Martin
played Hammond organ and built up an electronic tape to give the
effect John had described – using various organ recordings speeded
up, slowed down, electronically distorted, played backwards and
dipped in a bottle of Coke. Or something. Anyway it worked.

If it worked for Evans and Aspinall, it did so only after Martin double-speeded the organ, leaving Lennon 'to play the tune an octave down, and really slow', hoping to make the end product sound strangely strange but vaguely normal. And all for a song that Lennon 'didn't believe in . . . when we were recording it'. Despite such deprecation, work on 'Good Morning, Good Morning' and 'Mr Kite' would be spread over seven sessions, trying the patience of all concerned.

Meanwhile, McCartney continued to produce and record new songs with his usual aplomb, a whole lot less paranoia, and, sometimes, minimal input from his fellow Beatles. When he turned up on the first of February with a title-song for the album, 'Sgt. Pepper's Lonely Hearts Club Band', Harrison was relieved to think he'd finally got a part to play, with a juicy guitar lead already written in.

However, after seven hours spent trying to record Harrison's solo, McCartney decided he would play the solo himself and, unfazed by any possible recriminations, went ahead and dubbed on his own riff. In a 2004 *Uncut* conversation, McCartney admitted it was about now that he began to 'take charge' of the sessions, 'I was conscious that was happening . . . [And] there were moments when I was treating these world-class musicians like mere band members. In my defence, all I was concerned about was making a great record.'

He perhaps should have explained that to Harrison, whose first songwriting contribution to the sessions – a fortnight later – was a typically sour song, with at least one line that seemed like a 'pop' at Paul: 'It doesn't really matter what chords I play'. 'Only A Northern Song' also seemed designed to ridicule the original 'northern' concept for the album – which Harrison may or may not have been a party to – while expressing dissatisfaction with the way his own songs had been parcelled in with those of Lennon and McCartney, as part of Northern Songs. 'Only A Northern Song' was a song of independence from a man already looking for the exit sign:

George Harrison: I don't personally enjoy being a Beatle any more. All that sort of Beatle thing is trivial and unimportant. I'm fed up with

all this me, us, I, stuff and all the meaningless things we do. I'm
trying to work out solutions to the more important things in life. [1967]

If Lennon was fed up with his suburban existence, Harrison was
equally 'cheesed off' with his not-so-mundane life, married to a
gorgeous model, financially independent, and given the unique
privilege of working with the finest pop songwriters of their day.
Despite its truculent tone, though, 'Only A Northern Song' fit the
mood of the other songs recorded to date, and so Harrison must
have been more than a little bemused when George Martin told
him it wasn't going to make the cut:

George Martin: When[ever Harrison] brought a new song along . . .
I would say to myself, 'I wonder if it is going to be any better than
the last one?' It was in this light that I looked at the first number he
brought me for the *Sgt. Pepper* album, which was 'Only A Northern
Song'. I groaned inside when I heard it. We did make a recording
of it on 14 February, but I knew it was never going to make it. I had
to tell George that as far as *Pepper* was concerned, I did not think
his song would be good enough. [MoSP]

If they did have such a conversation, it was some way off, because
as late as 29 March – the penultimate recording session for *Pepper*
– Harrison was telling a female journalist that there would probably be two of his songs on the album. The quote above also implies
that Martin had some kind of veto on songs, which seems decidedly unlikely at this late stage. In truth, he was probably just the
messenger, and it was McCartney whose veto now came into play.

Tony Barrow: Paul's opinions and ideas tended to prevail with The
Beatles, particularly on matters of musical policy, such as whether
a new number was worth recording or whether the running order for
the group's stage show needed altering slightly. I didn't see any of
the others resist him.

Maybe Paul didn't take kindly to George's gentle lampooning of 'his' concept, which with its own title-track had now been expanded to include what Steve Turner depicts as 'a fictional Edwardian brass band transported through time into the psychedelic age'. That might be an overstatement of the role assigned to these Beatle alter-egos, but as McCartney says in *Many Years From Now*, 'I started to get this idea that [the] Beatles were in a park up north somewhere and it was very municipal, it was very council. I like that northern thing very much, which is what we were, where we're from.' Once he had the song, and got the others to agree that it would be the title-track, McCartney – ever the art-student – began to conceive of the kind of cover to accompany it:

> **Miles:** The original cover concept was northern dignitaries – the mayor with his chain and everything. The original idea was supposed to be a northern scene – the Lord Mayor presenting Sgt. Pepper's brass band with some kind of medals, with the floral clock, and all that northern stuff . . . It was very much Paul's idea, and he did a number of sketches; and then . . . it got transformed. The original idea was a northern thing . . . an English, working-class, northern version of a psychedelic [band].

Brimming with ideas, McCartney was back a week after recording the title-track with another brand-new song. With 'Fixing A Hole', though, he began to slowly-but-surely depart from any theme at all (unless constant references to rain were intended to mock southern stereotypes about 'the north'). His explanation for the song at the time seemed to suggest he was already looking to paper over the cracks:

> **Paul McCartney:** ['Fixing a Hole'] is just about . . . the hole in your make-up which lets the rain in, and stops your mind going where it will . . . If you're a junkie sitting in a room fixing a hole then that's what it will mean to you, but when I wrote it, I meant if there's a crack or the room is uncolourful, then I'll paint it. [1967]

The most unusual thing about 'Fixing A Hole' – which was done
with once-familiar ease in a single evening (overdubs on the twenty-
first notwithstanding) – was that it was recorded not at Abbey Road,
but at what Martin later dismissed as 'little more than a demonstra-
tion studio, in the heart of Tin Pan Alley . . . a low-ceilinged, boxy
little room with a low-ceilinged boxy little sound to it'. Regent Sound
Studio, on Denmark Place, may well have been everything Martin
claimed (Kinks producer Shel Talmy got even more to the point by
calling it 'a shit-hole'); but at least one contemporary producer, the
Stones' Andrew Loog Oldham, loved 'the Regent sound':

> **Andrew Loog Oldham:** [It] was no bigger than an average good-sized
> hotel room. The control room was the size of a hotel bathroom, but
> for us it was magic. The sound leaked, instrument to instrument, the
> right way. You'd hear the bottom end of [the] drums bleeding through
> [the] acoustic [guitar], and vice versa . . . Put them both together
> and you had a wall of noise.

McCartney evidently had something specific in mind; and it was
his decision. With Martin, Harrison and Starr in tow, he cut three
versions of the basic track and returned to Abbey Road, satisfied
with the evening's work. The following evening, he 'orchestrated'
the forty-musician overdub for 'A Day In The Life'. While for
Lennon, cloistered in his 'country' home, inspiration now came
from a cathode tube and capsules, McCartney was finding it in
more worldly places, on Hampstead Heath walking the dog ('Getting
Better'), or picking up a parking ticket from a not-so-pert parking
warden ('Lovely Rita').

But then, McCartney was still confining any substance abuse
to a smoke or seven, thus refraining from altering his mind in any
permanent way. Lennon, on the other hand, was hanging out with
Indica co-founder John Dunbar, 'down in Weybridge . . . [going,]
"No, I'm not going to mend your fucking bike, Julian," and snorting
up Owsley tabs and coke out of a kitchen pestle and mortar. And
. . . watching the TV'.

The contrast was reflected in the type of songs these partners-in-pop-preeminence were writing, which were almost night and day. As Miles told Steve Turner, 'Lennon was going through a very neurotic phase, whereas McCartney was on a roll. He had this nice house, a lovely music room and a beautiful girlfriend. He was in a very creative period and it happened to coincide with the recording of *Sgt. Pepper*.' Lennon certainly felt the album slipping away from him. In fact, he later told Miles that 'he always thought of it as Paul's record. He [admitted,] "I was very out of it then." . . . because that was when he was taking a tremendous amount of acid.' Though his competitive spirit would rear its head again before *Pepper* was finally put to bed, he felt he had already given of his best. As indeed he had:

> **John Lennon:** I got a little resentful later on about the album. I was living a more suburban life at the time, with a wife and a kid, while [Paul] was still tripping around town, hanging out and being a bachelor. He'd work something out for a song or an album and then suddenly call me and say, 'It's time to go into the studio. Write some songs.' He'd have all *his* prepared, ready with ideas and arrangements, while I would be starting from scratch. On *Sgt. Pepper*, which was his idea, too, I managed to come up with . . . 'Day in the Life' under the pressure of only ten days. Even so, I was in more at the start. Later on, I had sort of succumbed to marriage and eating. [1980]

In fact it had been Lennon who had been stockpiling (ideas for) songs the previous autumn, and McCartney who was 'starting from scratch'. But the latter was open to all the amazing sounds of the city at a remarkable time for English music, whereas Lennon merely felt threatened. So when the most original new band crossing psychedelia and pop came to the studio next door, he didn't want to know their name, let alone hear their numbers.

GAMES FOR MAY

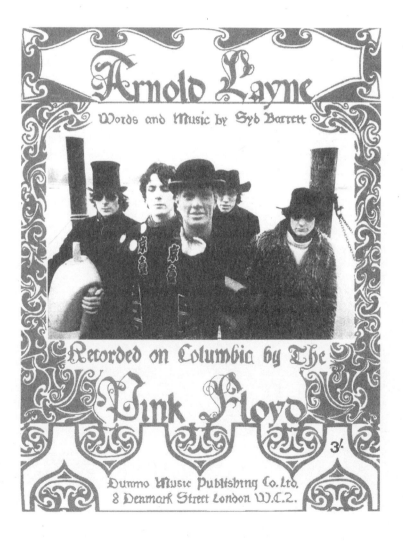

A man in a purple shirt called Norman arrived. He used to be one of their recording engineers and now had a group of his own, The Pink Floyd. Very politely he asked George Martin if his boys could possibly pop in to see The Beatles at work. George smiled, unhelpfully. Norman said perhaps he should ask John personally, as a favour. George Martin said no, that wouldn't work. But if by chance he and his boys popped in about eleven o'clock, he might just be able to see what he could do. They did pop in around eleven, and exchanged a few half-hearted hellos. –

Hunter Davies, *The Beatles: An Authorised Biography*

It was the evening of 21 March, 1967. The Beatles were putting the finishing touches to 'Getting Better' and 'Lovely Rita' in Studio Two. Hunter Davies had finally convinced the lads to let him see them at work in the studio. Meanwhile The Pink Floyd were across the hall, in Studio Three, working on the startlingly percussive 'Pow R Toc H' with their producer, Norman Smith, whom they had been 'badgering' to arrange an introduction – or so the story goes.

Davies's version of the fabled meeting between Floyd and the FabFour is the one generally quoted account, and he clearly suggests it was a fleeting rendezvous of no great import. But Davies was (and is) a professional biographer, not a music journalist, and was clearly ignorant of the Floyd. He was also seemingly unaware that Lennon was as high as Mr Kite, having unwisely ingested a tab of acid (having supposedly mistaken it for speed). As such, Lennon was in no fit condition to meet anyone, even someone like Syd Barrett, who could more than hold his own in the acid-consumption stakes.

One can't help but feel a certain irony that it was Syd who

played the straight man that night in Studio Two, and that it should be Lennon who was out to lunch, dinner and supper. But Syd probably still saw himself as the sorcerer's apprentice. If so, he was about to receive a glimpse of how intensive – and tedious – the wizards' work had become. According to Peter Jenner, 'We were in there for like an hour or two, and all they were doing was a fade. Endlessly.' It was apparent to all that there was a fundamental difference in the bands' respective approaches:

Jeff Jarrett [EMI engineer]: The Floyd were into creating moods and atmospheres with sound, whereas The Beatles were creating great songs and . . . would then spend a long time trying to create interesting sounds that helped enhance those songs.

McCartney already knew this. Unlike Lennon – who wouldn't actually hear the Floyd until the '14-Hour Technicolour Dream' at Alexandra Palace in late April – Macca had taken a rather active interest in Barrett's band since the previous October, when he had caught them at the *IT* launch; becoming a regular at the weekly UFO soirées where Floyd and The Soft Machine took it in turns to entertain the freaks. His sometime confidant Miles was already an advocate:

Miles: He knew I was keen on [Floyd]. We'd had a lot of conversations about trying to introduce modern electronics and ideas from other [musical] disciplines, really 'out there' jazz, [because] all these elements were the future of pop . . . As far as I was concerned this was the great interest in The Pink Floyd. They seemed to be pushing things in that direction, and that was probably why he came down to U-Fo.

Paul had been impressed enough by what he heard at the *IT* launch to pass on plaudits, a review in a November issue of *IT* referring to the band getting 'bigger amplifiers, new lights gear and a rave from Paul McCartney'. Once UFO was launched in late December, he became almost as much a fixture there as the Floyd. Indeed, his main memory of the club, in conversation with Jonathon Green two decades on, was seeing 'the early incarnation of the Floyd. They'd be down there [with] a lot of projections, lots of people sort of wandering about . . . It was all like a trippy adventure playground really.' And when he made his plea for tolerance of all things psychedelic on Granada TV at the end of January, it was largely for Floyd's benefit. So it would stretch the bounds of credulity if it took him a whole month from Floyd's first visit to Abbey Road, on 21 February, to check them out or say hello. In fact, McCartney took no time before stopping by.

> **Miles:** I remember going to a Beatles recording session, and [seeing] one of the Floyd's roadies, and he said they were recording there. So I think the first time any of The Beatles went to see them in the studio was when I took Paul through. I just said that they were there, and he said, 'Let's go and say hello.' It was just Paul and I . . . He'd [already] met them at UFO. They were standing around in the studio, shouting at the control booth window, because they didn't realise you could just talk into a live mike. I just remember Paul trying to make them feel at home.

The fact that the Cambridge lads acted so gauche about the workings of an EMI studio surely suggests this meeting took place the first time they ventured through the Abbey Road portals. McCartney was certainly at the studio on the evening of the twenty-first, laying down the final overdubs on 'Fixing A Hole', making for a light workload. Floyd, on the other hand, had much to do. Of course, Syd always had time for McCartney. According to Floyd engineer Peter Bown, the feeling was mutual: 'McCartney [told Barrett] he liked what he'd heard of the band and thought they were doing something unique and creative.' An endorsement par excellence, and one that their producer, Norman Smith, surely took on board.

It had been Smith's desire to do more than flip the fader at Beatles sessions that had brought him to this place. There can be

little doubting his ambition, given the way that he muscled Joe
Boyd out of the equation after Boyd had successfully captured the
band at Sound Techniques, in both pop-single guise ('Arnold Layne
b/w Candy And A Currant Bun'), and with two of their psychedelic extemporisations ('Interstellar Overdrive' and 'Nick's Boogie').
Boyd's big mistake was trying to tie the band to him, not just for
production, but for licensing any recordings as well. The Polydor
contract he showed to Andrew King and Peter Jenner would have
made Boyd, and his Witchseason Productions, an integral part of
any deal.[1]

King and Jenner turned to booking agent Bryan Morrison for
advice, and almost immediately found themselves on the end of
an EMI counter-offer. In Jenner's view, 'Morrison was a man who
saw things in a very straightforward way – you take the top money
from the top label.' Morrison perhaps forgot to mention that he
already knew an aspiring producer at EMI searching for a band to
make his name, and who wasn't squeamish, even after he caught
the cacophony first-hand. Smith's surprisingly forthright view of
that defining experience was that 'although their "music" did not
do an awful lot for me, their "light" show and general charisma did'.

In fact, once Smith brought the band to the attention of his
boss, Beecher Stevens, the negotiations proceeded without him.
There was already a single in the can, a rival offer on the table,
and (one assumes) the expressed endorsement of James Paul
McCartney. But Floyd's managers were keen to ensure that any
contract they signed made the recording of an album the priority,
not simply more pop singles. As Peter Jenner says, 'We were the
first band to be signed by EMI with an album deal. We didn't have
to have the hit singles first, before we were allowed to make an
album.'

There *were* strings, however, and one of them was attached to
Norman Smith. Stevens told Rick Sanders in 1974, 'One of the
boys in the group . . . seemed a bit strange, which is one reason I
wanted Norman Smith as their producer. I thought he was close
enough to their music to keep a firm hand on the sessions.' In fact,

Smith could hardly have been further from sharing the Floyd aesthetic. Yet, whatever their arrangement with AIR, EMI were never going to countenance an outside producer working with an inexperienced band like Floyd. And Smith had 'dibs'. There was also a general sense – shared by group management – that the Floyd needed someone who could bring out the undoubted pop sensibilities in Barrett's songs:

> **Peter Jenner:** [Norman] applied his professional expertise in the way that a lawyer does. His job was to produce a record. I don't remember him coming to talk to us [about the deal]. We got the word from EMI. [But] what I think that Norman did was he turned the songs into three-minute pieces, from being six-, seven-minute rambles. Joe did the same – but Norman more successfully . . . Syd did essentially write standard pop song structures, but then live they would improvise these long instrumental breaks. When Norman got hold of them, he thought, 'This ain't gonna work.'

Floyd's inexperience was certainly in evidence at that first session; and not just because they didn't know to use the studio mikes when talking to the control room. When they started recording 'Matilda Mother', one of Barrett's earlier compositions, the volume was instantly deafening. Engineer Peter Bown states, 'We wrecked four very expensive microphones that first night. They got louder and louder until everything was overloading and the mics just gave up the ghost.'

Also recorded that first night, at least according to the studio logs, were versions of 'Arnold Layne' and 'Candy And A Currant Bun'. Which seems unlikely, given that the Boyd-produced versions were already in the EMI pipeline for a mid-March release. Yet an acetate of the b-side, featuring the same basic track but with alternative lyrics, a different mix, a new vocal and an additional keyboard break, confirms that the song underwent some reconstructive surgery. According to Boyd, 'EMI made us go back and change the "I'm high, don't try to spoil my fun" [line].' In fact, the song underwent an entire reinvention at EMI's behest, changed from the utterly suggestive 'Let's Roll Another One' to the sweet-toothed 'Candy And A Currant Bun'.

Rather than market Floyd as England's first psychedelic band, EMI had decided they would do the exact opposite. Their first press release included the immortal claim, 'The Pink Floyd does not know what people mean by psychedelic pop, and are not trying to create hallucinatory effects on their audiences.' Quite why they were so concerned with any perceived meaning to the first Floyd b-side, after putting out an a-side deviant enough to be banned by Radio London, of all stations, remains a mystery. Thankfully, 'Arnold Layne' survived unscathed any post-production that did or did not take place on the twenty-first, and was left to the whims of the public, who embraced Barrett's pantie-sniffer to their bosom.

If the session on the twenty-first was little more than a dry-run, work on *Piper At The Gates of Dawn* started in earnest six days later, with a seven-hour session that did not end until 2.15 a.m. Again it was the recording crew who bore the brunt at this unearthly hour, having less recourse than Floyd to what Dylan liked to call 'powerful medicine'. This was probably the session when, according to drummer Nick Mason, 'We ran through our repertoire to select a number to start recording and to impress our new comrades. Regrettably they had all been on late sessions the day before. After thirty minutes Peter Bown had fallen asleep across the console, and Norman . . . followed suit a short while later.'

Roused from their slumbers, work began on 'Chapter 24', so named because the lyrics were lifted clean off (Wilhelm Reich's translation of) Chapter 24 in the I-Ching. Five takes sufficed and so, feeling that they were getting the hang of this recording lark, the Floyd decided to see if they could capture their signature piece, 'Interstellar Overdrive', which they already envisaged as the centre-piece of the album. The challenge was to get the sense of space and timelessness it had at UFO, yet rein the song in to some extent, lest it take over proceedings.

'Interstellar' was the one song attempted at the *Piper* sessions that the band had already recorded in a studio. In fact, they had done so twice, two and a half months apart, and on both occasions it had topped the fifteen-minute mark as they attempted to replicate that feel of a live performance in the studio (never an easy trick). The first studio version, recorded at the end of October at a tiny two-track studio in outer Herts. – Hemel Hempstead, to be precise – was then used as the soundtrack for an underground film. It was, as Andrew King asserts, 'very live – it was as they played it live'.

This audio journey – all fifteen minutes, eleven seconds of it – demonstrates a clear transatlantic analogue to what The Velvet Underground were doing in New York, during their stint with the Exploding Plastic Inevitable, when they too adapted a basic framework – they called it 'Melody Laughter' – around which they wove whatever sonic spell manifested itself. Where the Floyd were not so solid was in the way their rhythm-section tethered the song to any ostensible arrangement. Or not. The playing from Mason and Waters on the October recording failed to provide the necessary bed-Rock, and it proves hard work getting the song back to base. And yet according to Andrew King, 'Given the chance, Syd would have jammed the same chord sequence all night. Roger gave ['Interstellar Overdrive'] the dynamic boundaries within which Syd could run free.' If so, those 'dynamic boundaries' had yet to be established as of October 1966.

By the time Joe Boyd got them into Sound Techniques the following January, they had shows at All Saints, the Roundhouse and UFO under their multicoloured belts, and a proper engineer and producer to hold their hands. The result: a giant leap towards originality. Again the results were intended for a film soundtrack, to Peter Whitehead's pseudo-documentary depiction of swinging London, *Tonite Let's All Make Love In London*. Again restraint was not the order of the day since Whitehead intended to cherry-pick snippets for effect, painting pretty psychedelic pictures to while away the hours (yep, you guessed it, the film is another period piece best appreciated blitzed).

As such, the January 'Interstellar Overdrive' ran for close to seventeen minutes, an unprecedented length for any track (perhaps the closest comparison coming from those Barrett favourites Love, whose 'Revelation' would occupy the whole of the second side of *Da Capo*, without revealing a great deal). The Floyd also ran through another twelve-minute, UFO-style psychedelic jam, 'Nick's Boogie', for the sake of belated posterity.[2] This session was clearly intended to document the psychedelic Pink Floyd, not the would-be pop stars Boyd also effortlessly captured, two weeks later, on 'Arnold Layne', a recording Smith was unable to better.

Containing 'Overdrive' was Norman Smith's greatest challenge that spring. He already realised where the power-base in the band lay, '[Syd] really was in control. He was the only one doing any writing, he was the only one who I, as a producer, had to convince if I had any ideas.' But he was finding that Barrett had not only a mind of his own, but a contrary spirit, housed in that charming, youthful exterior. As Smith recently revealed, 'I always felt I was treading on thin ice the whole time, and I had to watch exactly what I said to Syd. He was always terribly fragile . . . [But] there was [also] a certain stubbornness in the man's make-up.' That stubborn streak did not manifest itself in verbal confrontation, as it could with a loose cannon like Lennon, but rather in a determination not to be blown off course by the ultra-straight Smith:

Norman Smith: He would be singing a song and I'd call him into the control room to give a few instructions. Then he'd go back out and not even sing the first part the same, let alone the bit I'd been talking about. Sometimes he even changed the words – he just had no discipline.

In fact, Barrett displayed real discipline at these sessions, crafting some of hippydom's most mind-manifesting manifestoes until they had all the surface sheen of highly accessible pop songs, showing himself to be more chameleon than popinjay. As EMI engineer Bown suggests, '[Syd] was less rigid about what could and couldn't be done. No-one really understood Pink Floyd, particularly Norman. Pink Floyd were different, and they were meant to be different.'

That initial EMI 'Interstellar Overdrive' was cut in two takes, both around the ten-minute mark, at the end of a long session. As with 'Arnold Layne', it condensed down and amped up the song, but inevitably it fell short of what the song could be in performance (Pete Townshend later dismissed the whole album as having 'so little to do with what they did live. It was like bubblegum – Mickey Mouse music', though the exact same 'criticism' could be levelled at The Who circa '67). It went back to what Jenner had told that sceptical female reporter from Canadian radio: 'If you had the sort of sound they're making in the clubs coming over the radio while you were doing the washing up, you'd probably scream!'

If the 27 February 'Interstellar Overdrive' was a muted cry, it was not the last such scream. When the band returned to Abbey Road on 16 March, after a bout of gigs and promotional work for 'Layne', they set about producing a more abridged version for a French EP, presumably believing our Continental cousins could not withstand the full ten-minute travelogue (actually, France was the only place in the world to issue The Rolling Stones' eleven-minute 'Goin' Home' as a two-sided single, so . . .). Using the basic track from 27 February, they tacked a freak-out ending on to the song in place of the usual burbling jump into hyperspace. But still they would not leave their signature song alone. Further brushstrokes would be applied at the mixing stage.

For now, it was necessary to return to some stranger stories from Barrett's burgeoning collection of fables. If he had complained in his first EMI press bio about 'having no time [any more] for reading fairy stories', he was still finding time to pen his own. Though Floyd were encountering little resistance from the label regarding their fastidious working methods and nocturnal lifestyle – The Beatles having prepared the way in both instances – their itinerary had nothing like the same flexibility as The Beatles'. They had most definitely *not* retired from the road. As Mason observes, 'We were still, quite often, using afternoon sessions and then actually going and doing gigs in the evening.'

The solution reached was to block-book a set of sessions in mid-March to break the back of the album. After a productive 16 March session, the band decided to spend three days the following week producing enough for an album-order to be pencilled in. By the time they met a spaced-out Lennon, and heard a little of what The Beatles were about to offer the world, Floyd had laid down five further forward-thrusts in four days of sustained studio-work, 'Flaming', 'The Gnome', Roger Waters's 'Take Up Thy Stethoscope', 'The Scarecrow' and 'Pow R Toc H'.

'Stethoscope' and 'Pow R' were 'old' stage favourites, but 'Flaming' was a recent addition to Barrett's book of song. Based on The Byrds' 'I Come and Stand at Every Door' – itself based on the ancient Orcadian folk-song, 'The Great Silkie of Sule Skerry' – it was not content to climb a mere eight miles. After Syd sang, 'Hey ho, here we go/ Ever so high', came an audio-representation of a psychedelic experience – supposedly based on a pill-popping picnic enjoyed on the banks of the River Cam in the autumn of 1965 – which gave the lie to EMI's claim that Barrett's band were 'not trying to create hallucinatory effects on their audiences'.

If the studio left them reliant on audio tools alone to create this netherworld of the senses – their light show and deafening PA being absent from the equation – Abbey Road studios was one of the best-equipped studios in the world when it came to sound effects, even if they had to be dubbed to four-track. In this pre-digital era, Floyd's Nick Mason was astonished to discover that the EMI 'empire owned vast quantities of instruments that were scattered around the studios . . . An extensive sound-effect library was also available, as well as purpose-built, tile-lined echo chambers that we especially favoured for recording footsteps.'

And though Norman Smith did not have George Martin's experience when it came to incorporating sound effects – utilised extensively on the comedy records which had made Martin's reputation at Parlophone – everyone on his team was au fait with ADT,

Bob Dylan tries to take it easy. Mayfair Hotel, 3 May, 1966.

A fresh-faced Pink Floyd prepare for the psychedelic explosion, 1967.
© Redferns, photographer John Rodgers

A study in self-assured nonchalance: Cream, 1967.
© Redferns, photographer Michael Ochs Archives

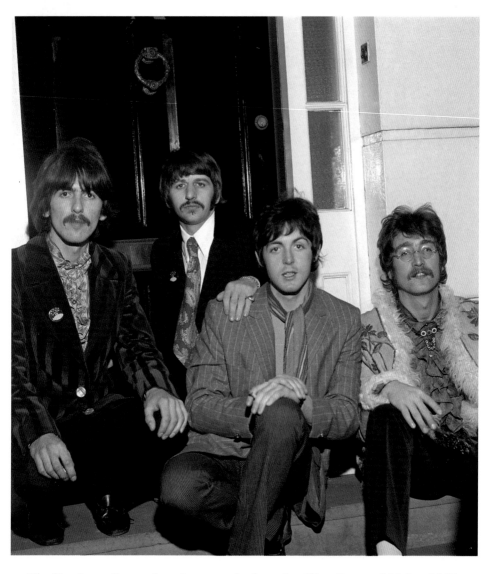

The Beatles strike a relaxed pose at the launch of *Sgt. Pepper*, 19 May, 1967.

The Fab Four show the world their new fold-out sleeve, 19 May, 1967.

Hendrix, The West End, London, England, the third rock from the sun, 1967.
© Redferns, photographer Mick Gold

The Move, stationary, 1967.
© *Redferns, photographer Jan Persson*

The Beach Boys get to grips with flower power (and sideburns), 1967.
© *Redferns / GAB Archives*

which was liberally applied to most Barrett vocals, especially on the more otherworldly songs likes 'Flaming' and 'Astronomy Domine'. The Binson Echorec was another tool which proved that the only difference between men and boys was the price of their toys, and was dolloped on with relish:

> **Nick Mason:** [The Echorec] can make almost any instrument sound as if it's been recorded by Thomas Edison himself, in terms of the way you get a build-up of white noise, but that [was] part of the attraction of it.

If The Beatles were experimenting with the sounds of the East, the Floyd preferred to dip into the West's equally rich traditions – combining folklore *and* classical music. 'The Gnome', a Grimm fairy-tale lyric, they gave an almost choral arrangement. Using a celeste (an organ stop that is intentionally tuned slightly off pitch) which someone had 'left in the studio from a previous session', the song acquired its ethereal, otherworldly sound. As Mason told John Cavanagh, this kind of spontaneity was a feature of these sessions, 'There's a sort of random air to *Piper*, which is just based on what was around at the time.'

Even before 21 March – when Floyd completed their sustained assault on the album, and got to meet the other Beatles – McCartney had evidently been keeping tabs (sic) on their progress. A passing reference to the sessions in that week's *Melody Maker* reported, 'Beatle Paul McCartney has already dropped in to several of the sessions'; while Andrew King remembers, 'McCartney was fairly matey. He would come into the studio occasionally while we were recording.' Was he worried the Floyd might get 'there' first?

With eight originals in the can – and with The Beatles still ten days away from concluding the session-work on *Sgt. Pepper* – it perhaps entered the Floyd's heads that they would have their own album, started just a month ago, ready to roll at much the same time as The Beatles' latest fab waxing – especially if the post-production on *Pepper* was as protracted as the sessions.

It was not to be. On the day Floyd completed a satisfactory basic track for 'Pow R Toc H' (which must be heard in mono, the stereo mix resembling a naked mollusc hanging from the shell of its mono self), the Floyd heard that their first single had entered the charts at thirty-three. As a result, they were obliged to leave much of the mixing to the Abbey Road team as they toured hotspots of hedonism like Barnstaple, Bromley and Bishop's Stortford, stopping off to pre-record a mimed rendition of 'Arnold Layne' for *Top of the Pops* on 4 April – along with The Move, who were similarly booked solid with live commitments. However, whereas 'I Can Hear The Grass Grow' continued to climb, 'Arnold Layne' slipped back and when *ToTP* was broadcast on the sixth, Floyd's performance went unused.

Still with no time off for bad behaviour, the band were obliged to hew another week out of their April schedule in order to record the two tracks needed for the album to go into post-production (and EMI's release schedule); at the same time making a stab at a second single to sit alongside the grander vinyl visitation. A gig on the fourteenth, in Newcastle-under-Lyme, was deemed an impractical distance away and was rearranged for May, leaving just two shows in easy reach of London, Tilbury in Essex and Brighton on the south coast, interrupting a week of rare respite from the road. It was full steam ahead on the express to Album Deadline.

Of the two *Piper* cuts recorded between 11 and 18 April, 'Astronomy Domine' proved the more problematic. Despite fourteen takes on the eleventh, it still required two further sessions, one devoted to overdubbing vocals and a new guitar part from Syd; a further evening being set aside to record the 'wild track' that would eventually give the song (and the album) such a striking opening. This comprised Peter Jenner reciting through a megaphone a composite of quotes from *The Observer Book of Spaceflight* that Syd had compiled. Finally, on the eighteenth, Barrett's vocals were treated with ADT and a mono mix was done, in expectation of a speedy conclusion to the album.

Clearly the attention to detail expended on this song suggested real determination to start the album as they meant to go on, with their very own psychedelic overture. The 11 April session may well have been the session where Bown recalls 'they had a lot of trouble getting things together in the studio', but if so it was their quest for perfection that was causing frustration, not their unfocused ways. On a good day, the band could easily produce a superlative single-take 'Astronomy Domine', as was demonstrated just a month later, when a live-in-the-studio version filmed for the BBC's *Look of the Week*, complete with atmospheric light show and Barrett as stage-director, superseded its hard-won studio-kin.

According to Cambridge college-friend Ian Moore, the inspiration for the song was another of Syd's early psychedelic trips, one in which he had a plum and an orange in either hand, and 'the plum was the planet Venus and the orange was Jupiter, [while] Syd was floating in space between them'. It couldn't have been further in content from the song they began the following day (and which follows it on the LP). Bearing the interesting title 'Percy the Ratcatcher', it was later renamed on the studio layout sheet 'Lucifer Sam – theme from the day in the life of Percy the Ratcatcher'. Seemingly concerning a Siamese cat with magical gifts, the song received the same loving attention to detail as its precursor, with much of one session (the eighteenth) devoted to layering the vocals to give them a slightly sibilant sound.

Also recorded on the eighteenth was a song that seems to have been marked out as a possible follow-up single ('See Emily Play' having not as yet been written). Later superseded, 'She Was A Millionaire' would be mentioned in relation to a *third* Floyd single at the end of July. Two of the three takes recorded on the eighteenth were marked as complete, both clocking in at exactly 4.06, suggesting that Floyd's efforts yielded something usable. However, the fact that there was no final mono mix made, nor additional overdubs during post-production sessions, suggests it was quickly sidelined, before it was simply forgotten (then misplaced).

There was now thirty-eight minutes' (i.e. a 1967 album's) worth of new material in the can, most of it already mixed to mono by

Smith and his assistants, all ready to introduce the commercial world to the previously subterranean sounds of psychedelia. And yet, the *Piper* project now stalled for almost a month while the band prepared for the two biggest shows of their career to date, a 14-Hour Technicolour Dream to be held at Alexandra Palace on the last Saturday of April (29) – at which Lennon finally got to hear what he'd been avoiding – and a special sit-down concert at the Queen Elizabeth Hall on Friday, 12 May, entitled 'Games For May'. Split over two halves, with an interval, it was presented as if it were the kind of classical recital more commonly held at QEH. The 'Games For May' concept also prompted Barrett to write a theme song for the event, perhaps his finest pop moment, 'See Emily Play'. But the resultant delay ensured that the album would not be ready until July at the earliest.

Though both shows were triumphs, generating glowing reviews and confirming their cutting-edge credentials, by the time the album did appear the band's talismanic leader had started to act *very* strange and the album – which would surely have benefited from any direct comparison drawn with a contemporaneous *Sgt. Pepper* – became more of an afterthought to many ex-teenyboppers' lysergic summer.

It is thus surprising to find Floyd manager Peter Jenner informing *Melody Maker* on 15 May that not only would the band 'complete the recording of their new single and their first LP this week', but that the single 'will be rush released on either May 26 or June 2, and the album will be issued in mid-June'. And he was absolutely on cue – sure enough, the album *was* completed the following Sunday, the album-closer 'Bike' being recorded over twelve takes in Studio Three. The band then hightailed it (with the emphasis on high) over to Chelsea's Sound Techniques, to put finishing touches to the single version of 'See Emily Play', which they'd recorded earlier in the week (probably on the eighteenth).

Amid all this activity, the Floyd had apparently found time to acquire one of the few perks that a contract with EMI proffered, an advance copy of the latest Beatles LP, *Sgt. Pepper's Lonely Hearts*

Club Band. According to June Bolan, who worked as Jenner's assistant and a shoulder for Barrett throughout 1967, 'that' evening (the twenty-second, one would have to suppose) the Floyd had a big party at Jenner's house to celebrate the release of the epoch-defining Beatles album, and the completion of their own humble invocation of the zeitgeist.

If their own crazy schedule, Barrett's thirst for perfection and a certain dilatoriness that probably reflected increasing drug use, stopped *Piper At The Gates of Dawn* going head to head with the Sergeant, it would still become the other essential book-end to this summer of sex and drugs, setting it to a genuine acid-rock soundtrack.

TAKE A TRIP

BEATLES NEW L.P.

MOST EXPENSIVE EVER PRODUCED?

THE current Beatles recording sessions are producing some very trendy clothes as well as forward-looking songs. The variety of musical instruments in the studio is only equalled by the varying styles of the Beatles suits, jackets, ties and shoes.

The new album will also be surely one of the most expensive ever produced. Messrs. Lennon, McCartney, Starr and Harrison, together with road managers, Neil Aspinall and Mal Evans, not forgetting recording manager, George Martin, plus engineers, doormen to keep out intruders, etc., have been spending every weekday night in E.M.I.'s No. 2 studio for the past month and there were dozens of sessions in earlier months too. The results, so far, have been "Strawberry Fields Forever" and "Penny Lane", their recent single, plus six additional tracks for the new album, which means that they are about half-way through.

EXPENSIVE

I estimate that the new LP will eventually cost something like £25,000 to produce! That's a lot of lolly, far more than any normal LP costs to produce, but we're talking, after all, about the princes of pop, and any Beatles album must sell at least a million, if not several, all over the world.

So E.M.I. are hardly likely to begrudge the Beatles studio time. Gone are the days when a track would be run through, rehearsed, arranged and a master tape recorded, all in two hours. Now they frequently arrive at the studio with only a vague theme or rough set of lyrics, which they then proceed to play about with, for hours, or often days.

Three guitars and a set of drums are all old hat and apparently considered incapable of backing a new Beatles song.

John, George and Paul discussing a particularly difficult lyric line for one of the songs on their new album. Note that George has shaved off his beard. That's Ravi Shankar's brother in the background, he's spending most nights in the studio with boys.

Experiment is everything. The night I was in the studio, George Martin spent half an hour, before the Beatles arrived, dropping spoons, pennies, and any other object he could think of, into a large cauldron of water. The bottom of the cauldron was lined with plastic sponge, so that just the resulting splonks, gesplashes and plops would be recorded by the microphone.

Then the fashion display began. Paul zipped into the studio, wearing a lemon yellow jacket, set off by a brightly striped tie. With only a pause to shake hands, he was behind Ringo's drum kit, demonstrating that if ever the other three Beatles decided to retire, he could do the whole job, songwriting, singing, harmonising with himself on the vocals, playing lead guitar, bass guitar, piano, organ, trumpet and drums.

Then George strolled in, with his Civil War moustache, but minus beard. With that beard he reminded me of an Afghanistan sheep-herder, but the illusion is now gone. His moustache was set off by a long, black, Mississippi gambler's jacket and black moccasins.

Ringo and John arrived next, having driven up together in John's Mini—with blacked-out windows, of course. The new moustache very much, but curiously they are much blacker than his medium-brown hair. So much so that some people say that

Sgt. Pepper is called the first concept album, but it doesn't go anywhere. All my contributions to the album have absolutely nothing to do with this idea of Sgt. Pepper and his band; but it works 'cause we said it worked. –

John Lennon, *Playboy*, 1980

On 25 February, The Beatles' new double a-side – 'Strawberry Fields Forever b/w Penny Lane' – appeared in the shops, confirming for all those with ears that psychedelic pop was the happenin' sound of a self-consciously turned-on town. Lennon also felt inspired enough to manifest his mind one more time, which was a stroke of luck as the *Pepper* sessions were in danger of becoming an excuse for learning the limits of four-track technology, not a reaffirmation of The Beatles' place on the slippery pop pole.

Two nights earlier, McCartney had produced one of his vignettes of urban life, 'Lovely Rita', a straightforward enough rewrite of 'Fortune Teller', yet still confusing enough to convince at least one American academic of the day that it was about 'a whore in Liverpool, who procures through her daytime trade as a meter-maid'. Yet even this ditty was not left in its live-in-studio state, spruced up by the odd instrumental overdub. An entire session in early March would be spent adding not only 'backing vocals' but what Martin disparagingly described as 'a selection . . . of weird and wonderful noises . . . on the play-out of the song', including the entire band playing 'paper and combs, as a mock brass section' (a trick later used by Johnny Rotten on the original studio version of 'Submission'). Martin was not very impressed:

George Martin: The anarchy that crept into the recording of 'Lovely Rita' was the beginning of the undisciplined, sometimes self-indulgent

way of working that became a bit boring during *Magical Mystery Tour*.
[MoSP]

At some point during these interminable sessions, Martin would
confide in Beatles publicist Tony Barrow 'that this [album] was the
most indulgent thing he and The Beatles ever did'. He went further,
stating, 'We are only able to do this kind of stuff because the group
is so uniquely successful that nobody among the EMI hierarchy
dare challenge what we are doing.' The one person in the echelons of EMI who might have convinced The Beatles to question
their working methods was Martin himself. But he, too, didn't 'dare
challenge what [they] are doing'.

Martin may well have found at least one ally if he *had* queried
the process. Lennon liked to think of himself as a doyen of the
weird and wacky, but he was a traditionalist at heart. When the
band did eventually decide to revert – or even, get back – to former
ways, he was a primary mover in such a 'retrograde' direction. For
now, his painful insecurities meant he was constantly looking for
affirmation of his worth from equally fucked-up, fair-weather friends.
As Barrow puts it in his memoir, John managed to convince himself
'that hallucinatory substances improved and accelerated [his]
creative thought processes. Friends who joined [him] in [his] chem-
ically-induced paradise actively encouraged . . . [this] belief, while
some of us looked on.'

Lennon was not alone in believing that the substances he was
ingesting 'opened up' his mind, even if his womb-like world supplied
the only subject matter he had the will to address for long enough
to yield a song. Barrow again cuts to the chase in describing the
man beneath that 'bullet-proof exterior' as 'pitifully insecure . . .
[someone] who doubted his own abilities and couldn't concentrate
long enough on his songwriting to complete more than a fraction
of his best work'.

The one full-time eyewitness to Lennon's withdrawal from the
world was his bemused wife, Cynthia Lennon, who later described
his routine thus, 'When he woke up he'd write a few words down

and then maybe go over to the piano. [But then] he'd listen to music, gawp at television and read newspapers. He was basically dropping out from what was happening.' If her husband was increasingly uncomfortable with reality, he still felt it his duty to scribble brief bulletins from the world he preferred to inhabit.

Many of these bulletins were ideas that went off with the nowhere man (Lennon almost bragged to Hunter Davies, 'Sometimes . . . I've let a few things slip away, which I *could* have caught if I'd been wanting something'). Yet there still remained occasional moments of crystalline clarity. Over several months, using three separate song 'ideas' – which, as he predicted to The Beatles biographer, 'turn[ed] out to be different parts of the same song' – Lennon worked on 'Strawberry Fields Forever's' equally psychedelic sequel, 'I Am The Walrus'.

Another such moment produced the following Lear-like couplet: 'Picture yourself in a boat on the river/ With tangerine trees and marmalade skies.' This time, though, he called his straighter friend, Paul, to come quick. The songwriters' symbiotic distillation of shared ideas was something Lennon described – at the end of his life – as having been 'functional, as well as musical'. Paul's input now would salvage this idea and give it to the Sergeant, allowing Lennon to sink back into his torpor again:

> **Paul McCartney:** We . . . went up to the music room at the top of the house and he played me the idea he had for it, starting with 'Picture yourself . . .' . . . and how this title would make a great psychedelic song. [1993]

The title from the outset, according to its composers, was 'Lucy in the Sky with Diamonds'. As Mal Evans explained in *Beatles Monthly*, the same month it appeared on album, 'John got [it] from his son! Julian brought home a painting he'd done at school and his father asked him what it was supposed to be. "It's Lucy in the sky with diamonds," explained Julian.' That there was such a painting is not in dispute. Mrs Lennon also remembers it well: 'I remember [Julian] coming home from school with [the drawing and showing it] to his Dad, who was sitting down . . . It was just a simple child-like drawing of a little girl in the sky with stars. It was the usual house and trees and stars and the little girl was Lucy, a girl from his school.' A chord was struck and Lennon kept the painting to show to his partner-in-song:

> **Paul McCartney:** I went up to John's house in Weybridge. When I arrived we were having a cup of tea, and he said, 'Look at this great drawing Julian's done. Look at the title!' He showed me a drawing on school paper, a five-by-seven-inch piece of paper, of a little girl with lots of stars, and right across the top there was written, in very neat child handwriting, I think in pencil, 'Lucy in the Sky with Diamonds'. [MYFN]

Forget Lennon Senior, here truly was a child prodigy! Born in May 1963, Julian was barely three and a half years old when he began entitling his early visual work. However, when the supposed drawing was reproduced, in Steve Turner's commendably thorough *Hard Day's Write*, there was no such handwriting, neat or otherwise; though in all other respects it seemed to match Paul's detailed description. In fact, so closely did it match Macca's memory that anyone cynically inclined might have doubted the likelihood of such a synergy.

As it happens, the illustration in question had already been rejected by Christie's, to whom it was offered for auction, because their Beatles expert simply didn't believe it was genuine – indeed, did not believe it was the work of *any* three-year old. All of which has a bearing because of the absolute determination with which Lennon and (especially) McCartney have insisted over the years that they wrote the song without the foggiest idea that Lucy – Sky – Diamond spelt LSD. Whodathunk?!

What *is* incontestable is that the song was called 'Lucy in the Sky with Diamonds' by the time EMI engineers rolled the tapes on 1 March. However, journalist Thomas Thompson witnessed the song as it evolved in performance throughout the previous night – without any tapes rolling! – and he called the song 'Lucy with the Diamond Eyes' in his account of the 'rehearsal' session in *Life* magazine. What he heard was still at night's end a work in progress. From his privileged eyrie, Thompson managed to depict The Beatles' new way of working on a song that, even after McCartney's initial input, still needed a belt and some braces:

> Paul and John explain to [Martin] that they have spent this day writing a song which they want to record tonight. 'All right, let's hear it,' he says. Paul pounds out a strong assortment of chords and John sings, falsetto, the melody *which is to be called 'Lucy in the Sky with Diamonds' [author's italics]*. They go through it half a dozen times while Martin nods, quickly familiarising himself with the composition and making notes. At this embryonic stage the song sounds like the early Beatles works . . . but before they are done with it . . . it will undergo extraordinary changes. 'Picture yourself in a boat on a river, with tangerine trees and marmalade skies,' sings John over and over again, while George Harrison begins finding a guitar accompaniment and Ringo . . . slaps out a rhythm . . . It begins absolutely from scratch . . . It is now almost midnight in the recording studio and after four hours of assault, 'Lucy in the Sky . . .' still sounds quite terrible. Fifth Beatle [!] Martin grimaces, 'We are light years away from anything tonight,' he shudders. 'They know it is awful now, and they're trying to straighten it out. It may be a week before they're pleased, if ever. They're always coming up with something new they've just learned, something I wouldn't dream of. They never cease to amaze me.' . . . [But by] the bone-weary hour of 2 a.m., 'Lucy with the Diamond Eyes' is beginning to take shape.

Of course, by the time the article appeared, in mid-June, the whole world – Thompson included – knew that the song was called 'Lucy in the Sky with Diamonds', so the former 'title' reads like a slip of the pen. Except that nothing like 'Lucy with the Diamond Eyes' appears in the final song (though it scans *exactly* with 'the girl with kaleidoscope eyes'). Thompson confirms that the songwriters had come straight from Weybridge to Abbey Road, but no mention is made in his piece of any unexpected change in tempo (the song jumps from 3/4 to 4/4 for the middle-section in which its eventual title appears). And according to Martin, 'John, as he often did, composed ['Lucy in the Sky . . .'] on the hoof; he had the introduction written, but little else as far as the melody went, until we actually got into the studio.'

All of which leads me to suspect that the middle-section was only added once the song was introduced to the band at Abbey Road. Could it be that this middle-section was a belated suggestion of McCartney's, as had been the case on 'A Day in the Life', and that it fitted his avowed intent, to write 'lyrics [that] were intentionally psychedelic'? Martin certainly considered it to be 'virtually two separate songs, the middle-section [having] a completely different tempo and . . . a completely different time signature to the opening'.

Not in dispute is the source of the song's opening image, 'Picture yourself in a boat on a river', which Lennon had taken from one of the few books he always held dear, *Through The Looking Glass (And What Alice Found There)* (specifically the passage in the chapter 'Wool and Water' where 'the boat was left to drift down the stream . . . while Alice forgot all about the Sheep and the knitting, as she bent over the side of the boat'). Lennon later admitted that he'd 'always wanted to write *Alice in Wonderland*'. He also intimated that the 'girl with kaleidoscope eyes' was his Johanna, and 'Lucy in the Sky' his vision:

John Lennon: It was Alice in the boat. She is buying an egg and it turns into Humpty-Dumpty. The woman serving in the shop turns into a sheep and the next minute they are rowing in a rowing boat somewhere, and I was visualising that. There was also the image of the female who would someday come save me – a 'girl with kaleidoscope eyes' who would come out of the sky.' [1980]

If Carroll's two child-like visions had long been an inspiration to Lennon, it was probably the Christmas 1966 BBC broadcast of Jonathan Miller's *Alice In Wonderland* that now set Lennon thinking along these lines. It seems inconceivable – given a cast culled from the ranks of The Goons, Beyond the Fringe and The Establishment; and music provided by, of all people, Ravi Shankar – that Lennon did not catch the production, or that he wasn't inspired to revisit Alice by Miller's landmark film.

But there were plenty of other influences at work on one of Lennon's most literate lyrics. Carroll loved his wordplay, but no more than his contemporary, Edward Lear, whose *Nonsense Verses* were still greatly loved when Lennon was a boy. Then there was that mainstay of Lennon's off-the-wall humour, Spike Milligan. Milligan, who had worked with George Martin, not only knew Lennon but actually attended at least one *Sgt. Pepper* session, where he indulged in the usual wordplay games with the young songwriter:

> **Spike Milligan:** John told me that some of his lyrics had been inspired by Goon Show dialogue. We used to talk about 'plasticine ties' in The Goon Show and this crept up in 'Lucy' as 'plasticine porters with looking glass ties'. I knew Lennon quite well. He used to talk a lot about comedy. He was a Goon Show freak. It all stopped when he married Yoko Ono . . . He never asked for me again. [HDW]

There were other influences, altogether more generational. The main one was Dylan, who had convinced Lennon never to be afraid of putting poetic sense ahead of the prosaic kind. As the Liver-pudlian told Cott, 'We've gone past those days when we wouldn't have used words because they didn't make any sense, or what we thought was sense . . . Dylan taught us a lot in this respect.' On a very basic level, 'Lucy in the Sky' was an attempt to write a pastoral English equivalent of Dylan's 'Mr Tambourine Man', a song both Lennon and McCartney adored. Even the boat on the river is as much Dylan's 'magic swirlin' ship' (itself a homage to Rimbaud's 'bateau ivre') as Alice's daydream.

Whereas Dylan was attempting to convey a consciousness-altering experience among the all-night revelries of the New Orleans Mardi Gras, where alcohol, speed and weed sufficed, Lennon had something a lot more kaleidoscopic in mind. He wanted to paint colours with sound. Not that he was the first to notice 'how acoustic perceptions, such as the noise of water gushing from a tap, or the spoken word, were transformed into optical illusions', when tripping on LSD. Actually Dr Albert Hoffman, the man who first synthesised the man-made drug, included said observation in his early notes. Lennon's compositional cohort was all for describing a psychedelic trip in song:

> **Paul McCartney:** When we were talking about 'cellophane flowers' and 'kaleidoscope eyes' and 'grow so incredibly high', we were talking about drug experiences, no doubt about it. [MYFN]

Yet McCartney was still writing from one side of the divide – the same one as the Dylan who wrote 'Mr Tambourine Man' (though *not* the one which revealed its definitive self to The Beatles at the Albert Hall) – and Lennon the other. Paul had yet to try LSD. As such, the 'drug experience' meant something entirely different to him. Hence, perhaps, his desire to portray 'Lucy in the Sky' as a drug-song, but not an acid-song. For him, it was no such thing. (This could be why he continues to make such a fuss about this 'accidental' association.) For the moment, Lennon's true ally in the band when it came to pushing an acidic agenda was Harrison:

> **George Harrison:** A lot of the lyrics that John was doing I could relate to. Having done this lysergic stuff together, I felt very connected to him. His lyrics often made me howl, because I felt I knew where they were coming from. [1996]

All three were on board, though, when it came to making Lucy/Alice sound like she'd had a 'drug experience'. Allan Moore, in his painfully dry monograph on the album, notices that 'the frequently asserted LSD references in the song are supported by "abnormalities" in texture and production: the drifting of the double-tracked voice; the [use of the] Indian tamboura; the phasing on the bass ... and, perhaps most notably, the general avoidance of a drum beat in the verses' first strains (notable for the emptiness of their texture), which allows a sense of impressions simply to waft in.' Ian MacDonald gets there quicker, attributing the recording's success to 'a glamorous production (voice and guitar through the Leslie cabinet; echo and varispeed on everything)', but surprisingly dismisses the song itself as 'poorly thought out'.

Neither MacDonald nor Moore really 'explains' the purpose of the strangely discordant bridge, which sounds as if Sgt. Pepper's Lonely Hearts Club Band have just gatecrashed a Beatles recording session. This time, though, the kitchen-sink proved an appropriate addition, and the song was rightly heralded by many as a highpoint of the album on its release. The Beatles certainly gave the song due diligence, spending three entire evening sessions (28 February through 2 March) getting it better.

Throughout that first evening they were also engaging with *Life* reporter Thomas Thompson about their hopes and fears for the album. The unerring confidence that oozed out of every McCartney pore was still intact as he helped bang 'Lucy' into shape, taking time out to tell Thompson, 'Sure, we're going to lose some fans. We lost them in Liverpool when we took off our leather jackets and put on suits ... [But] we've reached the point now where there are no barriers. Musically, now, this moment, tonight, this is where we are.' Harrison seemed equally happy with the direction the band was finally heading in, and unconcerned by any commercial consequences:

> **George Harrison:** We've only just discovered what we can do as musicians. What thresholds we can cross. It doesn't matter so much any more if we're No.1 or on the charts. It's all right if the people dislike us. Just don't deny us.

Thompson himself seemed to suspect that the most popular band in the world was taking some huge risk. A year after 'Tomorrow Never Knows' he suggested in print, 'They are stepping far ahead of their audience, recording music so complex and so unlike the music that made them successful that they could very likely lose the foundation of their support. But that possibility does not bother them in the least.' They became bothered the following week, when they found 'Strawberry Fields' stuck at number two, and looking unlikely to topple Engelbert Humperdinck's egregious assault on Ray Price's twangy 'original' of 'Release Me'.

McCartney put on his brave face for the media, telling Alan Freeman, 'We can't just stop where we are, or there's nothing left to do. We can go on trying to make popular records, [but] it can get dead dull if we're not trying to expand and move on into other things. Unless you're careful, you can be successful and unsuccessful at the same time.' He was still convinced that he could carry the band's new sound to the masses, but the news that 'Strawberry Fields b/w Penny Lane' had stalled at number two, where it stayed put for three consecutive weeks (March 4, 11 and 18) before dropping to five, couldn't help but raise questions about the potential market for their increasingly ornate album.

In fact, the remaining three songs McCartney contributed – 'Getting Better' (recorded on the ninth, the day the charts confirmed their forestalling), 'She's Leaving Home' and 'With A Little Help From My Friends' (both collaborations with Lennon) – could all have fit comfortably on either of *Pepper*'s two predecessors. Even 'She's Leaving Home', the most ambitious – and successful – of these cuts was very much in the vein of 'Eleanor Rigby', a number-one single just six months earlier.

Where 'She's Leaving Home' deviated from 'Eleanor Rigby' was in the way that it used a true story, culled from the newspapers, to depict *both* sides of a familiar tale of generational conflict; as opposed to hanging the powerful sense of loneliness everyone feels on a morbid tune, a fictional life and a single portentous question, 'Where do they all come from?' Lennon was not the only one whose lyric-writing was developing apace.

The story in question had featured in the 27 February edition of the *Daily Mail*, telling of the heartbreak Mr and Mrs Coe felt because their daughter, Melanie, had run away. Mr Coe was particularly bemused to find that she had left so many material possessions behind: 'I cannot imagine why she should run away. She has everything here. She is very keen on clothes but she left them all – even her fur coat!' Unlike with Tara Browne, McCartney had no knowledge of the Coes' personal circumstances save what he had read, but began writing the song almost immediately, bringing in Lennon to provide the dexterous little asides that are a counterpoint throughout the song, leading relentlessly to that final, heartbreaking, 'Bye bye'. In the finished song, John's voice becomes the echo to all that unfolds.

Despite its detached viewpoint, McCartney manages to seamlessly weave the feelings of the two parties – the girl and the parents – so successfully that Melanie Coe herself later admitted, 'The amazing thing about the song was how much it got right about my life.' For Macca, such facility came easily. As he points out in his authorised biography, 'Songs . . . don't have to exist for me. The feeling of them is enough.' Lennon stated a preference for songs of personal experience, but at this time was going to great pains to avoid those experiences that would have opened up his worldview.

'She's Leaving Home' was a new type of song, but the theme it addressed was the kind repeatedly addressed in BBC's contemporary *Play For Today* series, where gritty realism had become the order of the day. Here, in just three minutes nineteen seconds, McCartney (and Lennon) portray characters altogether more three-dimensional than Father MacKenzie or Eleanor Rigby, while its narrator – much like a good playwright – delicately avoids taking sides. Wilfred Mellers was one of the few critics to recognise the structural complexity of the song, and the tightrope it walks:

Throughout, ['She's Leaving Home'], though parodistic[!], is never destructive. The arching cello tune is as beautiful as it is comic; and

the irregular structure enacts the story, conveying not merely the fact
of the girl's departure but all the muddled hope, apprehension and
fear in the girl's heart, the fuddled incomprehension of the parents.

For once, that 'arching cello tune' had not been scored by The
Beatles' ever-ready arranger, George Martin, but by Mike Leander,
a jack of all arrangements (who, as noted, had recently scored the
horns on the Stones' 'Have You Seen Your Mother', only to see
them buried below C-level). Because of the increasing demands
The Beatles were making on his time (usually at twilight), Martin
had been juggling his other commitments throughout the winter
of 1967. Finally he found himself unable to do the string arrangement McCartney wanted, *when* he wanted it. Paul was unfazed,
making the call to Leander who, according to Martin, 'did a good
workmanlike job on the score'. Martin's tautological put-down hides
real hurt:

> **George Martin:** It obviously hadn't occurred to [Paul] that I would be
> upset. Years later, in fact, he said, 'I couldn't understand why it was
> so important to you. It was in my mind, and I wanted to get it out,
> get it down. That's all.' [MoSP]

Martin was clearly starting to believe he *was* the fifth Beatle; not
just a useful lieutenant, talented but certainly replaceable. In fact,
suspicion lurks that Macca quite deliberately turned the task over
to Leander. Even if he hadn't as yet realised Martin was polishing
up the regalia to a higher rank – and I suspect he had – the arrangement seems *consciously* syrupy. Martin would have made the whole
thing tasteful, but in order for the song to be both affecting *and*
parodic (*à la* 'When I'm 64'), it needed a little treacle. Leander
provided that.

McCartney confirms that he left Leander to his work, 'and then
reviewed it later, which I don't like as a practice . . . It didn't work
out badly. I don't like the echo on the harp, but that must be
George rather than Mike Leander.' Perhaps this was Martin's way

of kicking back. Yet McCartney had got his way; and the album now had its much-needed *big* ballad. And one from on high.

But if McCartney was trying to return the album to a commercial keel, Harrison seemed determined to steer it back off course. By the time Harrison appeared at the studio, song-in-hand, on 15 March – the same day they laid down the basic track for 'She's Leaving Home' – he seems to have decided he was no longer a Beatle, and it was high time he started recording a solo album of sitar music. Or rather, as he'd just suggested in an *IT* interview, he no longer felt The Beatles should define themselves by pop, and it was his duty to ensure that they go even further than their latest, faltering 45:

> **George Harrison:** You just go on and on and on until you go right out there. The thing is we *could* go there; there's times, I'm sure, where we hold back a lot with things like 'Strawberry Fields'. I know there's a lot of people who like that, who probably wouldn't have liked us a year ago. And then there's a lot of people who didn't like it, who did like us a year ago . . . We're losing a lot but we're gaining a lot, too. [1967]

Actually, Harrison seemed to have lost interest in most previous aspects of 'Beatle' music. As he informed Miles in that *IT* conversation, 'Indian music . . . has got everything in it. I still like electronics and all sorts of music . . . but Indian music is just untouchable.' And at one of the final *Sgt. Pepper* sessions, he warned *TeenSet's* Judith Sims, 'I'm going to be involved solely in Indian music for a long time . . . I think we've proved that electronic music can go with "pop" music, and we've also proved that Indian music can go with "pop" music, and we will prove that Indian and electronic and "pop" can all go together.'

The song he began recording on the fifteenth, 'Within You Without You', proved the exact opposite. Whereas *Revolver's* 'Love You To' worked, on one level, as a pop song played on Indian instruments, 'Within You, Without You' was an ex-pop guitarist renouncing the exterior world for the 'wisdom' of the East. As he told Miles, 'The way out is in.' Unfortunately, his new song had a set of lyrics that dumbed the homilies of Eastern philosophy down to the level of a Western nursery rhyme. As MacDonald states, the main problem with the song is its 'air of superiority and sanctimonious finger-wagging'.

In this, it was not alone. For all of Lennon's biting cynicism, the nastiest songs in The Beatles canon seemed to flow largely from the pen of George. *Revolver*'s 'Taxman' suggested he was just warming up, picking as a target the subject of entire books of folksongs down the ages. By 1968, though, he had divided the human race into 'Piggies' and the privileged few who had seen the lysergic light. 'Sour Milk Sea', another fabulous vat of vitriol, was demo-ed for *The White Album* but his fellow Beatles dissuaded him from sharing this warped worldview with their adoring millions, and he was obliged to give it to Jackie Lomax. He did finally manage to get 'I Me Mine' inserted on their swansong, *Let It Be*: though anyone reading *Melody Maker* back in December '67 already knew just how he felt about this world:

> **George Harrison:** I read somewhere that the next . . . Messiah, he'll come and he'll just be too much . . . The majority of people are going to believe and they'll be digging everything and he'll come and say, 'Yeah, baby, that's right,' and all those other people who are bastards they're gonna get something else. [1967]

By dividing the world into those who 'dig everything' and 'people who are bastards', Harrison came on as the bastard-child of Billy Graham and Austin Powers pontificating about *his* inner light – the kind which became 'profound' just by being set to sitar music. The 'inspiration' for 'Within You Without You' actually materialised when he was round at Klaus Voormann's house, playing that decadent Western instrument, the harmonium. But it didn't take long for it to be transposed into an Indian dirge:

George Harrison: Having the Indian things so much in my head it was bound to come out . . . [And] Klaus had a harmonium in his house, which I hadn't played before. I was doodling on it, playing to amuse myself, when 'Within You' started to come. The tune came first then I got the first sentence. It came out of what we'd been doing that evening – 'We were talking.' That's as far as I got that night. [HD]

When he presented the song to the whole band – along with that occasional fifth column, George Martin – the producer seemed surprisingly positive about his attempt to blend classical Western and Indian instruments, finding 'what George wanted to do with the song fascinating'. As ever, what Martin liked was a challenge. Recording tamboura, tabla, dilruba, swaramandal, violins, cellos and sitar into one mellifluous whole was certainly that. There was really only one thing missing – The Beatles.

On the album that was going to cement the band's identity, its most disaffected member was now given enough largesse to hang himself. Even Harrison admitted, in 1996, that the song 'stuck out a bit, really, on *Sgt. Pepper* because it had no relationship to anything else on that album'. Hence its appearance at the start of side two, allowing fans to move the needle directly on to track two.

George Martin: 'Within You Without You' I put at the start of side two because I couldn't think where else to put it. That and 'When I'm Sixty-Four' were the alien tracks to me. [1967]

'Within You Without You' was the final nail in the coffin of whatever concept supposedly wrapped everything together. And yet it made its first appearance at the same session as the artist who had been commissioned by McCartney's friend, Robert Fraser, to produce an album cover that would reinforce its ostensible theme. Peter Blake, who was already a well-respected man in the PopArt world, had come down to the studio to discuss a cover. According to *Beatles Monthly*, this initially consisted of 'John, Paul, George and

Ringo ... be[ing] photographed in some sort of Salvation Army uniforms'.

By this time McCartney was operating in full-on control-mode, pushing everyone – but mostly himself – to finish the album to his satisfaction before he flew to the States in early April, to see girlfriend-actress Jane Asher, who was touring there. Biographer Davies, who caught only the tailend of the *Sgt. Pepper* sessions, found a band 'gnawing away at the same song for stretches of up to ten hours. Paul often appears to be the leader in all this. This is mainly because someone has to say it's not good enough, let's do it once again. They all know it. But someone has to voice the instructions. Paul does it best, as he's still the keeny.' Abandoning his usual biographical detachment, Davies then tellingly observes how to his ears, 'the final, complicated, well-layered versions [often] seem to have drowned the initial simple melody'.

Lennon, the erstwhile bandleader, now seemed to be in some other place. On 20 March, Judith Sims turned up to see McCartney 'sat at the controls with George Martin, while John perched on a ledge near the speakers, in front of the large glass window looking into the studio. John was quiet then, apparently lost in his own thoughts.' The evening was spent overdubbing the vocals – lead, harmony and counter-harmony – to 'She's Leaving Home'.

The following night it was Hunter Davies who was required to be unobtrusive, sitting taking notes while McCartney put the finishing touches to 'Getting Better'. According to Davies, 'Paul instructed the technician on which levers to press, telling him what he wanted, how it should be done, which bits he liked best. George Martin looked on, giving advice where necessary. John stared into space.'

This time it became all too apparent to Paul and George that John was 'accidentally' tripping. When he went up on the roof to stare at the stars, they became concerned and quickly ushered him down, much to Martin's bemusement. Sims's prior account suggests that if he was tripping on the 21st, it was the second such 'accident' in two nights. In truth, Lennon was starting to unravel, and it fell to his fellow Beatles to pull him through. That night McCartney decided he would accompany Lennon back home and they would take acid together.

And lo, like that *Star Trek* episode where the entire crew of the Enterprise are sprayed with the diaspora of an alien flower,[1] which turns them into a bunch of love-sick beatniks – even the uptight Spock – McCartney seems to have suddenly understood what was so great about peace, love and understanding. His conversion was positively Pauline. Within a couple of months he was telling the trashy *Sunday People*, 'It was truly a religious experience. I had never realised what people were talking about when they said God is within you, that He is love and truth.'

He also started babbling about world peace – the first worrying presentiment of 'Pipes of Peace' from our Paul – telling Thomas Thompson in all seriousness that, 'if the politicians would take LSD there wouldn't be any more war, or poverty or famine'. Barely a fortnight later he would be in Los Angeles, staying with ex-employee and long-time friend Derek Taylor. When he described that night-trip with Lennon, he unnerved Taylor with his zealotry:

Derek Taylor: Paul and Mal [Evans] came to stay with us somewhere in the late spring of 1967 . . . Paul and Mal, this time, were full of tales of this here LSD and what it could do. Unrecognisable psyches on familiar heads and shoulders: the voice was Paul's but the tone was . . . God's? Paul said he and John had had 'this fantastic *thing*'; which really wasn't very informative, so I pressed him to flesh it out. 'Incredible, really, just locked into each other's eyes . . . Like, just *staring* and then saying, "I *know*, man" and then laughing . . . And it was great, you know.' . . . Realising he wasn't getting through, Paul said, 'You'll just have to try it.' [FYA]

Not everyone was quite so thrilled by Paul's recent revelation, or that familiar sense of separation it had brought to bear. The McCartney who surprised girlfriend Asher in Denver that April 'had changed so much. He was on LSD, which I hadn't shared. I was jealous of all [sic] the spiritual experiences he'd had with John.' When she returned to London, she found that Paul's place resembled a scene from *Jesus Christ Superstar*: 'There were fifteen people dropping in all day long. The house had changed and was full of stuff I didn't know about.' Cynthia Lennon was no longer the only partner shut off from the lysergic light.

Not surprisingly, Lennon and McCartney soon set about writing their first song celebrating this new drug-induced empathy. Yet 'With A Little Help From My Friends' hardly sounded like some multi-layered codex of hidden meanings. It certainly passed just about every appointed censor by, despite one line giving the game away – 'I get high with a little help from my friends.'

Perhaps fittingly, 'With A Little Help . . .' was the last new song The Beatles recorded for *Pepper*; before a band built on rock-solid friendships began to founder in the face of four increasingly independent existences. Tony Barrow is certainly of the opinion that, 'as *Sgt. Pepper* took shape . . . each one of the boys was working in his own interests. Their work was [also] increasingly self-centred.' The passage from 'With a Little Help . . .' to 'I Me Mine' would span a mere two years.

For now, the lads were content to send a little message to a friend in Woodstock, recuperating from a nasty motorcycle accident and – unbeknownst to the boys – starting to make the most rooted music of his life. 'I get high' was a key phrase that Dylan and The Beatles had long shared as a result of the American – at their first meeting – telling them how much he loved 'I Wanna Hold Your Hand', in particular its middle-eight, 'I get high, I get high'.

It was patiently explained that they were *actually* singing 'I can't hide, I can't hide'. As McCartney recalls, Dylan 'was rather amused by that. And we were amused that he was amused.' Having first got high in Dylan's presence, Lennon and McCartney now tipped their hat in the man's direction – home. In fact, as McCartney says in *Many Years From Now*, 'We were always sticking those little [in-jokes] in that we knew our friends would get; veiled references to drugs and to trips.' It was certainly one way to keep the song-writing process fun when writing to order.

'With A Little Help . . .' not only represented one last song for the Sergeant, it was a necessary vocal turn for Beatles drummer Ringo Starr, who had spent most of the sessions to date developing his chess skills. As McCartney told Hunter Davies, who was present when he and Lennon sat down and wrote the song, 'The last four songs of an album are usually pure slog. If we need four more we just have to get down and do them. They're not necessarily worse than ones done out of imagination. They're often better, because by that stage in an LP we know what sort of songs we want.'

What McCartney seems to have decided was to develop the concept of Sgt. Pepper's Lonely Hearts Club Band as band alter-egos, hoping to make Ringo into the club bandleader, Billy Shears. Starr later claimed that 'the original concept of *Pepper* was that it was gonna be like a stage show . . . We did it for the first couple of tracks and then it faded into an album.' In fact, the *Sergeant Pepper*/Billy Shears segue was the afterthought – not the album – a last-minute attempt to turn the album into something it never was.

The notion of segueing from 'Sergeant Pepper' into 'Billy Shears' song', then reprising the title-track, as well as the whole 'band playing concert in the park' album-cover idea, can all be dated to a single evening, 29 March, the penultimate *Pepper* session. Even if the session began with a series of attempts to tie up loose ends from previous sessions, a bewildering process to outsiders. *TeenSet's* Judith Sims, back for a second time, was one of these and thoroughly confused:

> This particular session was a hodge-podge of songs. They were learning new ones, making up new things, and adding bits and pieces to already-recorded numbers. It was thoroughly confusing; first they would work on words to one song, then instrumentals for another, back to instrumentals for the first, then an overdub or two on something else. I have no idea how they keep everything straight, but they do.

Sims seems to have been popular with the Liverpool lads, and was allowed to stay long enough to see the first performance of the new song 'Paul had written [sic], and presented to the others for the first time while I was there. Paul played through it on the piano, while the others looked over his shoulder and familiarised themselves with the words . . . and the rhythm. It's a bouncy, upbeat tune, the kind John calls a "Northern song".'

While they worked on ideas for an arrangement, Sims sat and chatted with Harrison, who still believed his own 'northern song' was a candidate for inclusion on *Pepper* (as it should have been). He also informed her that they intended to reprise the title-track. Actually, Harrison was more specific: 'The first track on the elpee is ['Sgt. Pepper'], and it stops in the middle of the song and picks up again as the last track on the record.'

Also there that evening was artist Peter Blake, who was presumably party to discussions about the way the band planned to tie such a tenuous theme together. By this time, it had been decided that the album would come in a double-sleeve (which made Blake misguidedly believe it was once intended to be a double album, à la *Blonde on Blonde*). According to Judith Sims, the cover at this stage was to feature 'a beach-type painting on the front (surrealistic), with spaces for photo groupings. The inside double spread would contain lyrics to the songs and funny punch-out noses, like Halloween masks.' The lyrics and the novelty items would survive, the 'beach-type painting' did not.

According to Blake, it was when he realised that 'the concept was to have the record like a concert with an overture, a song by Billy Shears . . . [and] ending on a reprise' that he suggested 'they had just played a concert in the park . . . and behind them was a crowd of fans who had been at the concert.' Such a suggestion cannot have been made any earlier than the twenty-ninth.

Until Blake made his suggestion, no-one seems to have had a clear enough idea of how to present these alter-egos visually. But the 'concert in the park' idea quickly took hold. When Blake explained that the 'crowd of fans' could be cut-outs, so that 'anybody, dead or alive, or even fictitious' could be included, they finally had something ambitious and arty enough for Paul. The sleeve would become the most famous album-cover in Rock, an image so iconic it still spawns a never-ending variety of parodies (a process that would begin before the year was out with The Mothers of Invention's *We're Only In It For The Money*).

The session on the twenty-ninth was the culmination of a number of disparate strands which had been flying around since work began back in November. Two days later, it was decided that 'Sgt. Pepper' would not be cut in two – as Harrison had implied – but would be reprised in a more rocking arrangement at album's end. And so the track was recorded again (and this time Harrison got to play lead). Perhaps the (relative) shortness of the album was already an issue,[2] or it was a belated replacement for Harrison's own 'Northern Song'.

The Beatles continued to have some fun with the LP format, leaving another serendipitous in-joke 'that we knew our friends would get' as the run-out groove at the end of the album, though it would only become a reality when the album was ready to be mastered on 21 April (i.e. after McCartney had returned from the States):

Paul McCartney: We were whacked out so much of the time in the sixties – just quite harmlessly, as we thought, it was quite innocent – but you would be at friends' houses, twelve at night, and *nobody* would be going to get up to change that record player. So we'd be *getting into* the little 'tick, tick, tick' . . . We were appreciating the run-out groove! We said, 'What if we put something, so that every time it did that, it said something?' So we put a little loop of conversation on. [1987]

According to Emerick, 'They [just] made funny noises, said random things; just nonsense. [Then] we chopped up the tape, put it back together, played it backwards.' This may well have been what the singer in a young band from Wolverhampton, The N'Betweens, heard while they were recording some songs with Norman Smith down the hall.[3] For Noddy Holder, as for many fans concerned by the whispers of experimentalism gone mad which had begun to circulate that spring, it all seemed rather odd, 'We could hear snatches of these weird sounds coming out, all these backward tape sounds, [and thought,] "What the hell are they playing at?"'

When the eighth Beatles album appeared, there was a great deal of speculation about what these snippets said – especially when played backwards (which was, of course, really forwards). Much to Macca's apparent consternation, it appeared to say something rather rude,[4] throwing into doubt the assertion that it was just some random audio cut-up.

A story was immediately inserted into *Beatles Monthly*, claiming that the loop was 'just a bit of jabbering conversation by The Beatles mixed up and distorted. Translated, it might well mean something like, "Thank you for listening. That's all for now. Please come to our next LP – you're all invited." Well, something like that anyway.' In other words, much like the message Jagger put at the end of 'Something Happened To Me Yesterday' ('If you're on your bike at night/ Wear a light') on the Stones' recent LP, *Between the Buttons* – only backwards and garbled. And not so cute.

This harmless piece of fun would come back to haunt McCartney when rumours ran riot in 1969 that he was dead, with most of the 'evidence' appearing to result from people playing their Beatles albums in reverse. For now, McCartney was feeling the natural high that comes with completion. He seems to have had no doubts that The Beatles' eighth album was all he wanted it to be, though its final sequence had yet to be resolved:

Paul McCartney: The weekend we finished the album is a bit of a blur . . . We all felt so exhilarated. *Pepper* had taken six months to make . . . When we first heard it back, we knew we'd pulled it off . . . something that would blow people's minds. [2004]

Like Dylan, before he jetted off on his world tour in early April 1966, McCartney arranged for acetates to be cut of the songs destined to make the final cut, intending to play them to the West Coast contingent of progressive pop when he got there the following week; after taking his actress girlfriend by surprise. He was leaving Martin behind, to mix and sequence the LP.

It seems extraordinary, looking back, that The Beatles still considered it part of the producer's job to sequence the albums they made, but it was assuredly the norm in 1967. Even albums which seem to have a somewhat greater conceptual unity than the slightly scatty Sergeant, say Astral Weeks – recorded by a newly solo Van Morrison the following year – was entirely sequenced by its producer, Lewis Merenstein. Even after months of pushing the envelope, it seemed The Beatles still thought of themselves as pop, and pop bands left such things to their producers.

What does not seem to have been in doubt was the way the album would now begin. As Martin says, 'We had to start with the song that gave the illusion of a concept', meaning the title-track; while the segue into Billy Shears was also a given (after Martin carefully snipped in audience noise from The Beatles' Hollywood Bowl shows to mask the join). After that, though, he seems to have been largely on his own and, occasionally, in the dark.

Most peculiar of all Martin's decisions was the one placing 'A Day In The Life', an obvious album-closer, after the title-track reprise; thus separating 'A Day In The Life' from its younger brother, 'Good Morning, Good Morning', and making the reprise redundant. Martin's argument, given in his book on the making of the album, was that 'the final chord of "A Day In The Life" was so final that it was obvious nothing else could follow it'. Which might be more convincing if the garbled gobbledygook on the run-out groove didn't follow it.

Again, Martin seemed to want his share of the plaudits. In a 1971 interview he seemingly implied he had imbued the album with some great conceit in the sequencing: 'Sgt. Pepper became a unit only when we put it together. It was designed that way. [But] it wasn't until I started piecing it together and cutting in sound effects and so on that it really became a whole.'

Initially, Martin was not so convinced he had pulled it off.

Recalling his feelings as he finalised the sequence for the album, 'It struck me that we had such a funny collection of songs, not really related to one another, all disparate numbers. Looking them over, I really did start to worry that we were being a bit preten-tious, a bit clever-clever.' Only when the album began to pick up a punnet of plaudits did his view begin to alter.

NEEDING HELP

Look! Listen! **VIBRATE!** **SMILE!**

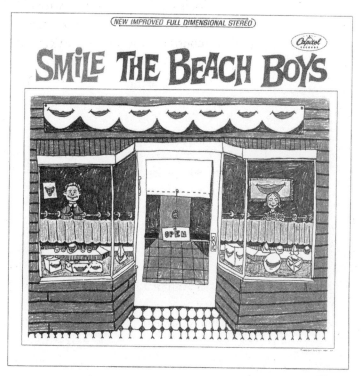

(D)T 2580

It's Brian, Dennis, Carl, Al and Mike's greatest ever! Contains "GOOD VIBRATIONS," their all-time biggest-selling single, other new and fantastic Beach Boys' songs...AND...an exciting full-color sketchbook look inside the world of Brian Wilson!

Some pills won't hurt you, but stimulate your mind.
Including the psychedelics. –

Brian Wilson, 1966

This is wonderful, no doubt, but it is fake, ersatz, instant
mysticism . . . I solved the secret of the universe last night,
but this morning I forgot what it was. –

Arthur Koestler, describing an LSD trip, op cit. *Acid Dreams*

Between September 1966 and March 1967, Lennon would produce his two defining compositions – 'Strawberry Fields Forever' and 'A Day in the Life' – as well as at least one more attempt to break on through, 'Lucy in the Sky with Diamonds'. Ironically, such extraordinary songs came at a time when he was finding songwriting a rather more difficult vocation than it had been when he and his partner had penned two albums a year, and still found time to tour the world. If he had been left to his own devices, it seems unlikely that these songs would have found suitable bed-partners, but as part of the *Pepper* amalgam of ideas they found themselves propped up on both sides.

Brian Wilson had no such luck. Having written three songs of similar stature – 'Good Vibrations', 'Heroes & Villains' and 'Surf's Up' – between February and October 1966, he found he was expected to match them to a portentous concept, *Smile*, and some more songs worthy of the same – all from his own pen (Wilson was – and presumably still is – loath to admit that much on the 2004 *Smile* smacks of filler). Wilson's problems were much the same as Lennon's – a debilitating cocktail of drugs, a band not always on the same wavelength, a plethora of hangers-on of debatable usefulness, and an insatiable desire to keep tinkering with what one had at the expense of further songs.

Fortunately, Lennon had a workaholic like McCartney, a consummate songwriter in his own right, to call on. Wilson had Van Dyke Parks – not even Macca's equal as a lyricist – and not even him for very long. By January 1967, Van Dyke Parks had been removed from the scene. Though Parks likes to believe he was fired 'by Mike Love' for writing 'words that were indecipherable and unnecessary', the truth seems to be that Wilson himself was starting to have his own doubts about Parks's lyrics (doubts that Love certainly happily fed). As David Anderle told *Crawdaddy*'s Paul Williams back in 1967, 'Van [Dyke Parks] was getting . . . too sophisticated, and in some areas Brian's music was not sophisticated enough. And so they started clashing on that.'

Wilson had no real use for Parks any more. He had the songs for *Smile*, save for one late addition, 'Love To Say Da-Da', which hardly needed a child prodigy to write it – just a child. Parks's disappearance was part of a general clear-out, sparked by Wilson's own paranoia, and stoked by third parties in and outside the band. Journalist Jules Siegel was another of those soon out on the street:

> **Jules Siegel:** He didn't trust [anyone] anymore, and with some of them he had good reason. With me, he had forgotten that I was a journalist, and the reason he got rid of me was because Anderle reminded him of that – because of a disagreement that David and I had about what I would and wouldn't write . . . After that [my girl-friend], I and Pynchon went to Studio A and Vosse was there, and he said, 'No, you're barred.'

Anderle wouldn't last much longer. For now Wilson clung to the chimerical notion that he would be able to get out of his Capitol Records contract, and set up his own Brother record label for future product; and Anderle was meant to make this happen. The decision, though, was out of his hands the minute it passed into the courts. And that minute came around on 28 February, when The Beach Boys filed suit in LA Superior Court against Capitol Records, for $225,000 in back royalties, but really as a means to force Capitol to renegotiate their existing contract.

It was a bad time to confront Capitol in court if Wilson was serious about going head to head with his labelmates from Liverpool. Until the legal matter was resolved, there would be no *Smile*, no 'Heroes & Villains', no crossing over to a new pop constituency. By the end of March a San Bernardino radio station was reporting that the new Beach Boys single 'is reportedly being held up until their legal suit with Capitol is settled'.

Whether this ongoing contractual dispute convinced Wilson he had yet more time to tinker, or he was just determined to fiddle away while Sunset Strip burned, is not clear. What is certain is that through January and February 1967 he was working harder than ever in the studio, but on songs he had already 'completed' the year before; but which were now subject to a whole new set of overdubs, rearrangements, and revisions. No wonder his fellow Beach Boys despaired of anything seeing the light of day.

At least three sessions were set aside for the others to dub their own vocals on to 'Heroes & Villains'. It was this song – first recorded back in May, then reworked in October *and* again in December – that ate up the most studio time (time Wilson would have to pay for out of his own pocket if he succeeded in escaping Capitol's clutches). It was now subject to six more sessions in January and February as Wilson continued to scrub till it shone. As if this were not bad enough, he had now decided that the song warranted a 'part two' – separate from 'Do You Dig Worms?', which already used the main musical motif (and was the kind of hash-humour that explained why Cheech & Chong started to sound funny if one smoked enough).

David Anderle: Brian was consumed with humour at the time and the importance of humour. He was fascinated with the idea of getting humour on to a disc and hot to get that disc out to the people.

Wilson wanted to match The Beatles in another department where The Beach Boys had not previously expressed concern –

issuing a single where *both* sides were worth investigating. As such, he abandoned a plan to issue 'Heroes & Villains' with a *Pet Sounds* leftover on the other side. Rather, he began work on a series of vocal chants based around 'Heroes & Villains', making the b-side a continuation of the a-side. However, the Desbutal doubts would not go away. When *NME's* Tracy Thomas interviewed him in early February, he told her he was 'doing the final mix on the a-side tonight, but I can't decide what to do with the other side'.

Even this 'final mix' of the a-side would be subject to one last final mix, an absolutely final and a definitively final mix – before being scrapped. Wilson no longer knew when to stop, the success of 'Good Vibrations' having turned any largesse from the label into a licence to never let go. And the drugs undoubtedly played their part. If LSD had opened him up to new ideas, it had never been his drug of choice. Like Dylan, that was speed. And like Dylan, speed was inexorably leading Wilson to the big crash, and years spent in recovery:

> **Jules Siegel:** [By] that point Brian was suffering from pretty severe paranoia – it was a classic amphetamine psychosis. He was taking a lot of amphetamines, in the form of Desbutal, which is methedrine and some barbiturate mixed together. That's a combination that's gonna fuck you up – if you take enough of it, you will feel like the walls are looking at you! There were a number of parts to his paranoia – some of [which] *were* valid – . . . [but] one of the effects of the amphetamine is the God-like feeling, combined with the fear. The things that you do, you see as having so much potency, which usually is your own delusion . . . A lot of it was just the effect of the amphetamines – you can't stop, you gotta get every thought out. The problem is when you crash, [just] how ugly and stupid and trivial it all looks – all you can see are the mistakes.

Van Dyke Parks, it seems, got out just in time. As he later observed, Wilson would go 'after take after take – a monotony of repeated takes – to get a performance that fell by the wayside because of maybe one eighth note . . . He was his own worst critic, and *everybody* suffered in the process.' He couldn't let go of any song till he'd achieved 'perfection', a notoriously indefinite concept at the best of times (one Dylan relinquished in his sleeve-notes to *Bringing It All Back Home* back in March 1965). As a horn player sarcastically observed during one of the *Smile* recording sessions, 'Perfect – just one more'; a by-word for Brian's methodology. At the same time, that whispering paranoia continued to hint of rival claimants ready to steal the man's thunder:

> **Derek Taylor:** Brian had become very, very competitive, so much so that it was no longer that healthy sort of competitive spirit thing. It was a mad possessive battle against the Stones and particularly The Beatles . . . He'd constantly be testing the strength of my devotion to the cause . . . He was always talking about a new plateau . . . all the time: 'The next record will create a new plateau for The Beach Boys in terms of creativity and acceptance.' Always these grand statements. [1975]

Taylor's presence merely served as a constant reminder of his former employers across the ocean. Indeed, Wilson began to suspect his publicist of a hidden agenda; one that his equally paranoid co-worker, Van Dyke Parks, developed into a full-blown conspiracy theory. This had The Beatles hearing *Smile* – an album that did not exist in even an embryonic sense when Parks got expelled from Eden – early on and extracting the essence Wilson had such trouble isolating himself:

> **Van Dyke Parks:** Derek Taylor was planted over here as a scout for The Beatles, to see what was going on on the West Coast, which had coopted New York City as the place of power . . . I think Derek Taylor facilitated The Beatles listening to *Smile* before the advent of *Sgt. Pepper*. Before that started, they heard *Smile* in part – the first eight-track – up at Armen Steiner's studio.

The desire to hide his lovely ideas away was an integral part of Brian's paranoia. No-one was allowed access to the process, not even his lyricist. So no-one else even knew how each track related to the ostensible concept, which shifted as often as the sands of time. By March 1967, without even the follow-up single to 'Good Vibrations' ready for release, Taylor was obliged to mount another press campaign, this time to explain away the non-appearance of, well, anything.

If Taylor had still only heard *Smile* 'in part' – or more accurately, in pieces – he was obliged to convince himself (and his readers) that 'the record is almost complete – almost. No-one is betting on any release date because it has been nearly complete for weeks . . . I have heard several of the sections, and ultimately they will become a masterly whole. But only when they're totally related and correctly shaped.' By April, he was obliged to change tack, representing 'Heroes & Villains' as 'tormented with over-elaboration and a score of second thoughts'. For 'Heroes & Villains', read the whole of *Smile*.

The presence of Paul McCartney at a Beach Boys session on 10 April did nothing to assuage the doubts that now plagued Mr Wilson's once-prodigious son. Indeed, according to one piece of tittle-tattle, reported in *NME* at the time, 'Brian Wilson is reported to have heard The Beatles LP track "A Day in the Life", and to be so knocked out that he has retired to live in a sauna bath, there to sweat out some more mind-jamming material for further Beach Boys discs.' The Lennon–McCartney composition was certainly everything Wilson had been hoping to achieve in a single four-minute song: audacious, adventurous, avant-garde, accessible.

The appearance of McCartney, acetates in hand, has come to be seen by Wilson apologists (a determined bunch of myth-makers, f'sure) as the final nail in the coffin they call *Smile*. In fact, this particular funeral-train had already run off the rails. As Siegel wrote, in his definitive article on the *Smile* sessions, (re)written during that long hot summer, 'Entire sequences of extraordinary power and beauty are missing in the finished version of the ['Heroes &

Villains'] single, and will undoubtedly be missing as well from *Smile* – victims of Brian's obsessive tinkering.'

By the time McCartney arrived in LA Wilson had a new obsession and a new single he wished to record to celebrate it – 'Vegatables'. It was this that McCartney heard, while contributing bass and/or backing vocals to a rendition of the traditional 'On Top of Old Smokey'. It was hardly 'Good Vibrations', and doubtless reassured him that there would be no nasty surprises in the Capitol release schedule. Wilson had no rough or ready version of *Smile* to trump the *Sgt. Pepper* acetate/s McCartney now played to him (and Taylor). Despite the imposed 'genius' tag, Dylan he was not.

In fact, having abandoned both parts of 'Heroes & Villains' in early March, Wilson did not return to any of the dozen songs he'd recorded for *Smile* back in 1966 during the weeks leading up to McCartney's arrival; nor would he return to them in the five weeks after his departure. Instead, he confined himself to working on what were probably both sides of another new 'single', 'Vegatables' and 'Love To Say Da-Da'.

This *could* mean that Wilson felt he had already completed those original twelve songs to his satisfaction, and was working on the two cuts needed to complete the project ('Vegatables' was certainly intended for *Smile*, and had been for some months before it was recorded).[1] According to *Smile* historian Domenic Priore, the 19 May session at Gold Star, which Wilson cancelled at the last minute, 'was intended as a compilation of the *Smile* album itself'. This seems like wishful thinking given the clearly unfinished nature of the material given release on bootleg in the late eighties and nineties. These merely served to confirm a suspicion voiced by Paul Williams, an early *Smile* advocate, in his review of the Beach Boys *Good Vibrations* boxed-set in 1993:

> Many of the tracks contain brief segments of truly extraordinary beauty
> and musical originality (it was hearing some of these tracks, as acetates,
> that got me and other visitors so excited). The presumption that Brian

was working on a masterpiece and would pull it off was based on the obvious ambitiousness and fecundity of the work in progress, and on the astonishing model of 'Good Vibrations', which seemed to prove that in the end Brian could take all these fragments and miraculously sew them together into a whole even greater than the sum of its parts. Maybe. Maybe not.

The studio logs suggest that Wilson had already abandoned *Smile* on or around 2 March, when 'Heroes & Villains' part two was finally put to bed – the same day The Beatles realised 'Lucy in the Sky with Diamonds' at Abbey Road. If, as Taylor suggested at the time, 'The Beach Boys' delays with product are the result of painful self-criticism' on the part of Brian Wilson, that process was seemingly nearing its end. 'Love To Say Da-Da', recorded between 16 and 18 May saw him regressing into the child of the man; while *Smile* itself was left still-born. By mid-May, the word was filtering out – the great project had been junked. Derek Taylor, in the 6 May issue of *Disc & Music Echo*, wrote its obituary (while pleading for The Beach Boys to still be allowed to enjoy an elevated place in pop's panoply):

> Every beautifully designed, finely-wrought inspirationally-welded piece of music made these last months by Brian and his Beach Boy craftsmen has been SCRAPPED . . . As an average fan of The Beach Boys I think it is bitterly disappointing. But it isn't as if one is bereft of the group's essential spirit . . . Switch off the lights, turn on *Pet Sounds* and you know that there are in The Beach Boys . . . elements which transcend the transitory Top 30, and which make nonsense of 'now music'.

For all of Taylor's heartfelt prose, he knew how high were the stakes Wilson had been playing for, and how much he had lost. Wilson's most plausible explanation for why the album was abandoned would come in an interview for his local LA paper, ten years after the fact, 'It got to the point where we were too selfishly artistic and weren't thinking about the public enough.' He had come round to Mike Love's point of view, after all.

When work began on the 'replacement' album, *Smiley Smile*, the day after the American release of *Sgt. Pepper*, all thoughts of making a Brian Wilson/Beach Boys album had receded. *Smiley Smile* was a Beach Boys album (it provided just the 'Good Vibrations' 45 and four re-recordings of *Smile* tracks, as reference points to its fated predecessor)[2]. It was also recorded in just six weeks. The new version of 'Heroes & Villains', recorded in three sessions, was rush-released in mid-July. *NME* felt that, though 'similar' to the million-selling 'Good Vibrations', it would 'not be so widely praised'. That certainly proved to be the case. Penny Valentine gave it both barrels in her July *Disc* review:

> Was The Beach Boys' latest single, 'Heroes & Villains', worth the complicated, rumour-infested nine-month wait . . . No! 'Heroes & Villains' is a cleverly-constructed, interesting record . . . But . . . the record as a whole . . . is disappointing . . . [After] spending more time on a single than anyone else in the history of pop music . . . [one] can't be blamed for expecting a veritable work of art!

Nor did the record prove as successful as any of The Beach Boys' 1966 singles, charting at twelve in the States and eight in the UK. Meanwhile, stories began to circulate of how costly the *Smile* recordings had been, and how little prospect there was of recouping those costs. At the same time, Brother Records was quietly forgotten as the boys skulked back to Capitol Records, surfboards in hand.

Amazingly, similar concerns had been voiced about the *Sgt. Pepper* sessions, with reports suggesting that the album had cost something like £25,000 to record. Unlike The Beach Boys, though, The Beatles' new EMI contract gave them unlimited studio time *at the label's expense*. The Sergeant, too, having taken an eternity to show his colours, generated those inevitable stories appearing to doubt whether *they* could deliver. Even the generally benign *Beat*

Instrumental ran a report in its April issue, entitled 'Most Expensive [Album] Ever Produced?', which emphasised just how strange some of these 'innovative' recording techniques seemed when viewed by those removed from the process:

> Three guitars and a set of drums are all old hat and apparently considered incapable of backing a new Beatles song. Experiment is everything. The night I was in the studio, George Martin spent half an hour, before The Beatles arrived, dropping spoons, pennies, and any other object he could think of into a large cauldron of water . . . [and] the resulting splonks, gesplashes and plops would be recorded by the microphone.

Quite what *Beat Instrumental's* roving reporter witnessed it is hard to say. Perhaps someone had dosed his cuppa. But such stories clearly riled McCartney, who had invested heart and soul in the Sergeant. As he later recalled to *Rolling Stone*, 'I remember before *Sgt. Pepper*, we were coming in for a lot of flak. People were saying, "The Beatles are finished. They're rubbish." Because we [apparently] weren't doing anything, we were just hiding away in the studios, out of our skulls, making this album.' In his biography, he became Eliza Doolittle, insisting that whenever he saw 'in one of the papers how The Beatles have dried up . . . I was sitting rubbing my hands, saying, "You just wait."'

On his trip through America in April Paul received much of the validation he'd been hoping for. When a few radio stations started playing 'A Day In The Life', presumably from an acetate he had provided, the response from listeners was ecstatic. Likewise, when he stopped off in San Francisco and played the songs to Jefferson Airplane – whose second album, *Surrealistic Pillow*, suggested San Francisco might really have a scene comprising more than drug-like jams to drugged-out fans – they were bowled over, under and around by what they heard. Roger McGuinn, too, got to hear the latest London bulletin, after Taylor brought McCartney to his house in LA, and they talked about experimental 16 mm film, new studio techniques and the joys of LSD.

Slowly, but surely, the word began to eke out – if *Smile* was a bust, *Sgt. Pepper* seemed like the real deal. Ever the West-Coast PR man, McCartney was turning his holiday into a business trip – the business of putting The Beatles back where they felt comfortable, leading the way. He returned in time to put the finishing touch to the LP – literally – the run-out groove, recorded on the twenty-first, being one last opportunity to demonstrate that 'experiment is everything'.

On Friday, 19 May, Brian Wilson cancelled the last of four consecutive sessions; designed to complete 'Love To Say Da-Da' and/or put together a provisional sequence for *Smile*. On the same day, at Brian Epstein's smart Chapel House townhouse, a select few were invited to the first preview party for *Pepper*; at which, according to Tony Barrow, 'In between *Sgt. Pepper* tracks, guests were treated to frequent plays of Procol Harum's sensational new single, "A Whiter Shade of Pale", which The Beatles had watched the group perform live at London's fashionable Speakeasy Club four nights earlier.' The Beatles again showed how they delighted in, nay thrived on, competition, the nonsensical 'Whiter Shade' sparking an equally random retort from Lennon, 'I Am The Walrus'.

Readers of *Disc & Music Echo* had already been permitted a sneak preview of the most eagerly awaited Beatles album, in the issue which appeared the previous day. Epstein, who had recently acquired a large stake in the music weekly, knew that there would not be the slightest hint of critical perspective in this *Disc* 'press release'. Sure enough, it was described as 'another masterpiece of musical genius.' The *Disc* description of individual tracks seemed almost designed to keep a lid on any comparisons with contemporaries; the title-track being 'slightly reminiscent of their early work' and the subject matter of 'Lucy in the Sky' hastily passed over in favour of the incisive observation that 'it includes some funny little background voices.'

Thankfully, fans would not have to wait much longer to make

up their own minds. The album was scheduled to be broadcast by the BBC in (almost) its entirety on the Saturday edition of *Where It's At*. Unfortunately, *Sgt. Pepper* was denied his knock-out punch when the BBC banned 'A Day In The Life' because – in a statement awash with the finest Beeb-like lingo – they decided it 'could be considered to have drug-taking implications'. So, were there any pop songs in the charts that week – and eligible for radio play – that might 'have [any] drug-taking implications'? Well, 'Purple Haze' and 'I Can Hear The Grass Grow', for starters . . .

The response to the ban from the two songwriters showed their different concerns. McCartney gave a plausibly prosaic explanation of the song, 'John woke up one morning and read the *Daily Mail*. The news stories gave him the idea for the song. The man goes upstairs on the bus for a smoke. Everybody does that sort of thing.' Lennon preferred to prick BBC pomposity, suggesting he could hip the officiate offender to their jive, 'I'd like to meet the man who banned this song of ours . . . [and] turn him on to what's happening.' It took George Melly, in his review of the album in *The Observer*, to state the blindingly obvious: 'I don't see how, despite The Beatles' denial, this [song] can be absolved from references to drug-taking: "I'd love to turn you on" surely means just that.'

The real question was how hard should one look for hidden meanings when encountering examples of so-called psychedelic pop. After all, what exactly did DJs *think* the repeated refrain, 'My friend Jack eats sugar lumps' – on The Smoke's 45, which charted earlier in spring – actually meant? And did EMI really believe that the title change for Pink Floyd's equally sweet 'Candy & A Currant Bun' hid its true subject matter from anyone who'd ever experienced 'the munchies'?

In reality, it had all become a game hip people played: let's see which drug references pass ultra-straight programme-controllers by – and which do not. And the freaks remained eight miles ahead. Who among those down UFO, the day after *Pepper*'s release, wouldn't have cracked up to hear that the Beeb had banned 'A

Day In The Life', but continued to blast 'Lucy in the Sky with Diamonds' across its monopolistic airwaves day and night?

That was the night that the Floyd returned to their alma mater for the first time in six weeks, no longer simply an underground phenomenon. 'Arnold Layne' had taken their name into the lower reaches of the charts, and the place was packed to its creaking rafters. As Boyd told Jonathon Green, 'You couldn't move in the club. [But] the people that came ... were different. It was the summer, tourists had started to come, kids were getting out of university, out of school, London was filling up.'

It was the first time those rafters resounded to the Floyd's follow-up 45, 'See Emily Play', which the band was still hoping might be rush-released by EMI (much as Track now rush-released Hendrix's follow-up to 'Purple Haze', 'The Wind Cries Mary'). It was also the night that most of the club's habitues heard about the imprisonment of its co-founder, John Hopkins, for nine months, for *possession* of an ounce of hash.

No-one in the visibly throbbing throng could have known that the stunning new song Floyd blasted out that night was written about a person whose 'wanton ways' may well have played their part in 'Hoppy's suspiciously disproportionate sentence. Emily Young, now a successful sculptress in her own right, was the fifteen-year-old daughter of Lord Kennet when she first began hanging out at the London Free School. Kennet, under his 'real' name, Wayland Young, had just published the book *Eros Denied*, which examined the history of Western society's fear of human sexuality, and the way that censorship and harassment had been used to deny free expression. His daughter, known to her friends as 'Far Out Em', seems to have taken him at his word; and began hanging out at this school for scandal with her American friend, Anjelica Huston, daughter of director John.

John Hopkins: Technically it was the London Free School that resulted in my going to jail . . . This was explained to me by Emily a year or two ago. She was at Holland Park Comprehensive, and with some

> of her mates, used to dash off to the free school at every opportun-
> ity, 'cause it was much more interesting . . . than what was happening
> in Holland Park. The Free School wasn't like a formal organisation,
> but we had a newsletter, and I was paying for the production of it,
> and my name was on [it] as secretary. Lord Kennet realised that his
> daughter was getting up to mischief at the London Free School. [And]
> I had a fairly high profile at the time, so apparently [someone] had
> a word with the local cops and they busted me. Which wasn't very
> difficult.

Kennet was quite right to be concerned. Barrett in his song suggests
that the still young Emily might 'lose [her] mind at play', which
clearly implies someone experimenting with drugs. And as Joe Boyd
points out in his autobiography, that 'phone call from the worried
and titled parent of a teenager . . . could have come from any one
of a number of sources'. Equally clearly, Ms Young was a free spirit,
and something about her struck a chord with Syd. And so, when
he was obliged to write a song for the Floyd's concert debut at the
Queen Elizabeth Hall, the so-called 'Games of May', he took her
as the epitome of the May Queen, swopping her schoolgirl uniform
for a 'gown that touches the ground' :

> **Pete Bown:** 'See Emily Play' was based on this schoolgirl. This English
> thing, the cult of the schoolgirl in the fetish uniform, has always been
> around . . . Emily was actually someone I went out with a couple of
> times . . . Some of these girls were seventeen or eighteen, . . . [but]
> English schoolgirls in the sixties were very forward looking.

By 21 May, when the Floyd recorded the final track for their debut
long-player, 'Bike', they had already decided that 'See Emily Play'
should be their follow-up single; and returned to Sound Techniques
– where 'Arnold Layne' had been recorded – the same evening to
put the finishing touches to another 'fetishistic' work.

   Their ex-producer Boyd has suggested that it was only after
Floyd 'spent a great deal of . . . EMI's money and a great deal of

EMI's studio time trying to get the sound I got down at Sound Techniques . . . [that they] ended up having to go down to Sound Techniques and getting the same engineer . . . in order to get the same sound'. In fact, there is no evidence 'See Emily Play' was ever attempted at EMI. Rather, Barrett seems to have been superstitious enough to believe that some studios have the right sound for a single, and some don't.

He would return to Sound Techniques for a third and last time in September, to record Floyd's next single – or so Syd believed. 'Scream Thy Last Scream', aka 'Old Woman In A Casket', proved far too disturbing for the doyens at EMI and was quietly sidelined. But it was at one of these Sound Techniques sessions that Barrett's old Cambridge friend and Joker's Wild guitarist Dave Gilmour turned up to say hi, only to find that 'Syd didn't seem to recognise me and just stared back . . . That was when he changed . . . He was a different person.'

Gilmour thinks this occurred while recording 'See Emily Play', but he is almost certainly mistaken. All the evidence suggests that Syd was still at the top of his game in May, as he recorded 'See Emily Play' in a single evening, and mixed it the 'following' night. Nor did his appearance the previous week on BBC's *Look of the Week* suggest the onset of psychosis, as a well-mannered, articulate Barrett first performed a stellar 'Astronomy Domine', and then responded to Hans Keller's pained query, 'Why must it be *so* loud?' in measured tones. He also still had the mental wherewithal to challenge producer Norman Smith when he tried to overcompensate for the 'pop' market by toning down the Floyd's more psychedelic transgressions.

One such disagreement may well have broken out over 'See Emily Play', which exists in an alternative form on acetate, where the thirty-two second psychedelic overdrive in mid-song (1.30 to 2.01 by my clock) surges to warp factor ten. On the single, though, Floyd pull back from the brink, though only just – as if Captain Smith had wrestled back the helm from Syd the space-invader.

Nonetheless, the single was the culmination of a remarkable

spring in the studio, and everyone at EMI had high hopes for the resulting record. Indeed, such high hopes that, as Peter Jenner says, 'The record company said, very smartly, Let's get this out before we release the album.' As a commercial move, it made all the sense in the world. But it allowed Barrett and the boys to play with the Piper a whole lot more; and it meant that by the time the single *was* in the charts, and the album was ready to roll, in mid-July, the Floyd's leader was already starting to 'lose [*his*] mind at play'.

TURNING THE
WORLD ON

In those days reviews weren't very important because we had it made whatever happened. Nowadays I'm sensitive as shit, and every review counts. But those days we were too big to touch. –

By 1970, when Lennon was interviewed by Jann Wenner for the magazine Wenner founded to write about rock music and the counter-culture, *Rolling Stone*, the close relationship between pop stars and those who wrote about them which The Beatles had enjoyed in those pre-*Pepper* years was but a distant memory. That relationship had been so intimate precisely because it was not critics who wrote for music papers in the early sixties, but reporters. Indeed, when Keith Altham wrote a slightly tongue-in-cheek story for *NME* in 1965 about Belfast's sullen sextet, Them, he was called in by owner Maurice Kinner and told, 'Had a call from [Them manager] Phil Solomon, close friend. He didn't like it. Don't do it again.'

After these self-same reporters became critics (or publicists) – Altham suggests – 'it did break down that relationship between the journalist and the star, [so] it meant that you didn't get the access, and the friendships broke down. The natural progression from that was that the PR was expected to provide a wall between the star and the media – and . . . if you erect a wall, the journalist has no alternative but to write on the wall.' That process began when The Beatles withdrew from touring, but was probably an inevitable by-product of the desire this generation of bands had to be treated seriously – which meant being criticised by their peers.

So Lennon may have felt immune from criticism in June 1967, but the days when The Beatles 'were too big to touch' were coming to an end. Even before the album was out, English pop critics were voicing doubts, and in somewhat sarcastic tones. Alan Walsh in

Melody Maker wrote one such early think-piece the week before *Sgt. Pepper* pushed everything from the pop pages. Entitled 'The Danger Facing Pop', it asked the question on the tip of many people's tongues:

> Four half-remembered people who in pre-psychedelic days used to be called The Beatles are about to present their latest work to the pop public: a new album, reported to be revolutionary . . . [Yet] the unworldly, almost god-like existence of Beatles 1967 does give rise to the question: is pop becoming too clever, too complex, too hip?

Those who had already heard the album were mostly keeping schtum. Graham Nash was the one early recipient prepared to address the same readers' concerns, reassuring them that, though *Pepper* 'on first hearing [is] a little disappointing, . . . on the second, third and fourth hearing, you realise that they know exactly where they are going, and that they are intelligent and thoughtful enough to try to take the fans along with them'. Not that Nash had been listening to the album in the same frame of mind as your average teenybopper, whose Dansette mono record player provided barely enough juice to blow a blender:

> **Graham Nash:** I got a quarter-inch [advance] tape of the album from Epstein, and I had The Turtles come over from America, and I got them extremely high on some incredible hash, and made sure they were completely in tune, and [then] played 'em the album. It changed them.

Nash's method of appreciating the album was readily adopted by those looking to turn on the LP as well as themselves. The album's reputation – then and now – could probably be divided between those who first heard it stoned, and those who did so straight. This was an issue from the day of release, making at least one critic question the faculties of those who equated psychedelics with greater perception. Richard Goldstein, in his contentious *New York Times* review, instigated the debate:

Some say The Beatles are head composers. To turn on, goes the reasoning, will admit the enlightened to a whole range of associations and subtleties unfathomable to the straight mind. My experience till now has been that what I like straight, I like all the time. The idea that certain progressions, tonal nuances and lyrical slights are comprehensible only to the turned-on smacks of critical fascism.

Yet The Beatles clearly expected many listeners would get high before they gave *Pepper* a spin. At least one important review – because of its exclusively ecstatic readership – concentrated almost entirely on appreciating *Sgt. Pepper* when stoned, in stereo. Said review was in *International Times*, the fortnightly underground newspaper co-founded by McCartney's friend Miles, which had already run two lengthy interviews with Beatles Paul and George about the need for change and growth, spiritually *and* musically:

One of the hang-ups on the pop scene is that too many groups have been writing 'psychedelic' music before they have achieved sufficient insight into its possibilities. The Beatles stay cool until they had thoroughly explored the potential of freak-out sounds: SERGEANT PEPPER'S LONELY HEARTS CLUB BAND is as flipped as its title implies. Tripping with this record is a mind-blowing experience. The record is a continuum of fantastic sound. There are no visible tracks: it is intended to be played right through from beginning to end. Devoted heads will use stereo equipment and earphones for effect. Freaky things are done with the recording channels on stereo versions of the record.

For The Beatles' traditional audience of teenagers, stereo sound was as remote a possibility as a psychedelic breakfast. And it was this audience that The Beatles still needed to cater for; having spent a great deal of time and effort getting the mono mix of *Pepper* righter than rain, while leaving the stereo version to the studio staff. As Martin tellingly observes, 'When I came to do the stereo mixes, there were no Beatles present. In 1967, very few people had stereo equipment. Almost everyone listened on mono; it was accepted as the standard. Stereo was strictly for hi-fi freaks.' Or just freaks.

Mono was also how The Beatles and their producer generally listened to the music when it was being made. As engineer Geoff Emerick points out, 'Almost all of The Beatles recording sessions – including those for *Sgt. Pepper* – were monitored in the control room through just one mono speaker . . . [save] when stereo mixing was being done.' Yet the mono edition – with its generally superior mixes[1] – has been out of print for years, superseded by a stereo version which The Beatles themselves barely gave the time of day.

Indeed, anyone looking to replicate the listening experience circa '67 should remember that almost everyone who reviewed the album, played the album, loved the album or hated the album in the summer of 1967, in the land of The Beatles, heard it in mono. Yet it is surely the stereo album Ian MacDonald is describing when he suggests its 'sound – in particular its use of various forms of echo and reverb – remains the most authentic aural simulation of the psychedelic experience ever created.' *This* album, though, was mixed by the squarest bunch of boffins going; while its main architect took his first tab just before he helped pen the album's last composition.

> **Paul McCartney:** When [Martin] was doing his TV programme on *Pepper*, he asked me, 'Do you know what caused *Pepper*?' I said, 'In one word, George . . . Pot.' [MYFN]

In other words, it was an album made by people who were high, but not hallucinating (save for Lennon's latterday lapse/s). The 'psychedelic experience' of which MacDonald enthuses was one that was largely *imposed* on the finished album, which with the possible exception of 'Lucy in the Sky with Diamonds' was intended to sound interesting to one and all, stoned and straight. Yet even in the land of the straights, *Pepper* was bound to generate comment.

As Derek Jewell pondered in his contemporary review for the *Sunday Times*, 'The Beatles are now producing performances, not music for frugging to. [So] will the kids follow?' Jewell presumably doubted that said 'kids' were reading his *Times* review. They had their music weeklies to tell them who was naughty and nice.

The music press certainly did its bit, talking up The Beatles' achievement, while giving them the benefit of the doubt. *Record Mirror*'s Peter Jones, one of the hipper hacks of the day, called *Pepper* 'tongue-in-cheek and clever. Not TOO clever, you under-stand – but once or twice right on the borderline.' He clearly realised something was happening, referring to the hole that McCartney felt like fixing as being 'either in Paul's head or in the ceiling . . . not too sure.' Nor was he in any doubt what a certain line in 'With A Little Help . . .' meant, though he refrained from spelling it out for the *Record Mirror* readership.

Probably Epstein's last useful act for the band was to organise another pre-release party-cum-press conference, where all four Beatles made themselves available to the press – as if it was still the good old days, when stars and scribes shared a shandy at the St James. Dressed in a suitably psychedelic array of outfits, the lads posed with the double-album sleeve, and in general went on a charm-offensive designed to put the press at ease. Harrison, who had recently complained to *IT* that the band wasn't experimental enough, told *Disc*:

> We're not trying to outwit the public. The whole idea is to try a little bit to lead people into different tastes. Then, the people with enough intelligence to understand what we're trying to do will get some pleasure.

The less circumspect Lennon suggested this change was bound to come: 'The people who have bought our records in the past must realise that we couldn't go on making the same type for ever.' Despite this, a lot of 'the people who bought [their] records in the past' were not converted to the cause, and over its next two issues the *Beatles Monthly*, the organ of the official fan club, let the disaffected (but still loyal) opposition have their say, led by a Scottish lass named Ann Craig:

> There are three tracks on *Sgt. Pepper* that are a bit too way-out for me, and I'm not . . . any denser than most Beatle people . . . In *Revolver* you showed how beautiful your songs could be; in *S.P.* you show how way-out they can be. Never get into a rut – but lovely songs last longer than esoteric ones, and I hope that your next single, though original of course, will be more akin to 'Here There & Everywhere' than 'Strawberry Fields'.

If not the most scientific of samples, the letters page in the July and August issues of *Beatles Monthly* suggested that it was almost exclusively girl-fans who felt let down by General Freak-Out's psychedelic sergeant. Jean Crosley was in no doubt as to the album's one true turkey, dismissing Harrison's contribution as 'just a crazy lot of noises with no tune at all'. On the other hand, Chrissie Wright thought Lennon the main culprit, for 'putting things like "Being for the Benefit of Mr Kite" and "Good Morning, Good Morning" on a record and pretending they're good music'. Jan Williams longed for 'The Beatles we used to know, before they went stark raving mad and started to write rubbish'; while Joanne Tremlett put all of Ann, Chrissie, Jan and Jean's concerns in a nutshell: 'The Beatles ought to stop being so clever and give us tunes we can enjoy.'

Could it be that The Beatles had overplayed their hand in (over)producing their new album? Certainly, for the *Beatles Monthly* to receive such a stream of feminine negativity suggested that any division between boy music and girl music – which The Beatles had done so much to dissipate – had returned with a vengeance. If the audiences at the underground clubs still had a welcome bevy of beatnik beauties, the 'head' music which Goldstein denigrated would increasingly resemble a boys own club.

Pop itself was up for grabs, with The Beatles' fellow Britpop exponents prepared to storm the breach. When *Disc* canvassed contemporaries in the immediate aftermath of *Sgt. Pepper*, they received quite a mixed bag of opinions. Pete Townshend, though positive himself, said he had 'never met so many mixed reactions about a record before. The Beatles are trying to see how deep they can get into their music without losing public interest.' It was a challenge he would have to meet himself in the coming year, as three consecutive singles – 'Magic Bus', 'I Can See For Miles' and 'Dogs' – all missed their mark.

Ray Davies, another A-list author of Britpop, seemed surprisingly uninterested in the Sergeant, insisting he'd 'only heard two tracks on the radio . . . [But] I'm sure The Beatles don't care if the songs don't appeal to their fans. [They] will say "We did it for ourselves."' In the process of putting finishing touches to his own daring departure, *Something Else* – the recording of which was completed by 12 June – he was to discover that releasing a set of thirteen wholly original songs was no longer enough. Jeff Beck, working on his own kind of *Truth*, was plain disinterested, 'I haven't heard the record and have no intention of doing so. It's not my type of music.'

The most acute assessment among *Disc*'s opinionated ones actually came from TV personality Simon Dee, who recognised that 'this is really another art form – not pop music'. Rock and pop were no longer as Siamese twins, joined by the hip. Whether this new 'art form' would be as popular as pop was a question cultural commentators were only too keen to ask. The album was certainly attracting a great deal of interest from quarters previously content to treat pop with ill-disguised disdain. No 'pop' album before *Pepper* had ever received the same blanket coverage across so many forums of popular opinion, high and low, some now obliged, perhaps for the first time, to adopt the voice of a rock critic. Not surprisingly, some fell foul of the temptation to puff up the album in order to pontificate about pop culture itself. Like the *Sunday Times*'s Derek Jewell:

> The Beatles . . . are using their unique freedom in the pop world to . . . enlarge its vocabulary in most exciting ways. The new LP . . . is

remarkable. Listening to its strange cadences, its sitar passages, its almost atonal propensities, the learned critic might easily assume derivations ranging from English 17th century music to Richard Strauss.

The *New Statesman* went one better, hiring an esteemed professor of music to share his thoughts. And though Wilfred Mellers was some way from writing published treatises on The Beatles (*Twilight of the Gods*) and Dylan (*Whiter Shade of Pale*), he was already reading a great deal into this particular collection of pop songs, calling the music 'quite sophisticated' and the lyrics 'close to recent Bob Dylan', which amounted to the same thing. He was also alone in spotting how 'irony . . . is usually present in the musical material itself: for instance the suddenly brisk refrain in Lucy . . . [and] the soupy cello soup and simultaneously uncomprehending duologue in "She's Leaving Home"'. Mellers even found a concept of sorts hidden away in the Sergeant's seamless grooves:

> The beautifully produced disc isn't just a collection of numbers but a whole of which the parts, if remarkably various, are related. This whole is about loneliness; and the period comedy of *Sergeant Pepper's Lonely Hearts Club Band*, which begins as a hilarious evocation of old-style camaraderie, [but] is gradually transformed as the 'lonely' elements are detached from the hearts, the club and the band.

If this was never a concept The Beatles considered, it made them seem all the smarter for that. Yet from the very off there were dissenting voices, who found no such conceptual integrity underlying another collection of songs; and the credentials of these carping critics were perhaps better than those who found only cause for celebration. Jazzman and raconteur George Melly, writing in the *Observer*, had reservations about both the musical side, with its 'tendency to overdo the curry powder', and the lyrical side, where 'the straight psychedelic excursions seem to confuse poetry with woolly nursery surrealism'. He also felt that the message of the album was singularly solipsistic, 'Look in, or look back, but don't, if you can avoid it, look out.' And yet, despite such caveats, Melly did think the album contained much that was exciting.

The same could not be said of Richard Goldstein – perhaps the most respected rock critic in America at the time – whose duty it was to review the album for *The New York Times*. Goldstein, an early champion of the likes of the Velvet Underground and Lovin' Spoonful, was hardly so strait-laced he needed a corset. And he was a fan of just about everything the FabFour had done to date. He also seemed to display an almost telepathic understanding of how the album came about, in what was still a rocket of a review:

> In *Revolver*, I found a simplicity and empathy that was staggering. But in *Sgt. Pepper* I sense an obsession with the surrogate magic of production, and a new sarcasm masquerading as cool . . . Much of the radicalism on this album has appeared elsewhere in a less sophisticated form. It was possible months ago to predict the emergence of the extended pop song, because it had already appeared in its infancy . . . Still, The Beatles will probably receive credit for most of the 'innovations' on this album, including, of course, the removal of 'banding', or space between the cuts. Unfortunately, there is no thematic development to justify this wholeness; at best, the songs are only vaguely related. In unadorned fact, The Beatles had composed a healthy chunk of this material before they thought of centralizing it . . . and the finished product shows this hesitant commitment to the idea of unity.

Such prescience concerning the circumstances surrounding *Sgt. Pepper* failed to stand Goldstein in good stead. The wrath that he brought down upon his head for statements like, 'The Beatles have given us a package of special effects, dazzling but ultimately fraudulent', was akin to someone questioning Christ's divinity at a convocation of Catholic priests. Yet Goldstein continued to argue his corner with a rare command of the actual issue – which was if *Pepper* professed to be Art, then it must be judged accordingly; not as another pretty pop confection, but as a Statement. And, by this criterion, he found the end result wanting:

> Hailed as progenitors of a pop avant-garde, [The Beatles] have been idolised as the most creative members of their generation. The pressure to create an album that is complex, profound and innovative must have been staggering . . . [And] the twelve new compositions in the album are as elaborately conceived as the cover. The sound is a pastiche of dissonance and lushness. The mood is mellow, even nostalgic. But, like the cover, the overall effect is busy, hip and cluttered. If being a critic were the same as being a listener, I could enjoy SPLHCB . . . [But] what I worship about The Beatles is their forging of rock into what is real. It made them artists; it made us fans; and it made me think like a critic when I turned on my radio.

No-one wrote 'pop' reviews like this. This was actual criticism, and, as such, tantamount to heresy. Too many people had invested their hopes and dreams, and not just for the future of pop, in these four lads to let them be roundly condemned for putting out an album that fell short of its 'revolutionary' hype. And just like the ranks of British fan club members who hated the album, those who leapt to its defence – in the *New York Times* letters page and the columns of the *Village Voice* – were nothing if not disparate in outlook (and, dare one say, critical faculties).

One pernicious little proselytiser proudly proclaimed himself to be an associate professor of music at St Lawrence University (which can't help but recall Eric Idle's Occasional Visiting Professor of Applied Narcotics at the University of Please Yourself, California, from Beatles 'mockdoc', *All You Need Is Cash*). He accused Goldstein of quoting 'out of context, two lines [in "Within You Without You"] that led him to the conclusion . . . that the song is not profound. (Is the song not lovely?)'. Quite how a string of non sequiturs can be quoted 'out of context' our associate professor never explains. Nor does the issue of whether something is 'lovely' have an iota of relevance as to whether it is profound. And there can be little doubt that Harrison hoped his tabla-raga would be considered both lovely *and* profound.

The debate was hotting up. And while Goldstein's review was level-headed and restrained (lest we forget, he did call 'A Day in the Life' 'an historic Pop event'), those who leapt to The Beatles' 'defence' were anything but. Even the *Village Voice*, Goldstein's home base for most of his working career, let a critic with no real Rock credentials before (and certainly none after) – Tom Phillips – write a review that read like a sophomore's teenage crush. The *Voice* then nailed an outlandish banner-headline to this lovesick puppy's mast, 'Beatles' *Pepper*: The Album as Art Form':

> I think The Beatles have scored a genuine breakthrough with *Sgt. Pepper*. Specifically, I think they've turned the record-album itself into an art-form . . . Unlike all past long-playing records that I know of, this one has a metaphorical structure, very much like a work of fiction . . . The band then is the world of performance, a world within a world created by and for its audience . . . Cuts two through eleven are widely disparate in mood and sound, but . . . the characters who appear form a gallery of Lonely Hearts, leading lives that range from quiet to raucous desperation. Among them are a solipsistic acid-head, an aging only child . . . and a nutty kid in love with a meter maid . . . My verdict: the most ambitious and most successful record album ever issued, and the most significant artistic event of 1967.

This was not pop criticism. It was the befuddled droolings of a man who found meaning wherever he looked, self-consciously passing his scattershot thoughts off as insight. Mr Phillips had had an epiphany – The Album as Art-Form. Two years and three months after *Bringing It All Back Home*! By the time he had his eureka moment, the bath-water was stone cold, but it didn't stop other culture-vultures adopting the mantra that *Pepper* was the first 'Rock' album. Perhaps Goldstein was destined to remain a prophet without honour.

Goldstein's fellow Rock critics – a motley bunch of renegade reporters and student drop-outs in these pre-*Rolling Stone* years – were content to participate in the blood-letting. Paul Williams, *Crawdaddy* editor and a father-figure for all Rock criticism, attacked him for 'trying too hard . . . *Sgt. Pepper* is a show, a delightful enter-tainment – if there's a message, it's Dig Yourself.' The *New Yorker's* Ellen Sander suggested that Richard was being a grouse for condemning the album as 'not all it was cracked up to be'. The only critic to saunter to Goldstein's defence was the marginalised Robert Christgau, then writing for the soon-to-be-extinct *Cheetah* (edited by Jules Siegel). Christgau couldn't quite bring himself to wholeheartedly agree with Goldstein's review, just his right to write it: 'Goldstein may have been wrong, but he wasn't that wrong. Sgt. Pepper is not the world's most perfect work of art . . . Sgt. Pepper is a consolidation, more intricate than Revolver, but not more substantial.'

And yet, for all the hubbub, there was a singular shortage of reviews from any other Rock critic in the aftermath of Goldstein's roasting. Perhaps no-one dared challenge such a rapidly hardening consensus. Actually, the forums open for any serious review remained few and far between. The Berkeley-based Jann Wenner discovered this when he submitted a two-thousand-word review to *Hi-fi* mag-azine, but had it rejected because, according to Derek Taylor, 'they said it contained too much hyperbole; nothing could be *that* good.' Wenner's response was to found *Rolling Stone*, where he could write what he liked, at least until the advertising revenue started to roll in.

In America, where the rockritic creed first grew wings, its orig-inal outlet, *Crawdaddy*, didn't give the album the benefit of Editor Williams's words of wisdom. He was too busy digging it. Instead, it couched its review in an overview on 'The State of The Beatles' in its October issue. Penned not by Meltzer, Pearlman or Landau – the cream of *Crawdaddy's* first crop of critics – but by the largely anonymous Don McNeill, the piece read like someone who was just grateful to have another Beatles album in his sweaty palms:

The Beatles are dead! Long live The Beatles! There they are, the metamorphosis complete, standing on the flowered grave of their former selves . . . One is tempted to call it a comeback. Throughout the winter, there was a sense of the inevitability of the downfall of The Beatles . . . But it can't be a comeback because they never left. Somehow, on the great pop pedestal of our time, right there in front of everyone . . . The Beatles have resolved the fact that they are The Beatles.

In the same month, *Hullabaloo* gave the album to the one other American Rock critic whose credentials equalled Goldstein's. Perhaps surprisingly Paul Nelson, ex-editor of *Little Sandy Review* and *Sing Out*, stout defender of Dylan's decision to go electric, and just about the hippest dude on the *Hullabaloo* staff, surrendered to the rococo charms of *Sgt. Pepper* without a fight, drawing a fine line from the single, to the album, to the promised land:

'Penny Lane' and 'Strawberry Fields Forever' served as perfect previews . . . for this album; they tied together its dual themes: a fond remembrance of the past and the celebration and realisation of the present and the future. *Sergeant Peppers Lonely Hearts Club Band* glories in the madcap vaudeville murder of the old Beatles . . . then resurrects them as a spangled and marvellous marching band of the mind . . . With this album, undoubtedly their masterpiece, The Beatles emerge, with Bob Dylan, as the major musical forces in the golden age of pop music. *SPLHCB* is that rarity among popular records: a completely realised, relaxed, and successful work of art.

By October 1967, when MacNeill's and Nelson's reviews rubber-stamped the view already adopted by America's mainstream media, it seemed that Melly's and Goldstein's cogent caveats were as straws in the critical wind. In the past year and a half, there had been a gradual coming together of elements in America's media and its intelligentsia, inside and outside academia, who wanted to imbue pop culture with capital-S Significance, and the Sergeant was a necessary recruit to their cause. For them, it was irrelevant whether *Pepper* reinvented the wheel. The world was now ready to get serious about pop, and that was what mattered.

It had been a long time coming. When Dylan had been providing an exemplary new set of standards in sounds, sequencing and songs through 1965–66; The Beach Boys were growing up to be men; and the wave of incisive English songwriters who followed in The Beatles' wake began to gaze beyond the three-minute single, intelligent commentary about pop music was decidedly hard to find. It even more rarely resided in the mainstream. As Ellen Sander observed in her memoir of the sixties, *Trips*:

> The line was drawn by adult tastemakers desperately scrambling for credibility after the fact and youth crossed it gaily. This phenomenon precipitated the emergence of peer group rock critics. The rock & roll press at the time consisted of anyone who was low enough on the staff totem pole to be sent out to cover a pop group.

Jazz critic Ralph J Gleason had written a defining article on the new music, 'The Children's Crusade', for West Coast culture-zine *Ramparts* in March 1966; but was otherwise obliged to confine his cultural nous to columns in the local *Chronicle*, at least until Jann Wenner came to him with his idea for a Bay Area-based bi-weekly Rock paper in the aftermath of *Pepper*.

Jules Siegel had also managed to convince his friend Arthur Kretchmer, the managing editor of *Cavalier*, a less risqué rival to *Playboy*, to let him 'put together an issue on Rock' in the fall of 1965, in which he 'laid out the cultural significance of Rock, and what it meant, and what it was part of. It's kinda sketchy and crude, but I was [already] beginning to develop the idea. At that point Rock was pretty much considered disreputable – for teenyboppers! ... That's how the *Saturday Evening Post* found out about me.' Though Siegel then got to write his famous Dylan cover story, the *Post* nixed his follow-up piece on Brian Wilson and *Smile*. There was still much pent-up prejudice at work here, treating what was happening musically with something akin to condescension.

The problem was even more acute in England, which had a thriving weekly music press, comprising four regular papers (*Disc, Melody Maker, NME* and *Record Mirror*), but very little in the way of sharp-edged criticism. The so-called 'in-depth' interviews with the stars of the day were anodyne affairs, and even a highly literate artist like Dylan was expected to answer asinine questionnaires, like *NME*'s 'Lifelines', detailing a few of his favourite things (for taste in music, he offered, 'Sort of peanut butter'). Hence the delight which greeted the appearance of *International Times* in October 1966, where the interviewer (invariably Miles) treated the likes of McCartney, Harrison and Townshend as intelligent individuals with opinions about all the great taboos – politics, religion and sex.

However, *IT* soon became distracted by the sort of culture it wanted to counter, preferring to address the social aspects of the underground. Even *Oz*, when it appeared in January 1967, failed to display more than a cursory interest in the sonic soundtrack to the sixties' social upheavals. And though the 'weeklies' began their slow passage into critical forums (a process not really completed until 1972, in *NME*'s case, and later still for its rivals), the response to *Pepper*, and The Beatles' subsequent musical career, from the UK music papers was markedly different from the American new wave of (initially) underground Rock periodicals like *Rolling Stone, Creem* and *Fusion*. In *Pop From The Beginning* (1969), Nik Cohn described The Beatles' relative reputations on either side of the Atlantic eighteen months after *Pepper* in the following terms:

> In America and in England, [The Beatles] have become two entirely separate things: in the States, where pop is followed with great solemnity by almost everyone intelligent under the age of thirty, there are still many people who take them seriously, who see them as divinities and hang upon their every utterance, while in England, where pop remains mostly entertainment, they're seen as cranks, millionaire eccentrics in the grand manner, vaguely regrettable, maybe, but quite harmless.

Cohn may be dramatising the differences between the two coun-
tries to substantiate his 'death of Pop' thesis, but there is much to
his contention. As pop became Rock (became Art), Stateside, *Sgt.
Pepper* was rubber-stamped as The Beatles' brightest beacon of artful-
ness. This process took place with surprising speed. By the third
week of September 1967, when *Time* magazine devoted its cover
and six pages to The Beatles' 'New Incarnation', the acceptance
of *Pepper* as Art was already set in critical concrete. By the time
Rolling Stone's first issue appeared, in December, it was a fait accompli
(certainly *Stone* continued to consider it so, even respectfully voting
the by-then-discredited artifact the best album of the last twenty
years in 1987).

Perhaps the reverberations the album caused in the States had
something to do with the fact that most US fans had never heard
a pukka Beatles album before. Richard Poirer, writing in 1967 for
the *Partisan Review*, an eminent political and literary journal coming
out of Boston University, called his article 'Learning from The
Beatles', but didn't learn enough to discover that they were from
an English port called Liverpool, or that the US albums were but
bastard runts of the UK albums, with as much relevance to their
artistic growth as a collection of their press-kits.

To Mr Poirer, *Sgt. Pepper* was 'the latest and most remarkable
of the thirteen [sic] albums composed and performed by The
Beatles since 1964 [sic]'. Not surprisingly, *Pepper* had a unity and
a completeness lacking in those previous twelve albums, because
it was the first time The Beatles had been able to insist that their
American label toe the line and issue their work unmutilated
(though the idea that American corporations could hack popular
English works to pieces and reassemble them abridged and out-
of-sorts, lingered until at least the seventies, when ABC found
themselves on the wrong end of a lawsuit from Monty Python for
doing to their TV programmes much like what Capitol had inflicted
on early Beatles LPs). In the decontextualised universe Poirer
lived in, *Sgt. Pepper* was bound to come across as a seismic statement:

> *Pepper* isn't in the line of continuous development; rather, it is an
> eruption . . . an astounding accomplishment . . . Nothing less is
> being claimed by these songs than that The Beatles now exist not
> merely as a phenomenon of entertainment but as a force of histor-
> ical consequence.

But in order for this album to be 'a force of historical consequence',
it required America's most august periodicals – *Time, Newsweek,
Life* and the *New Yorker* – to agree that something was happening,
and that the Sergeant knew what it was. *Life* got in there first, with
Thomas Thompson's incisive account of a single *Sgt. Pepper* session
for their 16 June issue. It was followed a week later by a *Newsweek*
review of the album, and even a *New Yorker* feature thereon. The
Newsweek review, by Jack Kroll, was suitably serious in tone, surprisingly suggesting The Beatles had come on in leaps and bounds from
Revolver, barely nine months earlier:

> *Pepper* is a rollicking, probing language-and-sound vaudeville, which
> grafts skin from all three brows – high, middle and low – into a
> pulsating collage about mid-century manners and madness . . . The
> Beatles have lost their innocence, certainly, but loss of innocence is
> increasingly their theme.

The *New Yorker* couldn't quite bring itself to wholeheartedly join
the revelry, so as an alternative canvassed the college campuses for
a consensus on this perplexing collection. Again, the emphasis was
on how much The Beatles had grown, and how intellectual they
– and their 'new' audience – had become. WMCA DJ Joe Brien
called it 'a terribly intellectual album. My youngest son is a freshman
at Yale. He tells me that the day the album was issued the entire
student body of Yale went out and bought it. Exactly the same
thing happened at Harvard.' Ah, the Ivy League stamp of approval!
    Meanwhile, the *New Yorker* went out and found their own
student, John Van Aalst, who admitted he was 'really more interested in classical music, but this Beatles record goes beyond the sound

of the record. It's technically interesting and imaginative. This is no longer computerised rock & roll ... It's an attempt to create music with meaning ... It conforms more to my conception of art.'

Even *Time* magazine – having singularly failed to review the album on its appearance – did a lengthy after-the-fact profile to compensate for its lack of cultural awareness, giving the album and the band a full five-page fanfare in a September cover story. It was still riddled with the kind of simplistic generalisations (see below) and factual howlers ('the [album] cover ... has THE BEATLES spelled out in flowers trimmed with marijuana plants') that had made Dylan rip a chunk off one of their reporters in London two years earlier. Coincidentally, the footage of this famous confrontation, included in DA Pennebaker's *Don't Look Back*, received its US premiere just a fortnight before *Pepper* was released. But despite a general disdain for *Time* among the attuned, it still had the cultural clout to get first-hand quotes from these increasingly recalcitrant pop revolutionaries:

> Messengers from beyond rock & roll, [The Beatles] are creating the most original, expressive and musically interesting sounds being heard in pop music ... leading an evolution in which the best of current post-rock sounds are becoming something that pop music has never been before: an art form ... The Beatles [have] moved on, absorbing and extending Bob Dylan's folk-rock hybrid ... They have transformed themselves ... to an experimental laboratory group, and they have staked out the recording studio as their own electronic rumpus room ... Says Paul: 'If we do have an orchestra, are we going to write them as a pseudo-classical thing, which has been done better by people who know how to make it sound like that – or are we going to do it like we write songs? ... The music has more to do with electronics now than ever before. To do those things a few years ago was a bit immoral. But electronics is no longer immoral.'

The endorsements kept coming, often from the most unlikely of sources. In Columbia University's own journal, Joan Peyser suggested that 'no notational system is capable of reproducing the complex nature of a Beatle record . . . What is preserved in the music is the performance itself; the record is the message . . . [For] Rock [now] is all-embracing, having absorbed elements of blues, folk, jazz, and the serious avant-garde.'

Unfortunately for Peyser, there were no 'performances' to be found on *Pepper*, only constructions from a series of performances, some ensemble, some solo (overdubbed). Such 'complexity' was a by-product of production techniques, not necessarily any greater fecundity of musical ideas than could be found on their former albums. It is clear that Peyser, in her piece published that autumn, was pushing for an aesthetic of Rock based on the values of *Sgt. Pepper*, a forlorn wish because it was an album made with already-redundant technology, using a methodology that did not lend itself to *instrumental* experimentation (and was not really necessary once eight-track became the norm). If it was now a dead-end street, it was one The Beatles had covered with a fine toothcomb.

Even The Beatles began to worry about the way that the album was now being interpreted within ever decreasing circles of obtuseness. McCartney, who had originally pushed the band in such a self-conscious direction, later recanted, saying he realised that it was 'around the time of *Sgt. Pepper* [that] you started to get the *New York Times* doing articles on [the music] trying to evaluate and analyse it. I think that kind of analysis killed a lot of stuff that was going on.' Paul's co-composer was quicker to the counter-punch. John still had that old anti-intellectual itch he liked to scratch every now and then – generally when his pretentious new paramour wasn't looking.

> **John Lennon:** It's nice when people like it, but when they start 'appreciating' it, getting great deep things out of it, making a thing of it, then it's a lot of shit. It proves what we've always thought about most sorts of so-called art. It's all a lot of shit . . . I bet Picasso sticks things in. I bet he's been laughing his balls off for the last eighty years. [HD]

But post-*Pepper* there was no way to get the burgeoning pop-culture industry back in the box marked pop; just as there was no way bands were going to go back to mono; or let their producers sequence their songs; or allow their label to issue any album save the one *they* wanted. At least all those 'peer group Rock critics' finally started getting invited to the right parties, which now had a smattering of Rock music played for its hipper guests. As McCartney told *Uncut*, thirty-seven years on, 'It was influential in a lot of ways, and not just musically. Suddenly, music writers had to find new ways to respond, because . . . they weren't dealing with Perry Como'. The real question – how would the other exponents of pop's progressive wing cope with the transition from pop to Rock which *Pepper*'s release had now codified – remained as yet unanswered.

SCREAM THY LAST SCREAM

Psychedelic pop, stamped and validated by The Beatles'
eighth album, needed a name to go with its now-serious
purpose. Richard Neville, in the 1969 memoir he wrote of
the era, *Playpower*, suggests that this 'new sort of music . . . was
[now] nicknamed acid-rock, after the famous Monterey Pop
Festival, and then instantly internationalised with the release of
. . . *Sgt. Pepper*'. In fact, acid-rock as a term post-dates both events,
though Neville is right to suggest it became 'flower power's jingle';

and a fitting one, as, like other forms of acid, it had the capacity to burn all with whom it came into contact.

The term itself was part of an attempted reclamation of Rock from British popsters and tunesmiths instigated by a Bay Area cabal of would-be trendsetters: journalists Ralph J Gleason and Jann Wenner (then writing for *Ramparts*); bands like Jefferson Airplane and The Grateful Dead; and a pair of local promoters, Bill Graham and Lou Adler. The last of these was largely responsible for the Monterey Pop Festival, scheduled for the weekend of the 16–18 June, precisely two weeks after *Pepper* gave the hippies a universal soundtrack.

The festival, originally the brainchild of Alan Pariser and Benny Shapiro, had been left to the likes of Derek Taylor, Lou Adler and The Mamas & the Papas' John Phillips to organise/realise. Not surprisingly, given Taylor's involvement, it was intended as not only a celebration of the West Coast vibe but also the best of British pop, with whom the LA bands certainly shared so much. Initially, Taylor intended to use the Monterey bill to present the three LA bands he'd filed under 'B' for 'Best' – his two clients, The Beach Boys and The Byrds, and the up-and-coming Buffalo Springfield.

For all three B-list bands, Monterey marked a watershed of sorts. For The Beach Boys, it could have been the moment when they staked a claim to the new psychedelic audience with the likes of 'Heroes & Villains' and 'Good Vibrations', both of which had already received live debuts. But the abandoning of *Smile* and (valid) concerns about what seemed like financial shenanigans behind the scenes caused them to pull out just as the bill was being finalised. Instead, they spent the days leading up to the festival putting finishing touches to 'Heroes & Villains' and 'Vegatables' – this time for real – as they hastily assembled their *Smile Lite* LP, issued the first week of September 1967 as *Smiley Smile*.

The sales figures for *Smiley Smile* confirmed, in black and white, one of the most spectacular falls from grace of any sixties band. The eleven-track album – save for its two already-released singles – sounded like a side-project the boys had slung together one weekend between *Today* and *Pet Sounds* to fulfil a contractual obligation to Capitol. The days of short-changing fans on album length – and without the year-old 'Good Vibrations', *Smiley Smile* would have clocked in at under twenty-five minutes – were over. *Sgt. Pepper* had started a trend for album-length albums that even American labels were helpless to prevent. The Beach Boys, and their label, proved hopelessly out of step. The album peaked at forty-one, signalling the end of The Beach Boys as serious commercial contenders for close to a decade.

Even Britain had slipped from The Beach Boys' grasp in the time it had taken The Beatles to put together *Sgt. Pepper*. When they returned in May 1967 – just six months after that most triumphant of tours – to headline a few more sold-out shows, culminating in the *NME* Pollwinners Concert, the reviewers were no longer disposed to be kind. Nick Jones, writing in *NME*, suggested that 'the polished perfection and the wealth of sound and orchestration that is . . . on their records [only served to make] the live Beach Boys group sound so comparably amateurish'.

The Boys' decision not to play Monterey may also have been bound up with a real inferiority complex, which the British critics weren't about to cure. After all, as Ralph J Gleason pointed out after the fact, the Monterey festival was 'a selective *Rock* festival with little nodding towards pop'. The County Fairgrounds still should have been an ideal environment for both The Byrds and Buffalo Springfield to display their own Rock credentials.

The Springfield were bathing in the spring success of their Top Ten single about the Sunset Strip riots, 'For What It's Worth' and live were producing some outlandishly elongated renditions of 'Bluebird' that would have made even The Move groove. But at the end of May, Neil Young suddenly announced he was jumping the rickety ship, apparently unhappy with the band's direction (or, more likely, his own lack of any final say). As such, when they arrived at the County Fairgrounds it was effectively the Stephen Stills Band, joined on harmony vocals by David Crosby, who had not endeared himself to his fellow Byrds by prefacing their rendition of 'He Was A Friend of Mine' with a rant about the cover-up concerning John F Kennedy's assassination:

> **Roger McGuinn:** I remember Crosby doing his diatribe about LSD and the Kennedy conspiracy theory. I don't know what the audience thought, but I didn't think that was cool . . . And he played with Buffalo Springfield, which was fine – [all] part of that camaraderie thing where we all helped each other – but I think it was the attitude with which he did it that was disturbing, because he did it as a spiteful gesture [to us] rather than a friendly thing with them . . . He really didn't want to be in the Byrds at that point.

Sure enough, Crosby was about to flutter away. Though Young would eventually realise his options remained rather limited, and skulk back to Springfield, the two bands were set on a collision course. Out of this would come a new, Crosby-less, countrified Byrds, who would follow The Beach Boys into a commercial wasteland with the ill-timed *Sweetheart of the Rodeo*; while on the other side of the picket fence, Crosby, Stills & Nash (and eventually Young) would become America's premier 'supergroup'.

The LA bands may have been under-represented at Monterey, but so were the English bands, though it was not for want of trying. Derek Taylor, in an early advance report of the festival, claimed that 'the organisers' were hoping to approach the likes of Donovan, the Stones, The Kinks and The Who, though in the end only the last of these made the trip. Joining The Who were a new incarnation of The Animals, which was now essentially Eric Burdon & friends, and The Jimi Hendrix Experience, whose leader was desperate to make his 'homecoming' as triumphant as his English debut.

If Burdon was riding high in the American charts with his valedictory to a misspent youth, 'When I Was Young', for Hendrix and The Who this was a much-needed opportunity to make their mark in the land of plenty of punters. For Hendrix, it was his first such opportunity; for The Who, possibly their last. And they responded accordingly. Quite simply, incontestably, they blew the West-Coast bands away. In one dynamic pincer movement on the Sunday night, The Who opened second-half proceedings, and Hendrix closed them in a blaze of glory.

Caught between The Who's raucous Rock and Hendrix's hard edge were The Grateful Dead, the local darlings of open-D tuning, who would later claim that they just didn't play well that night. In fact, they hadn't a prayer of playing catch-up with bands this tight, loud and dynamic, withering by comparison (they tried not to make the same mistake, appearing alongside real Rock bands, again).

Almost their only hope was getting the deadbeats who frequented their shows at the Fillmore to show some solidarity, but most of these had baulked at the cost of admission to the County Fairgrounds. So when the Dead heard 'that people in back of the arena were ripping out fences to get in', they began to demand, 'Let 'em in.' In one fell swoop, they ensured Monterey would be a one-off event (the city of Monterey demanded such an outlandish bond against damage insurance for any future event that the festival never happened again). The Dead still got creamed by two of the three best powerhouse trios in the world.

To those looking to propagate the new hippy ethic – or make a movie – Monterey was all peace and flowers (and I do not doubt that the vibe was extraordinary). As arch-cynic Keith Altham admits, 'I was almost beginning to believe it [at Monterey] – that love and peace might actually work, that they might actually be able to replace war and hate with something more worthwhile.' But its true significance lay in the fact that a bunch of Bay Area businessmen, bedecked in beads, drank their wine and set out to sell the San Francisco scene as where it was at – selling the pop world short in the process.

If the Dead were shown to be a support act at best, Moby Grape gave a short, energetic account of themselves, but to no avail. Their press-preview set at the Fillmore, ten days earlier, on the back of a CBS campaign intended to justify an outlandish advance, had already shown that hype alone would not sell coals to Newcastle. Quicksilver Messenger Service went over well with the locals, but left most of the world's journalists unimpressed. The real Bay Area winners were Jefferson Airplane, already taking a high-five with 'Somebody To Love', thus simply confirming their credentials via a truncated version of their full Fillmore set; and Big Brother & the Holding Company, fronted by the irrepressible Janis Joplin, a woman who had been dropped in a vat of the blues at birth, à la Obelix.

Joplin came across as such a force of nature during Big Brother's Saturday afternoon appearance – a lowly place for such a livewire, yet reflecting the band's relative position on the local scene – that a slot was made available for her on the Sunday night bill, on condition that they allow Pennebaker to film the set. Such was the power of what she produced that Dylan's manager, Albert Grossman, and Columbia president, Clive Davis, whisked her away from her current label, Mainstream; her band of big brothers; and this life, before anyone had realised how precious a Pearl she was.

But what Joplin was not was psychedelic. Sure, she took psychedelics, but then she'd have gulped down a fifth of cod liver oil if someone had told her she could get high on it. Joplin was an old-fashioned blues singer, fronting an old-fashioned electric jug band. And in this she was not so different from other SF aspirants. Jefferson Airplane were originally a folk-band; and when they tried to get truly psychedelic, on 1968's *After Bathing at Baxter's*, they made the Dead sound economical. The Grateful Dead was Jerry Garcia waking up to the fact that he was not going to be able to feed his assorted habits on the proceeds of a career in bluegrass. The most *psychedelic* bands in town – Moby Grape and Quicksilver Messenger Service – blew their wad before signing to the majors for big money (in the former's case, CBS; the latter's, Capitol).

In truth, the word on the San Francisco scene was a great big lie. There was nothing new about these bands – they did what folk and blues bands had always done, just for a whole lot longer. When the seriously psychedelic Pink Floyd reached the Bay Area, in early

November, they were stunned to find that San Franciscan psyche-delia meant drugs and lights, not sound and fury:

> **Nick Mason:** When we went to America on that first tour we were astonished at what we found, because . . . most of the San Francisco bands had a lot of country music in what they were doing, and I think we just assumed we'd be out there with people doing other versions of what we were doing. Big Brother were a real blues & country band, . . . and others that had sounded psychedelic [on record] turned out to be straight-forward pop bands.

Five days after their West-Coast debut, Pink Floyd were 'promoting' their third UK single, 'Apples & Oranges', by miming to it on *American Bandstand*. Syd, who 'wasn't into moving his lips that day', took them at their word. It had been four months since 'See Emily Play' had entered the UK charts, and Barrett had decided that he was no longer interested in being a pop star, something he had seemed to so enjoy during that first flush.

Back at the beginning of July – with *Pepper* still sticking to the roof of the album charts – 'See Emily Play' had constituted part of the same Top Thirty as 'A Whiter Shade of Pale' (Procol Harum – #1), 'Paper Sun' (Traffic – #5), 'Waterloo Sunset' (The Kinks – #15) and 'Strange Brew' (Cream – #19). It was an ex-traordinary cross-section of new styles in English music, all ostens-ibly drawing on the finest traditions of pop, but going somewhere else. And in each case, the bands were working on albums that sallied back and forth across the frontier separating pop from Rock.

The first to reach the finishing line were The Kinks, completing their first album not made under the direct tutelage of producer Shel Talmy in the second week of June. *Something Else*, though, was subject to unnecessary delays. Initially it was Ray Davies tinkering with the mix and the sequence, while his brother's solo debut 45, 'Death of a Clown', played catch-up with 'Waterloo Sunset', eventually reaching number three under its own steam. Then, with two hugely successful singles charting barely six weeks apart, Pye decided to allow a respectful distance before issuing the new Kinks album on 15 September. Yet despite such auspicious advance words, *Something Else* failed to chart at all (though when Pye hurriedly issued a budget compilation of earlier tracks, *Sunny Afternoon*, just two months later, it went Top Ten). Something was up. The Kinks fans only bought singles, it seemed. Or compilations of singles.

The fact that *Something Else* was a beautifully realised, quintessentially English suite of songs with a greater conceptual unity than *Sgt. Pepper*, and an album-closer fully the equal of 'A Day In The Life', counted for naught. The Britpop audience had become increasingly fickle, and whatever the Davies brothers hoped might happen, their record label lacked the vision to see beyond endless repackaging exercises and continuous chart singles. Sure enough, when brother Ray delivered the superb successor to 'Sunset', 'Autumn Almanac', Pye put it out just four weeks after *Something Else*, and fans lined up to buy the latest seven-inch instalment in Davies's disenchanted dialogue with the modern world.

Yet, when Traffic and Cream followed their single successes in '67 with end-of-year albums – *Mr Fantasy* and *Disraeli Gears* respectively – *their* audiences seemed to find no difficulty transferring their allegiance from single to LP. And Floyd, who were still leading the charge of the light-headed brigade, managed to replicate the success of their first two singles with *Piper At The Gates of Dawn*, which reached number six when it appeared in August. The Cambridge lads clearly shared with the likes of Traffic, Cream and Hendrix a determination to experiment across every front (whereas, according to Graham Nash, The Hollies made singles like 'Carrie Anne' (#3) as a 'commercial proposition', while an album like *Butterfly* served as 'our method of free-expression in music').

Like The Kinks, the Floyd had spent June applying the last brushstrokes to their work on the larger canvas. Even though producer Norman Smith would subsequently claim that 'once we had something down on the master tape, that was it as far as Syd was concerned, [because] he . . . wanted to put it out in its raw, unfinished state', work on *Piper* occupied a good six weeks after the 'completion' of its final cut, 'Bike'. Indeed, according to Nick Mason, 'We were . . . taking up unprecedented amounts of Abbey Road's studio resources . . . [so we] renegotiated our deal with EMI, taking a cut in our percentage from 8% to 5% in exchange for unlimited studio time.' Hardly the action of artists in a hurry.

At least one EMI engineer, Peter Bown, recalls Barrett taking a *very* active role in the mixing of songs like 'Chapter 24' and 'Interstellar Overdrive'. In the latter's case, the decision was made by Floyd to add another layer of sound 'live' to the basic track recorded back in February, presumably hoping to provide the same sensory overload the quartet could achieve in performance. And, even though, as Jenner points out, the Floyd 'were getting busier and busier, being dragged away, so it was [a case of] slipping [mixing sessions] in', they still insisted on being present as often as their helter-skelter schedule allowed. Finally, on 18 July, with 'See Emily Play' at eight in the singles chart, the album was mastered.

Two days later, the Floyd were playing the wilds of Elgin, to a crowd who clearly expected a pop band, one heckler offering the opinion, 'I could sing better in ma wee bath.' The band – Syd included – seemed to take it all in their stride, at least according to the *Disc* journalist along for the ride. However, the broadcast of *Top of the Pops* the same night – featuring Floyd's pre-recorded performance from earlier in the week – unveiled a Barrett no longer so stoic. According to Roger Waters, he turned up at the studio dishevelled and distracted, 'Syd didn't want to know. He got down there in an incredible state and said he was not going to do it.'

Apparently, Barrett was eventually persuaded to mime to 'Emily' one last time, but his next BBC session signalled the end of the happy-go-lucky pop star. The following Friday (28), the Floyd were scheduled to record a session for the *Saturday Club* radio show, but Barrett again seemed wholly disinterested. Indeed, according to the Light Entertainment Booking Manager, in a letter he penned to Peter Jenner demanding an explanation, he 'left the studio without [even] completing the recording of the first number'.

Rick Wright later told *Mojo*, 'He went missing for the whole weekend and when he reappeared again on the Monday, he was a totally different person.' In fact, Syd was at the UFO that night, for what was the final night of the original underground club. The Floyd were to be supported by a band with the not-so-envious tag of 'England's answer to Jefferson Airplane'. Fairport Convention would eventually leave Airplane in the dust but, as they had only been gigging for two months, not yet. According to another Floyd member, Barrett made it on stage, but only as a passenger from the astral plane:

> **Nick Mason:** Syd arrived [at UFO], but his arms hung by his side, with the occasional strumming. That was the night of doing [Saturday Club], which was the breakdown. But that wasn't the end of it all. That evening was something referred to four months later. [1974]

Joe Boyd, too, remembers an occasion at UFO where he ran across Syd in the scrum by the entrance, and as he looked into his eyes, realised there were 'black holes' where there had once been light. This incident has generally been dated to 2 June, which makes no sense. On further enquiry, Joe admits that what he *actually* remembers is 'the long gap since I had last seen Syd, and the huge excitement of them coming back to UFO after a long gap and all the success'. This fits the late July date a whole lot better. The gap between early June and late July was eight weeks (as opposed to six, from April to June), and the 'success' of 'See Emily Play' was on a whole other level to 'Arnold Layne''s fleeting incursion into the lower echelons of chartdom.

Boyd was shocked, but not totally surprised: 'It was obvious to me that if you did [LSD] every day, you were jeopardising the wires that held everything together in your mind.' Miles, that other UFO perennial, has a different theory. He suspects that the light show which had been so central to the early Floyd performances played its part in Barrett's breakdown:

Miles: They've done tests with schizophrenics [and strobes], and it triggers it. It could well be that Pink Floyd's own light system was driving him nuts. There were occasions at UFO he would go onstage and appear to be okay, and then next thing you know he was detuning and totally spaced out.

What seems quite clear – after one removes the wildly improbable from anything anecdotal – is that Barrett's mental collapse (for it was clearly that) was both sudden and unexpected, at least to the band itself, who were still surprisingly gauche when it came to experimenting with the mind-altering. Jenner, the one Floyd insider who had shared some of Syd's journeys into the inner hinterlands, went quickly into 'damage limitation' mode. He penned a prompt reply to the BBC Booking Manager, stating that Barrett had suffered a 'nervous collapse'. At the same time, he informed *Melody Maker* that 'Syd Barrett is suffering from "nervous exhaustion" and the group have withdrawn from all engagements booked for the month of August.'

It represented the worst kind of timing. The album they had worked so hard to perfect – and had come as close as any record has a right to be – appeared in the shops the first week in August. But by his own admission Barrett was no longer 'really here'. Despite this, the album was a commercial success, and though it was not about to challenge *Sgt. Pepper* in the end of year charts, *it* would be the album that signalled the next phase for a nascent English progressive Rock, stretching anyone still trundling through Pepperland to the limit.

And, collapse or no collapse, Barrett was back in the studio on 7 and 8 August, to record the next single. It was not going to be so easy to get off this treadmill. In fact, Jenner had already informed *Melody Maker*, back in July, that the follow-up single to 'See Emily Play' would be 'either "Old Woman With A Casket" or "Millionaire", both Syd Barrett songs.' The latter had already been recorded, during the *Piper* sessions. The former – better known to Floyd fans as the fabled 'Scream Thy Last Scream' – occupied these two days at Abbey Road.

'Scream Thy Last Scream' represented as dramatic a change in Syd's songwriting as the last *Top of the Pops* did in his personal appearance. Having delivered an album largely comprising adult fairy stories, here was an unrelenting examination of a psyche under assault – his own. However, it didn't seem like obvious single material. But then Barrett wasn't the only member of Floyd who was starting to doubt the whole pop process. The week before the August session, their bassist told a *Melody Maker* reporter he was tired of playing to audiences of single-buyers:

> **Roger Waters:** Perhaps we should stop trying to do our singles on-stage. Even The Beatles, when they worked live, sounded like their records. But the sort of records we make today are impossible to reproduce onstage so there is no point in trying. [1967]

Nick Mason also felt 'We were being hustled about to make hit singles. There's so many people saying it's important you start to think it's important.' If 'Scream Thy Last Scream' was hardly what EMI had in mind, Syd proved decidedly uncooperative about providing any alternatives. Mason believes he remembers Barrett and Smith having a 'talk about picking a follow-up to "Arnold Layne", and [Smith saying] that maybe "See Emily Play" should be the single. Syd reacted as if the word "single" was a nasty concept.' This is probably another Floydian memory playing tricks, and it was the idea of another 'poppy' follow-up to 'See Emily Play' that actually prompted Barrett's ire. Love had turned to hate.

> **Miles:** Syd was the only one who really saw it as they were gonna have hit singles, go on *Top of the Pops*, dress in Granny Takes A Trip clothes and get all the girls, and he *loved* that side of it. But his schizophrenic personality [meant] he [also] hated all that side of things, and all the trappings of fame. This had a lot to do with Syd's illness . . . But he was always very highly strung. He had a terrible attention deficit problem. He was *always* slightly out there.

Either way, Barrett's breakdown meant that recording *any* follow-up to their Top Ten single was never going to be a summer breeze. As Jenner recalls, 'It all became very fraught after that . . . Everything [had been] really easy and then everything became really difficult . . . The songs weren't there. We'd go in with half a song.' 'Scream Thy Last Scream' – for all its fragmentation – was a lot more than 'half a song', but it wasn't so much psychedelic as borderline psychotic:

> **Andrew King:** In our foolishness we thought we had to have a hit single and we put unrelenting pressure on Syd, and when he didn't come up with it we were thoroughly nasty to him . . . Things got to be very nasty in the studio, it would literally be Syd in one corner and the rest of the band in the other.

Barrett's solution was to again abandon Abbey Road for the singular solace of Sound Techniques, where he apparently spent three days in September reworking the maddening 'Scream Thy Last Scream'; as well as recording another, equally dissonant ditty, 'Vegetable Man', written after an innocuous comment from a journalist about becoming a 'vegetable' prompted Barrett to imagine someone already there.[1] As Jenner later recalled, 'Syd wrote "Vegetable Man" in my house. It was really uncanny. He sat there and just described himself.'

The songwriter and the producer had come to an impasse. Barrett was absolutely refusing to come up with anything commercial – even ridiculing the demands of the rabble with background crowd noises on 'Scream' that seemed to parody the ones which opened *Sgt. Pepper*. He had evidently been listening quite closely to The Beatles' so-called breakthrough. The next song he offered as a potential single, in early October, 'Jugband Blues', included an asymmetric bridge which represented in audio-form a mind crossing over into madness:

> **Peter Jenner:** The idea I think was that this brass band comes in and plays and then walks away again. It's that sort of thing like The

Beatles in that 'Good Morning, Good Morning' cockadoodledoo
session, [or] 'The Benefit of Mr Kite' and the hurdy-gurdy . . . that
sort of illustrative aspect [to] it. So in a sense the brass band was a
dream within the song. And I think Syd was aware of that, which
was why he didn't want them playing a [scored] part or playing in
time.

The real reference-point for Barrett here was surely the orchestral
segue on 'A Day In the Life' which, like 'Jugband Blues', used seemingly random precision to signify a transition from everyday existence to 'a dream within the song'. Syd's belief that the brass band
drafted in for the session shouldn't play along to a written part, or
play in a specified time-signature, again brought him into conflict
with Norman Smith, whose straighter sensibilities were offended.
Yet again, neither seemed prepared to give way. According to Cliff
Jones in his 1996 *Mojo* feature, it was Syd who finally snapped,
leaving Smith to it:

The two parts of ['Jugband Blues'] are bridged by a collage which
features the Salvation Army Band of North London who recorded
their albums at Abbey Road. Syd had asked Norman Smith for a
brass section to play through the bridge and wanted them to play
spontaneously, without music. Smith felt the bewildered musicians
should be properly scored. It was the only time Syd had a vociferous
disagreement with Smith [!], who finally agreed to record two versions,
one with his scored section and one with Syd's instruction to 'play
whatever you want'. Syd, tired of arguing, walked out, leaving Smith
to record the track his way.

Andrew King doesn't remember it that way. According to him, 'We
certainly did record them playing at random . . . but the Norman
Smith version won in the end.' Actually the only contemporary
description of the incident, by Alan Walsh in a December 1967
Melody Maker article, suggests it was Barrett who got his way, 'The
centre passage is almost free-form pop, with six members of the

Salvation Army on the recording session told to play what you like.' Perhaps Smith, like all good producers, took elements from both.

Walsh was personally blown away when he heard this 'poetic recitation by Barrett, with avant-garde sound effects by the group'. He was also surprised to have Peter Jenner telling him 'he had wanted to release [it] as their single, instead of "Apples & Oranges"'. EMI had succeeded in changing the Floyd's mind, suggesting it was too 'downbeat' until Barrett had relented and given them 'Apples & Oranges', which was almost a parody of the psychedelic single and his absolute last attempt to participate in the pop process.

When the single, not surprisingly, failed to ring enough registers, Syd was as unrepentant as can be, telling Walsh, 'All we can do is make records which we like. If the kids don't, then they won't buy it.' There was no doubting in which direction Barrett wanted to head – inward. A fortnight after he spoke – perfectly coherently – to Walsh, he was able to show the world what might have been, at what proved to be his final session with the Floyd. At the BBC's Maida Vale studios the four-piece recorded a *Top Gear* session in a single afternoon, comprising all three of Syd's post-*Piper* songs, 'Scream Thy Last Scream', 'Vegetable Man' and 'Jugband Blues' (this time featuring a bridge that was unmistakeably abstract), plus an audacious rearrangement of 'Pow R Toc H'. As Julian Palacios says, in his authoritative Barrett bio, *Lost in the Woods*, 'It's a wonderful session, and one that raises significant doubts about Barrett's "madness". In this relaxed setting, Barrett simply shines.'

By now, though, the lucid Barrett could come and go on an almost hourly basis, be coherent one minute and lost in the woods the next. Jonathan Cott, who was in England on a Fullbright scholarship while Jann Wenner passed him off as *Rolling Stone*'s 'European correspondent', was sent to interview Barrett, pending the US release of *Piper At The Gates of Dawn* (reprogrammed by Capitol to open with 'See Emily Play'). The Barrett Cott found 'was completely incoherent, and it was not possible to ask him a question [because of] the hallucinatory reality that he was in ... He didn't make one word of sense.' Yet even as those periods of lucidity began to diminish, and paranoia embraced him, he still had his moments. As Barrett's post-Floyd drummer Jerry Shirley told Kris DiLorenzo in the mid-seventies, 'For every ten things [Syd] says that are off-the-wall and odd, he'll say one thing that's completely coherent and right on the ball.'

As it is, Jenner believes that those songs recorded on 20 December at the Beeb should 'be compulsory hearing for anyone doing a course on mental breakdown ... Syd actually knew what was happening to him, "Jugband Blues" [being] the ultimate self-diagnosis on a state of schizophrenia.' He is undoubtedly right, and it may well be that the song-title itself was a little in-joke on Barrett's part, referring to another such song, 'Jugband Music', on the second Lovin' Spoonful album, which bears the immortal refrain, 'The doctor said, give him jugband music/ It seems to make him feel just fine.' Perhaps music was the only thing that made Barrett feel fine.

By now, Syd was certainly trying the patience of the still straight folk who constituted the remainder of the Cambridge combo. When, on their return from the US, he found out they had been sent on a package tour to promote the parody of a single he'd given the label, he was about ready to opt out altogether. He even seems to have reverted, at one point, to his 'Arnold Layne' persona. Roger Waters remembers these days thus, 'Syd was way out there. He thought he was a homosexual, and he'd get into the car in drag.' But no-one seemed prepared to call Syd's bluff, perhaps because as Kris DiLorenzo has remarked, 'During London's turbulent sixties scene it was difficult, especially in a love-and-drug stupor, to distinguish incipient dementia from contrived brinkmanship.'

When it came to 'contrived brinkmanship', though, Barrett had his work cut out on the package tour in question, which began at the capacious Royal Albert Hall on 14 November, three days before 'Apples & Oranges' went on sale. The to-die-for bill comprised The Jimi Hendrix Experience, The Move, Pink Floyd,

The Nice, Amen Corner and Eire Apparent; and though a similar bill four months earlier might have seen the Floyd co-headlining with Hendrix, their position on the posters and handbills was now firmly below the Brummies. In the interim, The Move had (almost) risen to the top of the charts with their magical successor to 'I Can Hear The Grass Grow', 'Flowers in the Rain' (kept off the number one shot by another sugary spoiler from Mr Humperdinck, 'The Last Waltz'). They also had their own head-case, in Ace Kefford, whose own experiments with drugs'n'drink permanently altered him:

> **Ace Kefford:** I was cracking up, just like Syd Barrett was. On the Hendrix tour, Syd never spoke to anyone. He could hardly move sometimes. He was on another planet. I was, too – but at least I always delivered the show.

Perhaps as an homage to Kefford, but more likely because he still wanted to write about going 'bonkers', Wood planned to make their next single 'Cherry Blossom Clinic' ('Lock me in and throw the key away'). However, Wood met the same wall of blank incomprehension as Barrett when presenting it to The Move's new label, Regal Zonophone; and just like 'Scream Thy Last Scream', 'Cherry Blossom Clinic' was rejected as a possible follow-up to chart success, ostensibly because he was poking fun at mental patients.

It was another fatal loss of momentum. 'Cherry Blossom Clinic', with its sardonic lyrics, nicely phased vocals and Beatlesque production, would almost certainly have given the band a pre-Christmas hit. The Move were meanwhile struggling to complete an album which would have comparable impact to their singles (hence, surely, Secunda's rather fabulous claim that the master tapes for the album had been stolen, so the songs would have to be 'redone'). It made the tour make-or-break for the band. Unfortunately, their brand of psych-pop sat uneasily between Hendrix's wild thing and Floyd's astral visitations. Barrett, evidently not wholly fried, predicted to *Melody Maker*'s Alan

Walsh in mid-tour, 'In the future groups are going to have to offer much more than just a pop show.' The Move proved unable to raise their game in the time allowed:

> **Carl Wayne:** It was horrible getting thrown in with all of the underground bands. Roy probably wanted to move on to a new music form. I felt uncomfortable playing pop songs in that company. That's why Trevor [eventually] went, as he wanted to play blues and something deeper than the pop we were churning out. Having to do 'Flowers in the Rain', 'Fire Brigade', and 'I Can Hear The Grass Grow', our three minute ditties – in which we could not clearly express ourselves – showed us as the manufactured group we really were. When we got on those tours we felt like fish out of water.

The one way The Move could yet affirm their underground credentials was with a live album (or EP). They decided they would record a show at their old alma mater, the Marquee, early in the new year, demonstrating that they could still take an audience higher and higher. However, as bassist Kefford confirms, 'not even' the resultant EP, *Something Else*, 'captures the essence of The Move properly. If they'd seen our act at these psychedelic shows, they'd understand why we had an underground following and were appreciated by musicians like Hendrix.' An LP from that night, with an unabridged 'Sunshine Help Me' and their stomping assault on 'Piece of My Heart' might have altered the general consensus, unlike the belated appearance of their eponymous debut LP – a pop album pure and simple. The departure (indeed, disappearance) of Kefford into a cornucopia of bad habits would leave him a wreck of a rocker, and The Move on the outside, looking on, unheralded exponents of the original underground.

Even then the whole of Hendrix's band remained fans. They loved the Move mélange of styles. Aside from sharing tours and all-night stands, the two bands even shared Olympic Studios in the autumn of 1967, as both worked on their respective albums (in Hendrix's case, his second, *Are You Experienced?*, having already rattled the right cages). 'You've Got Me Floating', on *Axis: Bold*

As *Love*, would actually find The Move doing their inimitable harmonies for the benefit of a hopped-up Hendrix.

Axis was certainly as psychedelic as anything post-*Piper* pop had to offer, songs like 'Spanish Castle Magic', 'If Six Was Nine' and the title-track showing that the Experience were gaining ground with every new gadget their guitarist brought to the endless party. Unfortunately, they had little opportunity to display any such development live. Like their fellow package-tour popsters, Hendrix's Experience were now expected to record a whole set of new songs while satiating fans who continued to demand the familiar old songs live, twice nightly. As Noel Redding complained in his memoir:

> When we sat down at Chas's on 7 November [1967] to hear the test pressing [to Axis], it sounded good. [Then] the next day the pressure started to begin the next LP. Each new LP may have meant new advances, but it also meant fresh material, which we could no longer polish live in front of an audience before recording. The crowds now demanded the tried, tested (and now boring for us) hits.

Hendrix was finding it hard to resist the demands of those paying fans and, ever the showman, continued to pull out all the stops (as footage from Blackpool in November, shot for a documentary film, testifies). By the end of the tour, which climaxed on 5 December in Glasgow, Jimi had decided that the only way out was to curtail touring activities altogether until the fans caught up with him. Given the pace he was moving at, this was not going to be easy, yet one way to bring it all back home was to refrain from issuing any single to accompany the December release of *Axis: Bold As Love*, letting the long-player stand alone, à la *Sergeant Pepper* (the title-track of which opened almost every Experience set on that autumn tour). As the guitar man told Alan Walsh the following summer:

> **Jimi Hendrix:** People were starting to take us for granted, abuse us. It was that what-cornflakes-for-breakfast scene. Pop slavery, really. I

felt we were in danger of becoming the American version of Dave
Dee . . . It's just not our scene. We decided we had to end that scene
and get into our own thing. I was tired of the attitude of fans . . . so
we decided the best way was to just cool the recording scene until
we were ready with something that we wanted everyone to hear.
[1968]

Hendrix was true to his word. He did not perform in Britain again
until February 1969, when he played the Albert Hall shows that
would mark a highly cinematic end to the original Experience.
Before 1967 was over, though, he had one more duty to perform,
headlining another spectacular at the cavernous Kensington
Olympia on 22 December, with his old pals The Pink Floyd, The
Move, The Who, The Soft Machine and, appropriately, Tomorrow.

If Olympia would prove to be Hendrix's last British gig for a
while, it was Syd Barrett's last major appearance, period.[2] He no
longer wanted to be a pop star. And since none of the other
Floydians had ever entirely embraced the pop audience, it was
crystal-meth clear that no-one in the band was interested in playing
the pop game any more. Indeed, when an article in the 16 December
issue of Melody Maker suggested that 'groups like Pink Floyd are
killing pop', it brought a swift response from the Floyd, Jenner
penning a lengthy letter to the paper which admitted to murdering
the genre, but for the greater good of music:

Yes, the Pink Floyd are killing pop music because there are a large
number of people whose minds are too closed to accept what the
Pink Floyd do as anything other than a threat to most people's ideas
as to what pop music is . . . The Floyd are not packaged, they just
are. Eighty% of Pink Floyd music is improvised. Many people don't
seem to realise this and many sets include numbers never played
before or since. So the Pink Floyd are largely unpredictable both to
the audience and themselves. They can be sublime. They can be
awful.

Jenner was carefully sidestepping the fact that those occasions when the band were 'awful' generally coincided with nights when Syd was on another planet. The commercial failure of 'Apples & Oranges', Barrett's not-so-incipient schizophrenia and the rest of the band's determination to carry on – as an *album* band – meant that the original psychedelic pop band ceased to exist after Olympia. Psych-pop had lost its reserve legion just as The Beatles (whose *Magical Mystery Tour* film was screened on BBC TV four days later) had lost their way in the Blue Jay.

For the still tripping troops, it was time to join those looking to move on. Hendrix, the Jeff Beck Group, Fleetwood Mac and Cream had all shown one way to go, by exploiting what seemed like a uniquely American taste for instrumental extemporisation. The fact that all of these bands, Jeff Beck included, had issued singles that were compact classics of the genre in 1967 – and had all enjoyed attendant Top Twenty success – no longer counted for much. It was time to leave the singles domain to The Move, The Hollies and The Kinks; oh and The Beatles, who had restored themselves to the top spot twice (with 'All You Need Is Love' and 'Hello Goodbye') in the past six months.

The first English pop-rock band to no longer think that the three-minute song could contain all they had to say was probably Cream. Their epiphany had occurred at Atlantic Studios in New York, while working on the follow-up to the successful pop concoction, 'I Feel Free'. It had its roots, not in some great desire for extemporisation, but in the band politics of a three-piece with enmity on all sides.

Back in March – just as 'I Feel Free' stopped garnering chart action – Cream had convened at Ryemuse Studios in London to demo half a dozen or so songs for their next album (and single). All five of the songs actually cut that day were single-length (the longest was 'SWLABR', at four and a half minutes), and all were written either entirely by Jack Bruce, or in tandem with poet/lyricist Pete Brown. Just two would end up on *Disraeli Gears*. The more psychedelic songs, like 'Hey Now Princess' and 'Weird of

Hermiston', would be given the elbow by Eric and Ginger. Jack is in no doubt as to why:

> **Jack Bruce:** The others were full of shit and jealousy. It goes back to the composer-credit thing. I think that was a lot of the reason why they couldn't hear 'Weird of Hermiston', which could have been a huge hit . . . They [just] didn't want to hear.

Still refusing to be blown off course, Bruce continued penning single material. When they convened at Atlantic's eight-track studios on or around 8 April, ostensibly to cut a new single, he played Clapton, Baker and producer Felix Pappalardi the undeniable 'Sunshine of Your Love', only to receive the same treatment all over again:

> **Jack Bruce:** It was a very difficult time for me. I was bringing . . . the best material that I'd written with Pete, and was very, very keen to have it recorded. But when we played it to the powers that be, they didn't like it. They said it's not happening. I'm talking about . . . stuff like . . . 'Sunshine of Your Love'.

Instead, they spent two days working on the traditional 'Lawdy Mama', which had been in their live set since Windsor. When that didn't work, they rewrote the song, with the help of their new producer and his girlfriend, Gail Collins, until it became 'Brain Stew'. Given Collins's own mental problems, 'Brain Stew' may have been appropriate, but seemed likely to cause comment. After a 'necessary' title-change, Cream finally had a song they were happy with. They had also found a studio they wanted to work in:

> **Ginger Baker:** 'Strange Brew' started off as a completely different song, 'Hey Lawdy Mama'. Then we changed the tempo with the backing track. In the end the backing track became 'Brain Stew' [and] eventually after three hours to 'Strange Brew' . . . We had all the engineers chipping in with suggestions. The recording session in

New York lasted five solid days, twelve hours a day, including Saturday and Sunday. You just can't get a studio for that length of time in England. You have to abide by what they say. [1967]

Cream returned to New York the following month, at which point work began on the follow-up to *Fresh Cream*. For reasons unknown, Cream had held back from releasing 'Strange Brew' as a single until they had another non-Bruce b-side ('Tales of Brave Ulysses'). And though they could easily have followed 'Strange Brew' – finally issued at the end of June – with the now-recorded 'Sunshine of Your Love', they refrained from any more singles until after the album appeared – which was not until December – at which point 'Sunshine' began to pick up airplay from America's new network of album-oriented FM stations. It was eventually issued in the US the following June, duly becoming their biggest hit. By then, Clapton had already 'Declare[d] War On Singles', informing *Melody Maker* the previous November:

We are very anti- the whole commercial market. The whole nature of the single-making process has caused us a lot of grief in the studio . . . Singles are an anachronism. To get any good music in a space of two or three minutes requires working to a formula . . . I hate all that rushing around trying to get a hit . . . And the promotion you get on singles is part of the system I would like to break down . . . People are brainwashed into thinking that the number one record represents the best music available . . . I'm a great believer in the theory that singles will become obsolete and LPs will take their place.

If LPs *were* supposed to replace singles, this doesn't explain why *Disraeli Gears* took six months to appear. By the time it did, Cream were no longer attempting anything resembling that original psych-blues fusion. The band's new spokesman, Clapton, was at great pains to emphasise that even the belated second album was 'not indicative of what we are doing now. When I hear it, I feel like I'm listening to another group. It's an LP of songs, and there's no extended improvisation ... anywhere. That's why we are rushing to do our next album.' Six weeks later, he had become even more explicit:

> Whereas the last LP was a collection of songs, the stuff we're writing now is really a series of jumping-off points, rather than just songs. I'm certain a lot of the numbers will be much longer on this new album. I mean you've got to have room to move about a bit – which is what you do on stage anyway, so why not on record? I suppose we could do a double LP!

Clapton's epiphany had come in America, on the band's third visit, in the autumn of 1967, when he had discovered that the American audiences not only weren't perturbed when they failed to play the latest single, but encouraged them to make every song the loudest, longest work-out this side of AMM. He excitedly informing *Hit Parader* on this tour that 'there are no arrangements, except for arrival and departure points. Sometimes we just play free for half an hour.' The Floyd had been playing twenty-minute extemporisations for a year or more by then; but not restricted to a drum solo, or some lead guitar wankfest (to use the technical term).

Predictably, Eric's expressed aim was to capture one such 'wankfest' on tape in the studio. Not surprisingly, this proved about as easy as capturing lightning in a bottle. The album of 'jumping-off points' that Clapton envisaged appeared nine months later, as *Wheels On Fire*, and a double-album it was. But it merely reflected the band's incipient personality crisis, comprising a nine-song studio album, largely composed by Bruce and Brown, and a live set which, save for Clapton's four-minute 'Crossroads', confirmed a theory Robert Christgau posited in print the month *Disraeli Gears* appeared:

> Popular songs rarely run over four minutes for a reason: Without a narrative (as in a ballad) or a great singer (like Mick Jagger) or a sophisticated but available structure ... it becomes geometrically more difficult to sustain interest at about that time. Not impossible,

> mind you – those attempts that succeed (like 'A Quick One' or 'Like a Rolling Stone') are marvellous indeed.

Cream would never succeed in capturing those magically mysterious extemporisations and making them part of a studio album – and the contradictions intrinsic to the band's make-up meant they barely made it into 1969. By then, they were a live act first, and a pop band a poor third. Contemporaries like The Kinks and The Who also now needed the revenue tours brought, after signing disastrous production deals with the same smooth-talker, Shel Talmy. Other British acts who now elected to prioritise live over studio commitments included Peter Green's Fleetwood Mac, Cream, the Jeff Beck Group and Jimmy Page's Yardbirds, who all told would transform the whole business of touring the States, giving the fans guitar-licks galore into the bargain.

None of these English outfits thought any longer in terms of singles, or felt the need to keep songs below that precious four-minute mark. In Hendrix's case, that difficult third album – recorded during respites from the road – was as elongated and as four-sided as The Beatles' first post-*Pepper* offering. Indeed, when a sixteen-minute, side-one version of 'Voodoo Chile' did not suffice, Hendrix offered a slighter return at the end of side four, thus clocking up another five minutes. The one song on *Electric Ladyland* that showed Hendrix could still rein himself in – and achieve a whole lot more – was pulled as a single, providing the last hit Hendrix enjoyed in his lifetime. It was a now-rare cover version drawn from his greatest inspiration, and the one figure who could still deflect rock from its chosen path.

'All Along The Watchtower' – which Hendrix began recording on 21 January, 1968 at Olympic – had first appeared the week after Christmas as part of another album bereft of any single.[3] *John Wesley Harding* was Dylan's first album in eighteen months. Recorded over three afternoon sessions in Nashville, with a familiar rhythm-section, and every song cut live in a handful of takes, it was the exact antithesis of *Electric Ladyland* – and every other album which attempted to out-psych *Pepper* in the past months. Robert Christgau opined at the time, 'This is not a better record than *Pepper*, but it should have better effect. It is a mature work that still shows room for rich development. If only it were so easy to say that of The Beatles.'

Actually, *John Wesley Harding* was a masterpiece of understatement, and the greater for that in an era of excess and hubris, in roughly equal measures. Dylan knew what he wanted to say. After spending a happy six months smoking weed and reliving the musical associations of a misspent youth with his, and The, Band, he had made something suitably subdued, suggesting that the healing had begun. But for all the dust of rumours that had suggested Dylan was a vegetable man, surrealist turns of phrase remained his to command, as a mordant set of sleeve-notes made abundantly clear even before the listener ventured far enough in to say they'd been there.

Should anyone have doubted that Dylan was making a statement as potentially revolutionary as its counterpoint – the Newport Folk Festival in 1965 – he had left another clue, on the front cover this time. Within days of the album's appearance fans began to wonder if they were seeing things, or were there really four Beatle faces discernible in the branches of a tree (with roots) in the top left hand corner of the original LP sleeve?[4]

And leaving aside the identity of the otherworldly companions posing alongside Dylan (a set of travelling minstrels from Bengal, as it happens), why had Dylan taken to wearing the selfsame jacket he had worn to keep him from the howling winds when Jerry Schatzberg snapped the cover for *Blonde on Blonde* two years earlier? Dylan wasn't saying. His one interview of the year, with old friend Happy Traum for *Sing Out*, merely confirmed the view of the 'little neighbour boy' on 'The Ballad of Frankie Lee & Judas Priest', 'Nothing is revealed.'

It would be another decade before the wider world found out what Dylan thought of the album The Beatles made after he accused McCartney of not wanting to be cute anymore. Dylan was nine months into the so-called 'Alimony Tour' when journalist Matt

Damsker caught up with him, and asked him what he thought he was doing issuing an album like *John Wesley Harding* after *Sgt. Pepper's Lonely Hearts Club Band*. Dylan's answer suggested he still preferred The Beatles when they were cute:

Bob Dylan: I didn't know how to record the way other people were recording, and didn't want to. The Beatles had just released *Sgt. Pepper*, which I didn't like at all . . . I thought that was a very indulgent album, though the songs on it were really good. I didn't think all that production was necessary, 'cause The Beatles had never done that before. [1978]

At least *John Wesley Harding* gave those elements of the new Rock constituency looking for an alternative to dropping out, or stretching out, another travelled road. And if any traveller missed this large signpost – bearing as its message, 'Get back to the country' – the songs Dylan had recorded in the Big Pink basement in West Saugerties in the months before *John Wesley Harding* were divided up between The Band and The Byrds on *Music From Big Pink* and *Sweetheart of the Rodeo*, as they too decided country-rock was the route back home.

But it was not Dylan's return to the arena that signalled the end of the psychedelic pop revolution. It wasn't even the first signs of debilitating habits, acquired in all innocence, which called time. It was the simultaneous release of the latest bulletins from the two bands who had set the pop agenda in the pre-psychedelic era, on 8 December, 1967 – The Beatles' *Magical Mystery Tour* 'double-EP' and The Rolling Stones' *Their Satanic Majesties Request*.

For The Rolling Stones it had been a nightmarish year, with studio sessions booked around court appearances and the occasional jail sentence. In the interim they made the unwise decision to out-psych The Beatles, issuing an album that found them catastrophically off-course, if not '2000 Light Years From Home'. Perhaps it was partially because they fired their manager and map-reader, Andrew Loog Oldham, at the start of the *Satanic* sessions:

Ian Stewart: All of a sudden they really wanted to get rid of [Oldham]. Before they started *Satanic Majesties* a lot of time was booked at Olympic. Andrew was supposed to be there as producer. And he was there, [but] only in a literal sense. We went in and played a lot of blues as badly as we could. Andrew just walked out.

The Olympic sessions trundled ever onwards. And as seven bootleg CDs of basic tracks from said sessions amply testifies, the Stones were stumbling in the dark. Working titles like 'Title 12', 'Title 15', 'Soul Blues', 'Blues #3', 'Five-Part Jam', 'Gold Painted Nails', 'Majesties Honky Tonk' and 'Fly My Kite' suggest they were making it up as they went along (as it happens, the first of these became '2000 Light Years From Home', the last 'The Lantern' – the others all proved dead-ends). Another nine-minute jam became the five-minute 'Gomper', while fifteen minutes of ever-changing time-signatures was reduced down to the false heartiness of 'Sing This All Together'. Just 'Citadel', '2000 Man' and 'She's A Rainbow' seemed to have been real songs before they ever crossed the river. At least one Stone felt that they were gathering musical moss:

Charlie Watts: Sometimes I think it was a miracle that we produced *anything* with all the emotional upheavals within the group. We had to find a new direction. The era that bred the Liverpool boom was over.

Their Satanic Majesties Request was the ultimate bad trip; and the same fans who had passed on 'We Love You' – that sardonic attempt at sympathy for the Stones, issued as a single in the summer – baulked at buying its long-playing counterpart. *Crawdaddy*'s Jon Landau suggested, 'They have been far too influenced by their musical inferiors', while Chris Welch prophesied in his *Melody Maker* review, that 'if sophisticated pop fans don't like it, well, it won't sell'. Well, they didn't, and it didn't. *Satanic Majesties* spent just six weeks in the album charts, drawing a line under the ostentatious use of sound effects as a substitute for songs of substance.

The Beatles found that they, too, were being judged by the British pop press in a harsher light as they continued to 'refine' the method that had seemed to work so well on Sgt. Pepper, following other trendsetters by stretching their songs to see if they snapped. In the six months immediately after Pepper bought them more time to innovate, The Beatles would make a handful of attempts to make geometrically challenged studio recordings. Once again, the results were largely buried in the back garden, with the octopus.

'It's All Too Much' – recorded in May 1967 – was the most successful of these studio work-outs, lasting some eight and a half minutes in its full studio guise. But by the time of its appearance on the Yellow Submarine LP it had been summarily trimmed of excess weight, all those handclaps being metaphorically stockpiled for the following year's 'Hey Jude'. The instrumental 'Flying' was another song that was allowed to meander away till nine minutes of tape had been utilised, but when it came to the Magical Mystery Tour soundtrack, was allowed just over two minutes to get airborne. Finally, Lennon's personal patchwork quilt, the absurdist 'You Know My Name', ran for six minutes, but still couldn't find its way home – at least not until 1970, when it appeared as the final Beatles b-side, again snipped down below the four-minute mark. Ian MacDonald concludes that the boys had begun to believe they could turn any kind of leaden leitmotif to gold:

> By mid-1967, their enthusiasm for 'random', which had begun as a sensible instinct for capitalising on fortuitous mistakes, was starting to degenerate into a readiness to accept more or less anything, however daft or irrelevant, as divinely dispensed.

Evidently, if the long song was what now separated the men from the boys, the FabFour were going to be stuck at the back of the class, despite continuing to churn out irrepressible pop standards like 'Hey Jude' and 'Get Back' that defied the odds, selling to the new Rock audience – for whom old habits still died hard – along with the younger pop audience. But when they plonked Lennon's most indulgent experiment to date, 'Revolution #9', on side four of their 1968 double-album, *The Beatles*, they only served to confirm Cohn's depiction of them as 'cranks . . . in the grand manner'.

For all of these attempts to record extended songs, when it came time to compile a soundtrack for their first television film, *Magical Mystery Tour*, The Beatles decided against compiling their second album of the year. *Magical Mystery Tour* lacked the same kind of ambition as *Sgt. Pepper*, though its six songs still took some six months to (write and) record. Indeed, it must have been a conscious decision *not* to turn the soundtrack into an album – which they could have done by using the eight-minute 'It's All Too Much', the six-minute 'You Know My Name', 'All Together Now' and the new a-side, 'Hello Goodbye', all recorded in the same time period. In the end, the record was neither an LP nor the single EP it could have been (by losing the two-minute instrumental 'Flying', and leaving 'I Am The Walrus' as the b-side to 'Hello Goodbye', issued independently three weeks before the double EP).

The decision to issue *Magical Mystery Tour* as a double EP – a format for which neither single nor LP charts catered – ensured that *Their Satanic Majesties Request* would not have to compete with it in the UK album charts (though in the States, where *Magical Mystery Tour was* an album, it staved off *Satanic Majesties*, staying at number one for seven weeks in the new year). The reception for *Magical Mystery Tour* in both incarnations was not as caustic as the one for its cinematic counterpart, nor the vinyl offering released by those other English high-rollers. But it still suggested that *Sgt. Pepper* was a one-off and that it was time to call a halt to the psychedelic productions and get back to something that appealed to both pop and Rock audiences. But *Pepper* had driven a wedge between the two, which would hold firm for the rest of the decade, and even when dislodged – by Punk – would continue to cast its long shadow.

PART THREE

1968 TO 2007

NOTHING TO GET HUNG ABOUT

*When I went out on tour with Wings [in 1972], we got to some
university somewhere, Nottingham I think, and one student said
to me, 'God, you know, man, around the time of* Sgt. Pepper, *we
really thought it was going to change the world. What happened?'
Looking at me as if it was . . . my fault –*

Paul McCartney, *Days In The Life*

As the sixties sped towards their violent conclusion, the
influence of the Sergeant seemed to be everywhere in pop
culture. The Album had arrived; and with it the kind of
Artwork that befitted a work of Art. Cream had even held up the
release of *Disraeli Gears* while prevaricating over its presentation,
and the double-sleeve to a single album became the norm with
more album-oriented acts, reflecting the clout the smart new bands
were determined to wield.

One now needed to fill all that space with something. How
about the words of wisdom to which one set the increasingly lengthy
songs on thy latest opus? For one true innovation *Pepper* can un-
reservedly be credited with – and which has endured to this day –
was printing its lyrics on the album-sleeve. By the end of the decade
even bands whose works were almost entirely music-orientated felt
that their lyrics were worthy of being rendered on the inner sleeve.
And by the early seventies, albums were coming with 'booklets' of
lyrics, notes, scrapbooks and discographies; while the sleeve artwork
graced many a bedsit in poster form. Where would it end?

Peter Blake, like his eighteenth-century namesake, had wrapped
the lyrics in his particular brand of illuminated art. This had driven
others to make the cover something other than a photo of the
band looking inscrutable. Whether covers to the likes of *Disraeli
Gears, Saucerful of Secrets, Axis: Bold As Love, Move* or *Music in a
Doll's House* could be said to reflect their contents was another issue.

And if imitation – albeit with satirical intent – was the sincerest form of flattery, then *Pepper's* was destined to be the most flattered record sleeve on the planet. Blake's whole design, coming out of the innately self-referential PopArt movement, lent itself to the send-up. When it *was* subject to its first parody, courtesy of The Mothers of Invention, McCartney even offered to help smooth away any permission problems (their leader, Frank Zappa, already knew how affected McCartney had been by their original *Freak Out*). The decision by these Mothers to mercilessly satirise the Sergeant was the first crack of the whip for the *Pepper* backlash which would, by the mid seventies, qualify as a movement in its own right; and which would become bound up with the revolution that sought to erase all that *Pepper* had wrought – Punk.

Not surprisingly, any backlash took time to gain momentum, as both the progressive and the pop proponents continued to doff their caps to those who had deranged assorted senses for the greater good. In fact, its initial impetus came from within The Beatles, where at least one of its two main architects was seeking to pull the *Lonely Hearts Club* edifice down, brick by brick. Lennon had always fancied himself to be something of an iconoclast. With *Sgt. Pepper* he finally had a target worthy of his bile – some of his finest work. By the album's first anniversary, he was not only dismissing much of it in the band's official biography, but selecting its finest jewels to cast aside:

> **John Lennon:** I actively dislike hearing bits of [my songs] which didn't come out right. There are bits of 'Lucy in the Sky' I don't like. Some of the sound in 'Mr Kite' isn't right. I like 'A Day in the Life', but it's not half as nice as I thought it was when we were doing it. I suppose we could have worked harder on it. But I couldn't be arsed doing any more. [1968]

For Lennon, it was a predictable reaction to the torpor into which he had sunk through 1967 and the first half of 1968, more than

the (occasionally dazzling) work he had somehow produced. He
was soon overtly questioning whether *Pepper* was the way ahead.
As Martin says in his account of the album's making, 'I thought
John had liked all the production techniques we had pioneered
on *Pepper*, but no sooner was it finished than he rebelled against
them. He wanted to get back to what he called "honesty" in
recording.' Nor was it simply hindsight revving away at Lennon.
The album was barely eighteen months old when he was telling
a press conference that he thought the Sergeant was a charlatan:

> **John Lennon:** The presentation was different . . . The packaging
> and the overall image was the difference, and the linking of the
> tracks. It still didn't make the songs any different . . . Our LPs
> reflect where we are at the moment, and *Pepper* reflected the
> changes we were going through and what we looked forward to.
> It was significant, I'm not putting it down, but it wasn't an opera
> . . . With *Sgt. Pepper* we wrapped the chocolates up in nice paper
> or wrapped two together. All we had, in fact, was still a box with
> chocolates. [1969]

If the sixties were now caught in hindsight's headlights, so were
The Beatles themselves, who had made it to decade's end in name
only (though that was still more than Brian Epstein, Brian Jones
or Meredith Hunter[1] could claim). The general sense of dissolu-
tion as of 31 December, 1969 was palpable; even before EMI
attempted to pass off an abandoned pre-*Abbey Road* album as the
boys' last word.

An attempt to 'get back' to the working methods that had
worked so well in the first half of the decade – rehearse a bunch
of songs informally, go into the studio and cut 'em live – had
shown that those days were long gone. So the results were put
on the backburner while McCartney disassembled its better ideas,
resurrecting them as a second-sided suite on *Pepper*'s conceptual
successor, *Abbey Road*. Typically, Lennon felt they should have
put out the ramshackle *Get Back & 12 Other Songs* instead, 'I

thought it [would've been] good to let it out and show people what had happened to us.'

The *Get Back* sessions – which felt like one sustained stint of dental repairwork for all four constituent parts of the fragmenting whole – had defeated even McCartney, who finally turned the tapes over to Phil Spector to play with. All parties had learnt the bloody hard way that you can't turn back the clock. Meanwhile, bootleggers attended to Lennon's wishes, taking a version of the original 'Glyn Johns version' of *Get Back* and issuing it under the ironic title *Kum Back* at the end of 1969, by which time it had been sidelined, replaced by the Spector mix (which in 2003 would itself be superseded by that CD oddity *Let It Be . . . Naked*, which managed to apply the Glyn Johns approach to the Phil Spector version).

Perhaps surprisingly, the subsequent *Abbey Road* sessions progressed with something like the FabFour's former ease. Harrison had got his hissy fit at the Twickenham rehearsals out of him (he'd quit the band for a few days in January 1969), Lennon was content to map out his first solo album and play his parts, while McCartney was no longer even pretending to care whether he ruffled his workshy co-workers' feathers.

If *Abbey Road* can be seen as a vindication of the working methods McCartney had wanted to adopt as far back as *Revolver*, it was put together in a way that reversed *Sgt. Pepper*'s methodology. The songs were centre stage. Where the songs he had to work with were scraps (and Lennon, in particular, had grown tired of writing anything as cliched as a middle-eight or a chorus about the time he went for a walk in Strawberry Fields), they were left as is, to be reconstituted as part of a surprisingly seamless ten-song segue with which the album – and The Beatles – signed off.

In fact, it is debatable whether anybody used the *Pepper* template to make an album ever again. Its influence on studio working methods from the eight-track era forward would be negligible. Though no-one is arguing with Abbey Road studio manager Jerry Boys when he calls it 'a very, very clever record', one is hard-pressed to substantiate his claim that 'in terms of creative use of recording [Sgt. Pepper] has been one of the major steps forward'. More like one step forward, two steps sideways. Yes, bands now felt they could spend months in the studio, but *not* compiling a catalogue of psyche-delic sound effects.

The very backwardness of the technology which had inspired the band's increasingly outlandish ideas was no longer an issue once the album appeared. By the end of 1967, there was no need to bounce from track to track like a game of table tennis, and without that essential spur to creativity most of the songs on *Pepper* would have *sounded* much like those on *Rubber Soul*, only not quite as good. The songs on *Pepper* were a layer-cake of ideas, not the musical meringue that multi-tracks now afforded and stereo sound-scapes demanded. Some bands couldn't wait to get away from British studios' 'traditional' working methods or the mono that made their songs move. As Carl Wayne complained to *Disc* in July 1967:

> In Britain you're limited to four-track apparatus. American equipment is so advanced and I hear it has reached a stage where stereo singles have been introduced ... But in Britain, it'll be some years yet, I suppose, before we have stereo singles ... [And] American engi-neers are so much more hip than the British ... 90% of engineers and recording managers in Britain regard their work as a nine to five job. They have no musical concept of what artists are trying for.

Unfortunately, the superior technology which enabled the post-*Pepper* progressives – even in England – to fill up eight, and indeed, less than two years later, sixteen tracks, with ever more ornate sounds, did not coincide with a commensurate increase in imag-ination. It merely prompted a lazy, short-cut method of recording – press a button and out come handclaps! – much as computer graphics have generally served to short-circuit the art of story-telling in the modern blockbuster movie. From the vantage point of forty years, most of the Prog-Rock output that separates *Pepper* from Punk only serves to show that technological innovation is no substitute for use of the cranium. Emulating *Pepper* was a long hard climb, and its wiser contemporaries were unsure as to the point:

> **John Sebastian:** I [had] just finished an album that was fairly compact in its arrangement and then hearing this incredible pile of tracks with stuff going backwards, entire orchestras playing very unconventionally, mechanical tricks which we'd never heard before, and it seemed like an almost insurmountable task to come up with anything even in the same ballpark.

Where *Pepper* did succeed in establishing a disturbing precedent – though it was one Dylan had already test-run on *Blonde on Blonde*, with stunning results – was the notion that one could turn up at (ever more expensive) recording studios with only the most notional idea of a song, and hope that inspiration would turn on its tap just because the meter is clicking. Not surprisingly, songwriters not equipped to buy the shoelaces their betters were not fit to tie for Lennon, McCartney or Dylan eventually proved that such a method worked about as often as a *Blonde on Blonde* comes along. The period from *Pepper* to *Tusk* would be a heyday for studio engineers and cocaine dealers, but pity the poor consumer who had stopped buying singles after the Summer of Love, thinking the LP format would now suffice.

The Beatles themselves – after six months sporadically working on *Magical Mystery Tour* failed to produce enough quality songs to fill even the kind of EP they used to put out for fun – abandoned the method with alacrity. When work started on the band's *magnum opus*, *The Beatles* (aka *The White Album*), in late May 1968, they famously recorded some twenty-seven demos at Harrison's home – the so-called Kinfauns tape – in a couple of afternoons, before inspecting the new eight-track facilities at Abbey Road. Even the teeth-pulling Twickenham sessions the following January were designed to ensure that when they visited St John's Wood, it would be with a set of songs they could craft into an album in double-quick time (and, in fairness, those *Let It Be* sessions *were* fast, just not fertile).

The Beatles were not the only ones who began to notice that an overt pop sensibility – i.e. keeping it short and brimful of ideas, amplifying a song's strengths, and turning its weaknesses to fuzz – was passing from the production process. (Nick Lowe codified this Britpop aesthetic when describing his idea of production in 1976 as taking 'a three-minute song, and every good bit and hook is pushed up on the faders, so that all you hear are the best parts leaping out at you.') A period of mourning had begun in and out of pop. Issued at decade's end was the first history of this amorphous beast, Nik Cohn's prescient *Pop From The Beginning* (later retitled *Awopbopaloobop*), in which he gave The Beatles the benefit of the doubt, but lamented the consequences of all they had wrought:

> They've added whole new dimensions to pop, they have introduced unthought-of sophistications, complexities and subtleties. And *Sgt. Pepper*, their best album, really was quite an impressive achievement. For all this I don't enjoy them much and I'm not convinced that they've been good for pop. *Sgt. Pepper* was genuinely a breakthrough – it was the first try ever at making a pop album into something more than just twelve songs bundled together at random. It was an overall concept, an attitude: we are the Lonely Hearts Club Band, everyone is, and these are our songs. It was ideas, allusions, pastiches, ironies. In other words, it was more than noise . . . So, if *Sgt. Pepper* passes, what am I grousing for? Well, it did work in itself, it was cool and clever and controlled. Only, it wasn't much like pop. It wasn't fast, flash, sexual, loud, vulgar, monstrous or violent. It made no myths.

Cohn had elucidated an aesthetic that would ultimately rebound on Rock in the guise of Punk – 'Art, it ain't'; or at least, when it sets out to 'be' Art, it rarely is; and its greatest moments – exemplified by that paean to anal sex, 'Tutti Frutti' – are only accidentally, and incidentally, Art. He posits that the best work in pop in the period addressed in his book were 'fast, flash, sexual, loud, vulgar', none of which epithets fit the *Pepper* platter. By the end of the seventies Cohn's suggestion that the Sergeant had somehow killed off all that was good and true in pop would become a common complaint.

Its would-be emulators didn't help matters. Cohn pointed out how, in its immediate aftermath, 'there have been little but pretensions. Groups like Family and The Nice in England, The Grateful Dead and Iron Butterfly in America ... could be knocking out three-chord rock and everyone would be happy. But after The Beatles and Bob Dylan, they've got into Art and so they've wallowed in third-form poetries, fifth-form philosophies, ninth-rate perceptions.' So was *Pepper* really to blame? Or would the Dead have made music for zombies anyway? Making *Pepper* the moment the worm turned on overlooks the fact that the whole direction of Britpop circa '66 suggested a burgeoning self-consciousness.

The Blue Meanies of criticdom had been there from day one of June 1967. Richard Goldstein, writing the week of its release for *The New York Times*, had predicted, with devastating accuracy, that 'when The Beatles' work as a whole is viewed in retrospect, *Rubber Soul* and *Revolver* will stand as their major contributions. When the slicks and tricks of production on this album no longer seem unusual, and the compositions are stripped to their musical and lyrical essentials, *Sgt. Pepper* will be Beatles baroque – an elaboration without improvement.' As the decade drew to a close, Goldstein's acolytes began to scribble asides in reviews and interviews, alluding to 'the *Pepper* effect'.

Cohn may have issued pop's first manifesto, but it still needed someone to put the whole of pop to date – *Pepper* included – in its historical context. Just so. The following year Charlie Gillett put meat on Cohn's polemical bones, publishing his seminal (and still in print) *The Sound of The City* (1970), which told the story of rock & roll, and its transition into pop, in almost academic detail. Gillett, though, barely departed from Cohn's carping tone at book's end when he took *Pepper* to task in an uncharacteristically animated way:

> Their impact reached its peak following the release of *Sergeant Pepper's Lonely Hearts Club Band* in 1967, which presented a suite of songs in a specific order . . . Many of the songs were obscurely surreal and seemed, as Lennon insisted, rather too casually put together to justify the intensely philosophical interpretations that were read into them. The record showed the group at its most removed from the material . . . [Though] they no longer had anything much to say, [they] amused themselves by seeing how many different ways they could say nothing.

Evidently, Cohn was not the only critic who resented his expulsion from that pop Eden, or thought he saw its serpent wearing a Sergeant's regalia. If young bookworms were discovering discontent at every turn of the page, America's most iconoclastic critic, Lester Bangs, was also lending his voice to the hubbub of these malcontents; choosing perhaps the most important essay on Rock to date to lob another verbal grenade at the besieged Sergeant.

Tiring of the corset-like remit to which *Rolling Stone* made its contributors adhere, Bangs asked *Creem* if he could review the second Stooges album for them in December 1970. Unfettered, Bangs turned his album review into a 10,000-word, three-part screed on the future course of rock & roll, which he subtitled 'A Program for Mass Liberation in the Form of a Stooges Review'. In it, he predicted Punk, and set the agenda for a thousand similar articles in the first half of the new decade. He also fired another early broadside at the late-period Beatles:

> 1967 brought *Sgt. Pepper* and psychedelia: the former, after our initial acid-vibes infatuation with it, threatened to herald an era of rock-as-movie-soundtrack, [while] the latter suggest[ed] the

possibility of real (if most likely unconscious) breakthrough in all the fuzztone and groping space jams.

Not surprisingly, Bangs believed in Piperland more than Pepperland. Later on in his article-cum-manifesto, Bangs went on to suggest that the only way forward was for the new Rock bands to 'somehow, some of them somewhere, escape the folk/*Sgt. Pepper* virus'. The demise of the most important band of the sixties had hit him hard. But this was no time to brood about The Velvet Underground. A young Jonathan Richman certainly didn't. When he was asked to supply his favourite albums of the sixties for an end-of-decade poll in *Fusion*, he found room for just one Beatles 'album', *Meet The* . . . (also Kurt Cobain's favourite Beatles 'album') – then placed it third, beneath the first two VU LPs. Richman was one of the first to 'escape the Sgt. Pepper virus' as he went in search of the Modern World.

Those looking for apostasy on the road to Altamont found the high-profile *Pepper* an easy way to explain away the transition from 'All You Need Is Love' to 'Gimme Shelter' in two and a half years. And the early seventies certainly had its share of Jeremiahs, hungover from the swingin' sixties and predicting hard rain. And most of 'em now seemed to be following Cohn and Gillett's lead, writing their own history of pop and/or Rock. Karl Dallas, *Melody Maker*'s folk correspondent for a number of years, wrote his *Singers of an Empty Day* the year after Gillett. Sub-titled 'Last Sacraments for the Superstars', Dallas hoped to deliver just that to the 'star-system' which had made The Beatles seem so important then, and so inconsequential now. For Dallas, the Sergeant had lost his sheen:

> At the time it seemed the most integrated, the most perfect rock record ever made . . . but later as the Lonely Hearts Club Band began to break up visibly, it could be seen that what was happening was four separate trips . . . [while] the total concept of *Sgt. Pepper* was really [just] an expansion of what had already been said perfectly, in musical terms, in 'Strawberry Fields Forever' and 'Penny Lane'.

If Dallas had taken a sabbatical from his weekly column in Britain's most prestigious pop paper to write his valedictory, Mike Jahn had surrendered the hot spot previously occupied by Richard Goldstein – that of *The New York Times* Rock critic – to write his own *Story of Rock, from Elvis Presley to the Rolling Stones* (1973). Adhering largely to his predecessor's point of view, Jahn sprinkled yet more hot coals on *Pepper*:

> Goldstein was proved right, for only a few years after its release, the Golden Album of 1967 was regarded by most serious observers as a flimsy period piece. The only songs from it which have survived are two innocuous good-time songs, 'A Little Help from My Friends' and 'When I'm 64', and one gem of a composition, 'A Day in the Life', the album's feature piece. The rest of it was a triumph of form over substance; a super-elaborate piece of confection designed to appeal to the then-current 'underground' inclination toward the cryptic and the baroque.

Perhaps the final stamp of validation for these former heretics came with the publication of a different kind of Rock history, the encyclopaedic *NME Book of Rock*, which had been first published in weekly instalments in 1973 (with a parody of *Pepper* for its cover), before being given its own perfect-bound form in 1975. Coming at a time when *NME* was championing a new kind of rock journalism – fiercely opinionated, elitist, contemptuous of all star-trappings, and obsessed with authenticity – the verdict of the world's most forward-thinking music paper had really begun to matter.

NME's verdict on *Pepper* was assuredly neo-revisionist: advocating that, despite being 'traditionally regarded as [the] apex of their career ... hindsight has come to regard it somewhat less favourably. Conceived through media of drugs and Eastern mysticism, it is a patchy, inconsistent album, even though it contains [the] most important song the band ever recorded.' In other words, a vindication of what Richard Goldstein wrote back when.

If this was the view of the *'new' Musical Express* – as expressed through the likes of Charles Shaar Murray, Lester Bangs and Nick Kent – the old *NME* still clung to the same rock from which *Pepper* had been hewed, and the year after its *Book of Rock* went all revisionist, the rest of the staff voted *Sgt. Pepper* equal first (along with *Blonde on Blonde*) in their first critics' poll of 100 Great Albums of Our Time, published on the seventh anniversary of *Pepper*'s release. The conformists, it seemed, still held the bridge. The following month a prolonged strike at the newspaper swept most of those on said bridge overboard, and when *NME* returned it was more determined than ever to denigrate any sacrament the sixties had spewed forth.

One of the figures whose contribution was redeemed by this wholesale re-evaluation was Syd Barrett. Another was Brian Wilson. In both cases, *NME* editor Nick Logan elected to let Nick Kent write what he wanted about these lost souls (and in 1975, both seemed lost for good). In the latter's case, Kent ended up writing so much that Logan was obliged to spread it over three issues. At the end of it, he had not only restored Wilson from bit-player to leading role in the transformation of sixties pop, but had laid much of the blame for *Smile*'s absence at The Beatles' door:

> The release of *Sgt. Pepper* [was] so ecstatically received, so lauded as the last word in rock genius that it alone symbolically transformed that whole year into a closed shop for comparable coups. *Sgt. Pepper* was such an achievement that nothing could possibly follow it, and Brian Wilson who desperately craved – nay, demanded and expected – the same impact for his work, instinctively knew that however great *Smile* might be, its release on the heels of *Pepper* would merely place it as an also-ran by comparison.

Kent was another ex-Bedfordian looking for a cultural kiss. Focusing almost exclusively on those who had played with fire and gone down in flames, Kent was a naysayer to all received wisdom; and the most important critical voice in the run-up to Punk. He wasn't, however, willing to participate in an Anglo–American poll of some forty-seven 'critics' who'd been asked to contribute to the *Critics' Choice Top 200 Albums* for a book by DJ Paul Gambaccini in Year Zero, aka 1977.

Nor was Lester Bangs on 'Gambo''s list, despite being at the height of his influence, contributing regularly to *NME*, the *Village Voice* and assorted punk 'zines. Bangs' view of *Pepper* had not diluted with time, and when he provided a summation of the birth of punk-rock for a book on Blondie (of all bands!) in 1980, he gleefully pointed out that 'Louie Louie' had 'already lasted longer than *Sgt. Pepper*! Who in the hell does any songs from that album anymore? Yet, a few years ago, some people were saying *Sgt. Pepper* will endure a hundred years.'

No way was Gambaccini about to let such a challenging view of Rock hold sway in *his* 'critics' choice'. On the other hand, a marketing manager, a programme director at a radio station and a chart compiler were all vouchsafed by the compiler as worthy contributors to a *critics'* poll of favourite albums. Omitting the likes of Paul Nelson, Paul Williams, Richard Goldstein, Charles Shaar Murray, Lester Bangs and Tony Parsons from his chosen few, Gambaccini preferred the opinions of sixteen DJs and industry people with no critical credentials (and precious little taste). Published in 1978, Gambaccini's book once again proclaimed that *Pepper* was the best – but only by letting a piratical band of rogue DJs rig the sales. Of the thirty-one bona-fide critics enlisted, just Chris Welch, John Tobler and Simon Frith included *Pepper* in their Top Ten albums; whereas of the sixteen outsiders, fully half voted *Pepper* among their top four albums of all time (including 'Gambo' himself), with three voting it number one.

This still left, among those polled, the likes of Jonathan Cott, Giovanni Dadomo, Robert Christgau, Cameron Crowe, Charlie Gillett, Clive James, Lenny Kaye, Greil Marcus, Dave Marsh, Lisa Robinson, Ed Ward, Ellen Willis and Richard Williams, who all chose not to give *Pepper* the time of day. In case anyone thought its exclusion from so many worthies* selections a series of slips of the pen, the publication of two important American collections the following year, Greil Marcus's *Stranded* (in which twenty eminent US critics picked one album they'd take to a desert island), and *The Rolling Stone Record Guide* (co-edited by Marsh), both gave the Sergeant a sound pasting.

In Dr Marcus's case, the omission of *Pepper* from 'his' desert-island collection said a great deal in and of itself. But Greil went further. In his own annotated discography at book's end, entitled 'Treasure Island', he described the album as one that 'strangled on its own conceits; [but] after those conceits were vindicated by world-wide acclaim, John, Paul, George & Ringo made ['I Am The Walrus'], [which was] radical where The Greatest Album of All Time was contrived ... *Sgt. Pepper* was a Day-Glo tombstone for its time.' The verdict of the *Rolling Stone Record Guide* was no less revisionist (even if it still received four stars!):

> *Sgt. Pepper* may well be the best-known pop album of all time. Its release was greeted with an effusion of paeans citing it as a bridge between pop and art. But *Sgt. Pepper* was really a thickly detailed, somewhat stiff collection of generally less-than-great Beatles tunes vaguely moulded into a whole. It was not, as many speculated, a concept album, but rather an ornately produced and speciously unified pop work.

But perhaps the most damaging depiction of this 'speciously unified pop work' in American terms arrived the previous year, when Robert Stigwood put out the film of the album of the turkey of an idea, *Sergeant Pepper's Lonely Hearts Club Band – The Movie*. As if determined to show he, too, did drugs in the sixties, Epstein's ex-partner cast Peter Frampton as Billy Shears – on the back of the inexplicably stupendous sales of *Frampton Comes Alive* – and The Bee Gees became the Lonely Hearts Club Band, a bubblegum Beatles.

The premise of the movie was both formulaic and redundant. In the words of *Time Out*, 'This crass moral pantomime is ... an allegory of big business versus simple music and love . . . centred around "Heartland", home town of the Lonely Hearts Club Band . . . The Bee Gees and little Peter Frampton fight off evil which materialises as punks, litter and a sadly unfunny Frankie Howerd.' Which sounds an awful lot like a premise George Dunning had already contributed to Beatles iconography in 1968 with his animated film, the quaintly queer *Yellow Submarine*; wherein The Beatles jump into their yellow submarine and travel to Pepperland to defeat the Blue Meanies, and restore the Hearts Club Band back to life (à la *The Lion, The Witch & The Wardrobe*). But that was then; this was now, maaaan. And if the Blue Meanies had mutated into a bunch of punks, meanies of another hue had been sent to review the film.

Even the double-album soundtrack of Beatles tunes performed by Frampton, The Bee Gees and friends – on which *Abbey Road* was as well represented as *Sgt. Pepper* – and which could have set a certain tone for some ersatz nostalgia, stank to the high heavens; prompting its own set of stinking reviews (of which Roy Carr in NME takes the rich tea: 'It sucks and that's it . . . To think we fought the psychedelic wars for this!'). The sour smell of failure prompted some to question the merits of the original brand.

Just four months earlier, US TV audiences had been regaled with the 'true' story of the *pre*-Fab Four, as ex-Python Eric Idle and ex-Bonzo Neil Innes unveiled their inspired seventy-five minute mockdoc of The Rutles, a movie-length spin-off from a five-minute sketch written for Idle's post-Python TV series, *Rutland Weekend Television*. If Idle aspired to gentle parody, *All You Need Is Cash* proved even more iconoclastic than Stigwood's po-faced Sergeant. With George Harrison's help, Idle set about deflating just about every Beatlesque myth going (so successfully that when his good friend Harrison – who appears as an interviewer in Idle's film – was asked what it was like being in The Beatles, he said it was *exactly* like The Rutles).

Sergeant Rutter's Lonely Darts Club Band, as the cherished artifact became in Rutland, was not spared Idle's hand, being sardonically described as 'a millstone in pop music history'. Ouch, ouch, ouch. Likewise, when Idle depicted the 'Yoko Ono' character as Chastity, a Nazi whose 'father started World War II', he was playing on a popular stereotype with the lightest of hands. Yet perhaps the real highpoint of the entire exercise was 'Cheese and Onion', Neil Innes's word-perfect parody of the psychedelic Lennon – 'I have always thought in the back of my mind/ Cheese and onion' – which he delivered with such Lennon-like inflection that the song appeared on a number of Beatles bootleg albums as a 'lost' outtake.

For all of the genuine affection that shines through Idle's (and Innes's) treatment, The Rutles declared open season on the Beatle myth, especially back in Blighty, where it received its TV premiere on 27 March, 1978, at the height of Punk. Idle even slipped in a reference to McCartney's shall-we-say tendency to appropriate trends for his own musical ends, Macca's Rutle replica, Dirk, forming a punk band after their break-up, The Punk Floyd. A month later, McCartney informed Roy Carr he had written his own punk paean, 'Boil Crisis', the opening lines of which suggested he got the joke: 'One night in the life of a kid named Sid/ He scored with a broad in a pyramid . . .'

For the homeland punks, though, The Beatles were part of the problem, make no mistake. The Clash weren't joking when they made '1977' (aka Year Zero) the b-side to their first single; nor when they proclaimed: 'No Beatles, Elvis or The Rolling Stones/ In 1977'. As for The Sex Pistols, they fired their one reliable songwriter in February 1977 because they found him listening to The Beatles!

Suffice it to say, no self-respecting punk was covering anything the Sergeant had up his sleeve. If The Beatles were given the time of day, it was usually an act of de(con)struction, like what The Damned dished out on their rendition of 'Help!', b-side to the 'first' UK Punk single, 'New Rose'. And when Siouxsie & the Banshees did 'Helter-Skelter' it became an unrecognisable dirge that only went dervish at its Mansonesque climax. The ethos of punk was firmly ephemeral, fixated on the seven-inch single and so DIY that when The Clash recorded their first album – which was being paid for by CBS, after all – engineer Simon Humphrey found that they were 'hostile to anything that had been employed as a technique pre-punk. So, if there was like a harmony part, or a double-tracked guitar, or even dropping in [a vocal] . . . they'd think you were trying to polish them up, or break down the whole punk ethic.' If it was a technique from *Pepper*'s palette, it was anti-punk.

And yet, one Beatle seemed to retain a certain kudos among punks simply by keeping his head down, and keeping out of the news. Lennon, the primary author of *Sgt. Pepper*'s key expression of revolutionary intent, had stayed an angry young man somewhat longer than the others. *Imagine*'s 'Gimme Some Truth' could have become a punk anthem in its own right if it had been covered by, say, The Punk Floyd. All that changed, though, with the release of *Double Fantasy* (1980), an album that delighted in the unalloyed joys of changing nappies and nights spent at home, i.e. the very things that had sent Lennon doolally and drug-addled back in 1967. It received perhaps its most scathing reception from the post-punk English music papers, Charles Shaar Murray firing a number of verbal volleys in its direction from his safe European home:

> The trouble with music that is self-centred to the point of utter solipsism is that one cannot criticise the art without criticising the life on which the art is based . . . It sounds like a great life, but unfortunately it makes a lousy record . . . Now bliss off.

Much like the poor journalist who, the day before Princess Diana's death, suggested if she had an IQ five points lower she'd have to be watered daily, Mr Murray suddenly found himself having to hide in King's Reach Tower when – a fortnight after his (perfectly spot-on) review was published – Mark Chapman decided verbal volleys would not suffice, and took out his hatred of the world on the one pop star who actually gave him the time of day.

ALL CHANGE!

If one event returned the whole Beatles mythology to the top of the slide it was the murder of Lennon. The suddenness of this full-stop made a re-evaluation of Lennon's place in history inevitable; and with it, The Beatles' own legacy. It also made it easy for Lennon's many apologists to cast Paul as the stage villain, and get a chorus of boos and hisses from all pantomime populists.

Not that McCartney had been helping his cause greatly in the last couple of years. The release of the unspeakable 'Mull of Kintyre' in November 1977 – which proceeded to outsell all Beatles 45s – was the end of the line for many. In interviews, he was having to become increasingly defensive about his current work, which had lost much of its edge, even if he insisted it hadn't. He remained determined to claim he was the same man represented on the 1976 double-album Beatles anthology, *Rock'n'Roll Music*, which seemed to have been *designed* to emphasise his role as the true rocker in the band. As late as 1978 he was even telling NME's Roy Carr, 'We do keep talking about going in the studio and cutting a no-nonsense rock & roll album, to just get it out of our system.' Instead he came up with *London Town*, a commercially safe outlet for his most balladic set of songs since *McCartney*.

Yet he seemed genuinely offended when *Melody Maker*'s Colin Irwin asked him in March 1978 how he responded to accusations of being 'wimpish and sentimental', telling him in no uncertain terms to 'Piss off!' After Irwin continued his line of questioning, an exasperated ex-Beatle asked, 'Is there *anything* you like about us?' The burden of being a former Fab was making him as crabby as Atlas after a hard day's night. The following month he told Carr, 'To me The Beatles are just old newspaper clippings.' By the time of Wings' last tour, in December 1979, the arch-advocate seemed reluctant to carry the weight of his own sixties legacy, playing just five Beatles songs in the 21-song sets.[2]

However, if McCartney had hoped to carve a post-Beatle career that would compare in quality if not impact to those myth-shrouded music-makers, the combination of the disbandment of Wings and

Lennon's premature death at the onset of the eighties pretty much consigned the man to years of bad press and unkind comparisons – to which Lennon no longer needed to add anything because every time McCartney did add anything, it was ritualistically pilloried.

John Winston's perfectly immense contribution to these cultural revolutionaries continued to grow ever greater in the afterlife of favour he now enjoyed. The man who had run out of things to say barely three years after The Beatles break-up – disappearing into a drink-fuelled depression that outlasted the punk interregnum – became in the popular imagination the tortured genius he had so long delineated himself to be.

The reputation of *Sgt. Pepper* – which was, 'A Day in the Life' excepted, seen as primarily Paul's work – could only continue to suffer in the process. For the Sergeant, the process of 'going in and out of style' would take time to complete the anti-hype cycle and return to favour, especially in England, where punk bands had as profound an effect on its native pop as the Beat groups who came before them.

In fact, when *NME* decided to canvass its own critics for a second time, in November 1985, for a second definitive (sic) list of the 100 Greatest Albums, *Pepper* had not merely slipped from its high berth, it had fallen overboard. While *Revolver* held up well (from fourth to eleventh – faring no worse than *Blonde on Blonde*, from first equal to eighth), that joint champion of the 1974 poll *Sgt. Pepper* was the new nowhere man. *Rubber Soul* suffered almost as badly, descending from fifteen to ninety-eight (below the likes of *Swordfishtrombones* [sixth], *Searching for the Young Soul Rebels* [thirty-four] and *Steve McQueen* [ninety-one]).

If Gambaccini's *Critics' Choice* book had suggested someone frigging with the rigging, the *NME* of the mid-eighties seemed no less guilty of dubious practices to make its post-punk point. In 1986, the entrenched English weeklies stood alone in failing to recognise that even the furthest tentacles of post-punk were grasping at reeds, and that the mid-sixties output of its pedigree pop performers had still to be bettered. The act that continued to outsell all others was about to enter the digital age, and with it a whole new audience they could charm. Twenty years on, Brian Epstein, Brian Jones, Jimi Hendrix, John Lennon and Lester Bangs were no more, but the Sergeant was still kicking, and due a digital spring clean.

REVOLVING

Sgt. Pepper typifies the year of 1967 and, as such, must rank as a masterpiece, for surely the prime objective for any piece of music is that it captures the time of its recording. –

Mark Lewisohn, *Recording Sessions*, 1988

Its track-for-track quality . . . these days makes Revolver *a more common choice as The Beatles' best album . . . [but] it's* Sgt. Pepper *that most authentically conjures up the elusive 'spirit of '67' . . . Embedded in its time in a way that* Revolver *isn't,* Sgt. Pepper, *appropriately approached, continues to be an active generator of 'period vibes'. If you want a contact high with the spirit of '67, a taste of the Universal Love vibe as it was then widely felt,* Sgt. Pepper *is the place to go. –*

Ian MacDonald, 'The Psychedelic Beatles: Love and Drugs', *The People's Music*, 2003

By 1986, the compact disc was three years old, and looking like it was here to stay. Launched with the catch-phrase 'perfect sound forever', it was so perfect that its 16-bit, 44.1 KHz processor would be redundant in less than a decade; as for forever, by the end of the nineties 'CD rot' was a term any collector had come to know all too well as certain CDs began to acquire an additional audio backdrop, as of a man shovelling gravel. But the time had arrived to make the most popular catalogue in pop history available in the digital domain, ready or not, introducing the songs to a new audience and digital sound to an old audience.

The digital format not only codified the Rock canon for consumption as a commodity, pure and simple (i.e. as pop), it allowed a new generation of music fans to hear the sounds of the

cities in an entirely different context – one that polished everything till it gleamed like a new penny. This suited The Beatles,
whose irrepressible hooks and hammy harmonies came through
bright and clear. By the mid-eighties, they were ripe for rediscovery.

It was agreed that the first four albums would appear on CD
in their original mono, the titles from *Help!* onwards in stereo
(though everything through to *Pepper* had been made with mono
in mind). Once the decision was made to issue all albums – save
Magical Mystery Tour – in their original UK configuration; two CDs
of 'stray' single and EP tracks (*Past Masters*) were required. Now
all that was necessary was for someone to tweak the tapes, and for
EMI to decide on a release schedule.

Called in *after* the initial set of CDs to 'clean up' The Beatles'
musty old analogue masters was their old sidekick, George Martin.
He had stood aside and watched Mike Jarrett do direct digital transfers of the first four LPs from their mono masters, a process that
apparently took just twelve hours per LP. As soon as Martin came
on board, though, the studio bills immediately rose as he made
good on his threat to remix *Help* and *Rubber Soul* as 'those early
stereos were not very good'.

Martin was reserving judgement on *Sgt. Pepper*, due to appear
as a stand-alone title a couple of months after the spring '87 release
of *Help*, *Rubber Soul* and *Revolver*. On the horizon loomed an
anniversary even Essex Music couldn't help but notice – the twentieth anniversary of the most famous 'millstone in pop music history',
an album which everyone knew opened with the words, 'It was
twenty years ago today . . .' As such, before they even issued the
first batch of Beatle CDs, the release schedule was being shuffled
around just one date, 1 June, 1987, and the release of *Sgt. Pepper*
on CD.

Compact disc itself seemed a strangely futuristic medium for
these oh-so-familiar vinyl artifacts. Much was made in the media
of how great it would all sound when bereft of the crackles and
pops that even the most carefully tended vinyl acquired in the still
of night. So when the first Beatle CDs began to appear in winter

1987, not everyone heard an audible sigh, as of a deflating balloon, as folk-with-ears began to realise that it wasn't only the disc that was compact, so was the sound. As in, where has all the top-end gone? On this evidence, the dynamic range of this digital alternative was about as good as cassette (minus the hiss). The notorious 'Abbey Road Roll-Off' had just made its first appearance.[1]

Some wondered whether perhaps those early albums just weren't very well recorded. Certainly for those who had grown up hearing them in (panned, mile-wide) stereo – and, if American, in a wholly random order – the immediacy of these mono mixes took some getting used to. The proof of the amazing pudding would be in the mid-sixties masterpieces. Everyone knew that *Rubber Soul* and *Revolver* sounded great in stereo, mono, or underwater. So when they appeared, and still sounded in need of a sonic scrub – even after Martin remixed the former because of 'deficiencies' in the stereo mix (which begs the question, why stereo then?) – people began to express concerns about the deficiencies of digital as a medium for this music.

Most of this disquiet, though, took place away from the that's-entertainment mainstream media, i.e. in hi-fi monthlies or industry magazines like *Billboard* and *ICE*. Most of the new breed of men's monthlies were just happy to be invited to the party. And there was a newcomer which seemed particularly keen to please when it came to John, Paul, George and Ringo: a monthly music mag, launched in September 1986, that called itself *Q*. *Q* targeted the mature music fan (i.e. those whose musical tastes were largely set in *Stone*), and revelled in gadgetry and an *NME*-induced smugness. It was beside itself at the prospect of an entire Beatle catalogue to coo about, laying the ground for some serious supplication with a Paul McCartney interview in issue one that was about as combative as a Swiss general.

By the time *Sgt. Pepper* appeared – right on cue, and housed in its very own slipcase, like a prized hardback first edition – *Q* had lined up its own two-part history of the Sergeant by the eminently qualified Steve Turner. Turner's proved to be the most authoritative article on the history of the album to date, and possibly the finest piece of journalism Q ever published. He had done interviews with participants and observers, assembled his observations, marshalled his facts, and come up with a credible chronology and critique of the album – all just in time, for the mills of Hype had begun to roll again. Not only was Turner's piece measured and mannered, but editor Ellen turned the album over to that shameless iconoclast Charles Shaar Murray for re-view. CSM called it generally right, depicting the album as a mixed blessing, though once again at editorial stage it mysteriously acquired a four-star rating:

> Sgt. Pepper . . . has been both hailed as rock's definitive masterpiece and attacked as the incarnation of the moment when the music went off the rails almost for good . . . It is an album immovably fixed in time, as 'dated' a record as anything in pop, and it only very occasionally transcends its status as a curio, a period piece . . . The sheer sonic ingenuity deployed on these sessions taught everybody, for better or worse, to hear music differently. Prior to Pepper, recording was by definition a documentation of an event which had taken place in the past. After Pepper, it became the creation of an event which might never have been able to take place. Like it or not, it was the record which changed the rules.

Such balance was entirely absent in Pepper's own CD notes. Ignoring the etiquette that it is generally bad form to praise oneself to the skies, the attendant text called itself the product of 'perhaps the most creative 129 days in the history of rock music'. If CSM had weighed up the pros and cons, EMI had simply employed the most willing sleeve-note writer they could find wading through the tape library. Mark Lewisohn was a Beatles historian par excellence, his authoritative chronology of the band's performances, The Beatles Live! (1986) one of the finest works of original research in Rock's notoriously imprecise history. But what Lewisohn knew about cultural or musical context could be written on a postage stamp, and still leave room for the complete works of Wittgenstein. He had burrowed so deep into the FabFour's forest, he had long forgotten there was a world beyond their woods.

Lewisohn remembered 1967 well enough. It was the post-*Pepper* world he remained a tad hazy about. But since he had spent the past couple of years going through every Beatle tape in the Abbey Road hold, and relied on EMI to endorse the eventual result, a lavish coffee-table book, he was an obliging nominee for the new post of EMI Minister of Propaganda. The 1988 appearance of his mammoth, beautifully presented history of *The Beatles' Recording Sessions* – which might be more accurately termed *The Beatles' In-House EMI Recording Sessions* – gave a stamp of authority to all subsequent Lewisohn pronouncements, irrespective of any ongoing contextual void.

Fortunately for EMI, Lewisohn was not the only one hoping to make 1987 the year *Pepper* was restored to its 'rightful' place in pop history. Paul Gambaccini was back for another uncritical edition of *Critics' Choice Top 200 Albums* and – surprise, surprise – still there in top spot, after all these years, was *Pepper*. And once again our compiler was obliged to rely on some of the States' most resolutely uninformed industry figures to bolster the album's showing.

Also appearing on the stands in August 1987 was an 'anniversary' edition of *Rolling Stone* (three months early), featuring 'The 100 Best Albums of the Last Twenty Years'. Actually, it was necessary to make it the last twenty *and a half* years, in order to place *Sgt. Pepper*, an album released five months before the first issue of Wenner's magazine, at number one (not that such niceties disturbed its publisher – a subsequent poll of the best albums of the eighties put The Clash's *London Calling* at #1, and *that* record was released in 1979). A delighted McCartney came down from his counting-house to give *Stone* some pearls before bedtime; and to remind everyone just who had been calling the Sergeant's shots:

> Still, today . . . it sounds full of ideas . . . I haven't heard anything
> this year as inventive . . . [But] *Pepper* was probably the one Beatle

album I can say was my idea . . . We were into Cage and Stockhausen,
those kind of people. Obviously, once you allow yourself that kind of
freedom . . . well, Cage is appreciating silence, isn't he?

The *Rolling Stone* poll was taken from just seventeen staff writers,
overlooking every ex-writer who'd made the magazine's name
(Nelson, Marcus, Crowe &c.), but still seemed as stuck in the magazine's late sixties heyday as its owner. With thirty-one of the top
fifty albums having been issued between 1967 and 1972 the poll
emphasised just how many American pop writers missed the sixties.
For them, writing 'in a decade of political conservatism and stifling
musical formats, of sexual fear and obsession with the past, the
hopeful message of *Sgt. Pepper*[!] . . . is much more urgent now than
it was twenty years ago'.

Also revisiting that summer lovefest from a two-decade remove
were Granada TV, the ITV station whose region covered Liverpool.
They'd commissioned an hour-long documentary entitled *It Was
Twenty Years Ago . . .*, and then recruited ex-love adult and PR king
Derek Taylor as a consultant. Taylor promptly decided to write a
book about his favourite year, calling on the many friends still
beholden to him. Though he had spent '67 on the other side of the
(pop) world, his was a much-needed insider's account, liberally
embellished with the recollections of a reconciled George Harrison.

If *It Was Twenty Years Ago . . .* was adopted as the catch-phrase
for this wave of sixties nostalgia, it also gave a new record label in
Italy, not historically the home of great labels, an idea for an
imprint. Under the 'It Was *More Than* Twenty Years Ago' banner
Bulldog Records began to release an astonishing array of live
concerts previously the sole domain of bootleggers. The difference
was that Bulldog was a legitimate label – at least in its land of
origin – exploiting a loophole in European copyright that would
become known as the 'protection gap'.[2] Bulldog's first release was
the fabled 1966 *Beatles at Budokan* concert, a gleaming recording
of a latterday by-numbers Beatles performance. Their next release
was the so-called *Dylan at the Royal Albert Hall* concert, where Judas

came face to face with some disenchanted disciples. Whatever next? Studio outtakes!?

As it happens, yes. A superb digital dub of around fourteen uncirculated studio outtakes was being discreetly hawked around collector circles just as the protection gap yawned open. A few months later, in the summer of 1988, Mark Lewisohn's authoritative *Recording Sessions* appeared on bookstands, setting Beatle fans drooling at the thought of all this unissued booty. It was closely followed by two thirty-minute CDs of Beatles studio outtakes that sounded better than anything the official label had yet managed to release themselves. *Ultra Rare Trax* vols 1 & 2, issued by the German 'protection gap' label Swingin' Pig, were everything the recent EMI CD remasters were not: revelatory sounding, these genuinely new outtakes provided a more vital insight into The Beatles' working methods than all of Lewisohn's pages of prose. And the word on the wire was that this was only the tip of the Abbey Road iceberg. A worried EMI exec., who spoke to *ICE* about the set, thought the selection of tracks a little odd:

> **Mike Howlett:** What amazes me is that there are lots of other peculiarities [in the vaults]. Those that have surfaced [on these CDs] are interesting, but not devastatingly so. There are other things, that have not surfaced, that I find even more interesting. I don't want to say what they are, but there are differences that would send collectors screaming up the wall! And I hope they're *not* going to be in future volumes.

Even after Lewisohn had pulled back the shutters on EMI's unreleased booty, Howlett's statement seemed scarcely credible. What were these 'differences that would send collectors screaming up the wall'? Certainly nothing that had featured in the two projects undertaken in the first half of the eighties by EMI engineer John Barrett (whose dubs, as it happens, had provided most of the material on *Ultra Rare Trax*).

It was Barrett who had been asked to catalogue the Beatles

tapes at Abbey Road while undertaking chemotherapy in 1982;
and had pushed EMI to open its portals to the public for the first
time in 1983, putting on a special show to commemorate the twentieth anniversary of The Beatles at Abbey Road. Here, for the first
time, fans heard radically different mixes and 'new' takes of songs
as seminal as 'Ticket to Ride', 'Norwegian Wood', 'Rain', 'Strawberry
Fields Forever', 'A Day In The Life' and 'Hey Jude' in studio-like
sound. Though security was tight, the ingenuity of collectors
prevailed and a dub was made of material played during the show.

Shortly after Barrett had completed his tape-research he lost
his battle with cancer. Ex-EMI engineer Geoff Emerick, fresh from
producing Elvis Costello's masterful *Imperial Bedroom*, was now
enlisted to compile an album of unreleased Beatles rarities for
possible release. The album he compiled, *Sessions*, comprised just
thirteen tracks, three of which were alternative takes of released
songs ('While My Guitar Gently Weeps', 'I'm Looking Through
You' and 'One After 909'), while the remaining ten comprised songs
given to other artists as unworthy of the Beatle imprimatur, early
cover versions and a couple of examples of the post-*Pepper* Beatles
'goofing around' in the studio ('What's the New, Mary Jane?' and
'Christmas Time Is Here Again'). Nothing on it would have rewritten
the Beatle book, nor sent 'collectors screaming up the wall'. Though
the project was assigned a 1985 release date, it was more in hope
than expectation. The Beatles duly exercised their veto.

Ultra Rare Trax 1 & 2, unlike *Sessions*, concentrated on alternative takes (though it did include seven songs from the abandoned *Sessions* LP). This was the way to go because The Beatles
didn't generally reject usable songs. Even their alternative takes
only served to show just how unerring was their judgement when
it came to what to keep from a recording (Dylan, take note). The
(ultimately six) *Ultra Rare Trax* volumes, and their subsequent
'protection gap' heirs, helped reveal elements of 'the process',
without locating that perfect prototype The Beatles themselves
unwittingly overlooked. Thus, on its first volume, *Ultra Rare Trax*
included for the first time the original take twenty-six of 'Strawberry

Fields Forever', at the correct speed and without the edit from take seven interposed – a collector's wet-dream but sounding plain 'wrong' to the general music fan.

Clearly Beatles fan Barrett had understood such nuances. Indeed, as more and more of his private hoard began to appear – every single tape being bootlegged, post-*Anthology*, on the *Mythology* boxed-sets and Vigotone's *Turn Me On Dead Man*, *Get Back* and *Another Sessions* CD series – it became clear that there was surprisingly little exciting 'new' material in the vaults. It also became evident that, of all the many sessions The Beatles had undertaken for EMI, the least interesting/revealing were the *Sgt. Pepper* sessions, from which almost nothing ever emerged on bootleg. Even Barrett's own hoard contained just his own remix of 'A Day In The Life' (for the 1983 Abbey Road Show) and a contemporary, correct-speed mono mix of 'When I'm 64'.

A great deal of what went on at Abbey Road in the winter of 1967 *could* have been of unquestionable interest to the music historian. The Beatles, after all, were doing something they had rarely done before, working out arrangements to songs which they had never played, *in studio conditions*. Yet it apparently never occurred to Martin and co. that these 'runthroughs' might be worthy of preservation, even as a single-track 'live' running tape.[3] What resides in Abbey Road's archive are attempts at finished takes along with the various mixes made before, during and after overdubs. In other words, the final stage/s of the process. Documenting the creation of a song like 'Lucy in the Sky with Diamonds', a bareboned idea at the point of studio-entry, simply hadn't occurred to them.

At the same time as the bootleggers lifted a lid on those Abbey Road sessions, it became apparent that tapes *had* been rolling at every turn during the making (and unmaking) of Brian Wilson's aborted *Smile*. The bootleggers were again first to answer the collectors' calls, a famous Japanese single-CD appearing in November 1989; which *Smile* authority Dwight Cavanagh was still calling, five years later, 'The most surprising and best quality unofficial release of the *Smile* recordings ever'. It featured fifteen minutes of

'Good Vibrations' (including two complete versions), seven minutes of new material for 'Heroes & Villains', the instrumental first movement of 'Surf's Up' (along with Brian's full solo rendition), plus a version of 'Mrs Leary's Cow' with the 'Heroes & Villains' 'intro'. If not quite the motherlode, this single non-Capitol CD suggested full session tapes might yet be pregnant with unrealised possibilities.

Its appearance simultaneously supplied the first faint doubts that *Smile* had *ever* been a viable concern. As *ICE* wrote at the time, 'Those hearing *Smile* here for the first time will be left wondering what all the fuss was about, since it sounds exactly like what it is: a collection of scraps from an unfinished project.' Capitol promptly decided to provide service with a *Smile* cut or two of their own, plumping for an alternative take of 'Heroes & Villains' and their own edit of assorted 'Good Vibrations' on to an otherwise unexceptional 1990 CD 'two-fer' of *Smiley Smile* and *Wild Honey*.

Seemingly unwilling to spring further surprises, Capitol required another nudge. It came in 1992, when a three-album vinyl bootleg added to the illicit booty with uncirculated, realised takes of 'Wonderful', 'Love To Say Da-Da' and 'Barnyard'. It prompted a concerted response from Capitol the following year, with the most thorough trawl of Beach Boys tapes to date resulting in a thirty-five minute edit of *Smile* outtakes, which were placed on a fifth, 'bonus' disc to The Beach Boys boxed-set, *Good Vibrations*. Unfortunately, it appeared to confirm that Wilson was nowhere near completing an album to rival *Revolver*, let alone its psychedelic successor. Paul Williams, who had yearned to hear this stuff (again) for sixteen years or more, was brave enough to use his revived *Crawdaddy* to admit he had called it wrong back in sixty-seven:

> Putting aside the myth (which David Anderle and I certainly helped create, in our published conversation way back a long time ago) of the genius artist frustrated on the brink of his greatest masterwork, these tracks are clearly the work of someone very stoned, a powerful

creative artist very much under the influence of marijuana and amphetamines . . . Being stoned definitely promotes original and unusual ideas in creative people, and it also serves to make one less inhibited about exploring and using those ideas. This is genuine, this is a plus. On the minus side, being stoned often makes dumb ideas seem terrific; it makes you laugh at things other people wouldn't see the humour in (not a problem unless you've decided to record an album that includes 'lots of humour'); and while (especially fuelled by amphetamines) it gives you plenty of energy to start things, it very often leaves you without the energy to finish them . . . [And though] there are moments of great sensitivity and deep feeling on these *Smile* tracks (notably Brian's vocal performances on 'Wonderful' and 'Surf's Up') . . . in its overall character it is not at all a 'heart' album (as *Pet Sounds* certainly is); rather it is, and was clearly meant to be, a sort of three-ring circus of flashy musical ideas and avant-garde entertainment.

Meanwhile – by remaining essentially exempt from the wholesale bootlegging that the CD era encouraged – *Sgt. Pepper* continued to bathe in its own '129 days of genius' myth; first propagated by someone who *had* heard the studio tapes and was still impressed by those occasional shards of inspiration. When George Martin supervised a one-hour documentary on the making of *Pepper* in 1993 – presumably intended for the twenty-fifth anniversary, but broadcast a year late – he was equally careful not to roll away the stone, playing but the briefest snippets of the (better) songs-in-prototype.

The participation of every surviving Beatle could have ensured a fascinating insight into the *Pepper* process. However, everyone from the editor down carefully skirted the issue of whether those perpetual onlookers Harrison and Starkey were really blown away by the results. By now, it was being taken as read that this was an album for the ages. McCartney certainly seemed to have abandoned any doubts, even dusting off the title-track on his return to touring in 1989–90, complete with Abbey Road audience noise; before recording a post-Fab 1993 soundcheck rendition of 'Fixing a Hole' – broadcast later on his *Oobu Joobu* radio series – that more than matched its original guise.

George Martin's companion volume, *With A Little Help From My Friends: The Making of Sgt. Pepper* – a balanced and remarkably well-recollected account of the sessions – also missed its deadline, only appearing in 1994. It thus came out alongside a couple of other tomes that seemed to suggest the Sergeant could do no wrong. The more well-received of these was Ian MacDonald's *Revolution In The Head*. Subtitled 'The Beatles' Records & The Sixties', there was no mistaking the wistfulness at the heart of MacDonald's worldview, expressed in an introduction that was one long eulogy for that 'disappearing decade':

> The Sixties seem like a golden age to us because, relative to now, they were. At their heart, the counter-cultural revolt against acquisitive selfishness . . . looks in retrospect like a last gasp of the Western soul . . . Till hard drugs are legalised, the old world will retain some moral hold on us; but when they are . . . the last ties will be cut with our former way of life, far away from us on the other side of the sun-flooded chasm of the Sixties.

One can almost hear someone piping away at the gates of Eden. Of necessity, The Beatles' career now needed to be represented by a gentle arc Going Up (1962–65), Reaching The Top (1966–67) and Coming Down (everything post-*Pepper*). So MacDonald not only reordered the work so that it appeared in order of recording (a chronology by composition being impractical), but conveniently redefined the work of other contributors to the sounds of the sixties to fit his rose-tinted contact lenses. Apparently, 'the quality of [Dylan's] work went into permanent decline' after the motorcycle accident, i.e. the year *before* he wrote 'This Wheel's On Fire', 'I Shall Be Released', 'I'm Not There', 'All Along The Watchtower', 'Dear Landlord' and another couple of dozen classics in six months of scribbling.

While MacDonald constantly reiterated the importance of *Pepper*

– 'It was a major cultural event'; 'The psychic shiver which *Sgt. Pepper* sent through the world was nothing less than a cinematic dissolve from one Zeitgeist to another' – he conveniently refrained from addressing the thorny question; were its *songs* actually as good as what came before? Even a later essay of his, concerned solely with 'The Beatles and Psychedelia' (see chapter heading), implied its sheer cultural importance rendered any such question moot.

The book caught its own zeitgeist, racking up rave reviews, some of which even managed to praise MacDonald's 'scholarship'. Yet *Revolution In The Head* involved no original research, even the studio 'info' being culled wholesale from Lewisohn. It was a highly subjective, at times wildly contentious, engagingly written plea for The Beatles' (undeniable) place in cultural history.

On the other hand, when a matter of weeks later Steve Turner published his own history of The Beatles' songs, *Hard Day's Write*, which displayed original research on every page, the reviews were altogether more mixed. Turner's 'error' was not having a concomitant cosmography attendant to his thorough account of the *history* of each and every Beatle song. MacDonald's model, requiring as it did nothing but an opinion about a song and a shorthand list of titles, spawned its own mini-industry of Songs Explained books, though not one successor had MacDonald's command of his milieu or grasp of musical finesse. Turner's premise, which took too much effort to replicate, remained an oddity in its field of endeavour.

If Martin, MacDonald and Turner were all trying their darnedest to place *Pepper* in some kind of context, the other contentious collection to give *Pepper* pride of place that year was merely an unwelcome presentiment of the post-modern virus that would soon infect every avenue of the mass media. In Colin Larkin's *The Guinness All-Time Top 1000 Albums* every opinion held equal weight, and transparency of methodology was for squares. Readers were left to wonder whether *The Guinness All-Time Top 1000 Albums* were arrived at after a thousand Guinnesses, or simply if you needed a stiff Guinness to even open the book.

Once again, a singularly ill-qualified editor was setting himself up as a pseudo-authority who by canvassing everyone in his phonebook, could 'demonstrate' that *Sgt. Pepper* was the greatest 'Rock and Pop' album of All-Time. What Larkin went to great pains to leave unexplained was, according to whom? His was the first such poll to take the views of critics and members of the general public, and to put them in the same statistical blender. The result was an unpalatable goo. Any poll putting Simply Red's *Stars* as the thirty-fourth greatest Rock/pop album of all time clearly incorporated the input of people with all the musical taste of the congenitally cloth-eared. But Larkin was unfazed by any negative feedback, continuing to compile ever more statistically unsound compendiums from the views of the great throng every coupla years, then passing them off as some kind of (un)critical consensus.

At the same time, the critical edifice that had placed *Pepper* at the back of The Beatles' mid-period masterclass was starting to weaken. Allowing that *Pepper* had enough moments to warrant a place in the mid-range of its third Top 100 poll, *NME*'s critics put it at an appropriate thirty-three in their 1993 assessment of greatness. By 1995, it had slipped again, according to the new favourite fix for Rock reactionaries, *Mojo*, whose own cabal of critics put *Pepper* no higher than fifty-one.

But *Mojo* wasn't about to let their own set of critics have the final say. Ostensibly in the interests of fairness – but actually to find out what its readers liked, and then attempt to mirror their every opinion – the new voice of the UK Rock press decided to let its (generally well-informed) readers have their say. The results appeared in the January 1996 issue. But even the *Mojo* readership still contained an annoyingly high number who could be relied on to vote for the last album they enjoyed or the first album they bought. Of those not so inclined, there were still plenty of folk voting for what they thought they should be voting for. Not that any of this harmed The Beatles, who came first, third, fourth and sixth (*Pepper* trailing behind *Rubber Soul*, *Revolver* and *The White Album*); telling us, one, that *Mojo* had a lot of Beatles fans amongst its readers; and, two, that The Beatles were assuredly back on people's minds.

By 1996, *Sgt. Pepper* and its living creators were enjoying the afterglow of a Britpop revival that at times resembled Beatlemania. When Oasis played to half a million people over a weekend at Knebworth in the summer of 1996, it was The Beatles live all over again as even on the radio broadcast it was hard to hear Liam over the singalong crowd's renditions of every tune in their repertoire. One couldn't help but think Shea Stadium (named after the famous revolutionary, Shea Stadium – really). The Knebworth encore was a fitting nod, too: 'I Am The Walrus'.

The Beatles were also back on pop fans' minds because of their own cunning plans. In 1995 the surviving members (plus Yoko Ono) had finally agreed that the time was ripe to rape the vaults and rewrite the past. After the success of EMI's 2-CD edit of Great Dane's 9-CD boxed-set of Beatles BBC recordings the previous Christmas, they concocted a plan for the *Anthology* to end all anthologies: three two-CD sets of (mostly) unreleased recordings, a six-part TV history of the band that could then be issued on VHS (and ultimately DVD), and a coffee-table volume hefty enough to weaken less sturdy recipients. Derek Taylor reflected a pervasive optimism that it could all come round again:

> **Derek Taylor:** We're extremely gratified that this thing has become so valid. If you like, there's the Britpop coincidence of Oasis and Blur and whatever. There's quite a drift in fashion as well. There are very few detractors around Britain, and a lot of young supporters.

In November 1995, prior to the year-long assault on punters' wallets that was *Anthology*, the product was presaged by some wildly optimistic predictions of TV audiences (fifty million in the US) and CD sales (seven million worldwide for each CD *Anthology*), based on the apparent revelation that 78% of families in the United States were aware of the band (which merely begs the question, 'And the other 22%??'); and that The Beatles were the all-time favourite group for VH-1 watchers. These figures merely told Capitol which couch-potatoes might not actively turn off a programme about The Beatles; not how many might purchase six CDs' worth of songs that in most cases anyone interested already owned in a superior form.

These modern marketeers also found that their spreadsheets had failed to inform them of the downside if punters thought the first 2-CD set stunk, or that the knock-on effect on sales of the remaining two sets might be not so negligible. Hence, why every reissue label before *Anthology* had issued any archival raids as lavish, expensive, one-time-purchase, boxed-sets like Dylan's *The Bootleg Series* or Eric Clapton's *Crossroads*.

Reaching for the 78% of folk who'd heard of the most famous band of all time, EMI forgot to tell the unenlightened that what they would be buying was a bunch of home demos, audition tapes (bad enough to get them rejected by the hippest label on the block), dodgy rehearsal recordings of dubious provenance,[4] annoying snippets of conversation that would never repay repeated listenings, oh, and composite 'takes' of unfinished and/or inferior versions of familiar favourites. In other words, every single mistake made by previous official compilers of 'bootleg' material contained on a single set.

Anthology 1, issued just in time for Thanksgiving, was one cold turkey. Advance CDs of the second volume, which contained the same annoying thread of interview snippets, were hastily re-edited to allow the CDs to flow more easily. After all, the second volume pulled out all the big guns – unbootlegged, 'unbelievable' outtakes from 1965 through 1967, including alternatives of both 'Strawberry Fields' and 'Penny Lane', plus no less than eight uncirculated alternatives from the *Sgt. Pepper* sessions. Before its release, though, dissenting voices were already questioning the validity of the exercise. One Beatle expert had this to say to *ICE*:

> The controversial thing about the material on Volume Two is that much of it is outtakes that never existed. There are several instances of 'a bit of take five added to take six, finished off with a remixed

version of the master . . .' In effect, they're creating new Beatles
performances in the mid-nineties using scraps from the sixties . . .
It means that you're getting stuff that never existed before. A bootlegger might call them 'outfakes'.

EMI only came clean about the 'outfakes' in the annotation
contained within the booklet (and even then, often only obliquely).
They were presenting bootleg material to millions of consumers
who had heard of The Beatles, but for whom bootlegs came in a
still. Without an aesthetic understanding as to the underlying point
of the exercise, they resembled bystanders at a patent medicine
show. The label had transformed the amount of supposedly worthwhile unreleased Beatles material in their vaults, in the decade
since Emerick compiled his thirteen-track *Sessions* album, into six
full-length CDs that could have all but accommodated the band's
entire official sixties output. As to the seven songs from the *Pepper*
sessions on *Anthology 2*, they were presented thus:

'A Day In The Life' – was, and I quote, a 'composite mix [that]
embraces the best of the unreleased outtakes'; and, as such, considerably less interesting than the oft-bootlegged rough mix of take
six.

'Good Morning, Good Morning' – a genuinely interesting early
take (eight), with alternate Lennon vocal, pre-overdubs. An illu-
minating insight into what *Pepper* might have sounded like with
less gimmickry.

'Only A Northern Song' – 'Take 3 . . . with unused vocal tracks
overdubbed on to a separate "reduction", Take 12, flown in'; and,
after all this, only marginally different from the released version.

'Being For The Benefit of Mr Kite' – after two brief snippets
(takes one and two – both incomplete), we arrive at Take 7, which
'formed the basis for the eventual master . . . crossfaded with an
organ and calliope effects tape prepared on 20th February'.

'Lucy in the Sky with Diamonds' – 'is a unique combination of
some of the different takes and sounds that comprised the original

master of "Lucy in the Sky with Diamonds" . . . newly remixed.'
Nuff said.

'Within You Without You' – The basic track, minus Harrison's
vocal, remixed. Er, pourquoi?

'Sgt. Pepper's Lonely Hearts Club Band (reprise)' – an earlier,
inferior take of the reprise version with a guide vocal. Strictly
bootleg fare.

For all their early hopes of another season of Beatlemania, the
reaction to the *Anthologies* was disappointing – commercially *and*
critically. Plans for a deluxe boxed-set, with an extra CD, as a
Christmas 1996 release were quietly forgotten, and when the
videos were reissued in the DVD format, in 2003, there was a
discernible lack of fanfare (despite the addition of some highly
worthwhile bonus material). The one-book coffee-table also found
itself subject to endless delays, not appearing until 2000, when it
went from Christmas bestseller to New Year sale bargain bins in
the twinkling of an eye.

Showing the inner workings of The Beatles' studio work in a
sensible boxed-set – judiciously selected by someone other than
the original producer, who remained too close to the process – utilising state-of-the-art remixes of the important songs for which no
notable alternative take could be found, intelligently annotated
and colourfully packaged, would have been both a welcome gesture
to collectors and a necessary consolidation of the canon (especially
if it had been topped off with an official release of *Get Back & 12
Other Songs*). But it was the post-*Pepper* Beatles who signed off on
the *Anthology* concept, and in the process demonstrated that they
never quite trusted EMI enough to surrender any of the control
wrestled back from the label in stages, starting in 1967.

Meanwhile that exemplary, extant canon remained resolutely
'retro', with EMI and Apple increasingly bemused by the bootleggers' ability to produce better-sounding CD versions of the official
albums working from vinyl or 3 $^3/_4$" tape than *they* could from so-
called master tapes. One particularly business-like German bootlegger

had systematically issued every Beatles album up to *The White Album* in its alternative mix (stereo up to *For Sale*, then mono), filled up each CD with alternative takes and outtakes, packaged them in pleasantly tactile digipaks and still had them 'on the streets' for under a 'tenner', i.e. five pounds cheaper than the official equivalent, which were bereft of bonuses, thinly packaged and sonically inferior.

The Japanese, not surprisingly, elected to go one step further. After (re)issuing 2-CD sets documenting each series of Beatles sessions on the Secret Trax label,[5] putting every single circulating mix and alternative take in one place, with meticulous annotation; they duly released the entire official catalogue in mini-album sleeves, using the now ultra-rare Mobile Fidelity half-speed-master vinyl boxed-set, which had been de-clicked with typical Japanese care. The results put the official CDs to shame, with many collectors filing their EMI editions away in the cellar, in a cupboard marked 'Beware the Leopard'.

In 1999 came the first sign that The Beatles were aware of the inferior nature of the product they continued to collect royalties on, with a revamped, remastered, remixed, resplendent soundtrack CD for the *Yellow Submarine* film. Four of the Sergeant's songs – the title-track, 'Lucy', 'With a Little Help' and 'When I'm 64' – were released from their sickly subterranean homes. In the clear light of digital day, they had never sounded so good. Fans eagerly anticipated the rest of the catalogue following hard on its heels, preferably before the Internet changed consumer patterns irrevocably, at the expense of all forms of intellectual property.

Instead, the label's unimaginative response was to revert to the original, 1986 masters for a release that merely reshuffled the existing canon. A single CD of Beatles *Number Ones* always seemed like a bizarre substitute for a CD of *all* twenty-two Beatles UK singles, a legitimate exercise, and one EMI had already undertaken for the deluxe singles-on-CD boxed-set (1992). Even more offensive to the band's history has been the ongoing release of the American variants of early Beatles albums in stereo/mono configurations, at full price; flying in the face of everything the band have ever said about these anachronistic abortions.

The one time EMI have done something creative with the canon, post-*Anthology* – the release of *Let It Be . . . Naked* (2003) – McCartney (and co.) refused to okay including the *Get Back* LP as a bonus disc, preferring to waste a second CD on a twenty-minute audio-verite document of mid-song disagreements. Meanwhile, the Sergeant remained strictly stereo, even after its thirtieth anniversary in 1997, when Pink Floyd did the decent thing, issuing their not-so-flawed masterpiece of psychedelia, *Piper At The Gates of Dawn*, in its original mono; along with a companion CD EP of the remaining three singles from Barrett's time with the band.

Now was the time to send *Pepper* back in time. Yet The Beatles prevaricated; preferring to supervise the DVD release of *Anthology* (which at least provided a few genuinely startling 5.1 mixes). By this time technology was starting to make decisions for them, on behalf of (non-)consumers already deciding what was worth preserving in the increasingly popular MP3 format, to play on the latest portable record-collection carriers. When the iPod arrived, it seemed to be all over bar the twisting (on the record companies' part) and the shouting (on the consumers').

With the barbarians not so much at the gate as on the Web, the industry woke up. Rather than letting every download be one more consumer lost to piracy (cough), the labels reluctantly began putting their music 'on line'. The Beatles, though, with surely the most valuable catalogue in hyperspace, continued to hold out and consumers were obliged to make their own transfers, from EMI's top-end-free CDs, or from superior 'pirate' versions (or even vinyl itself).

In the face of this wholesale consumer defection from the album medium, the very format *Pepper* had validated in its day, one might have expected the Sergeant to be on the slide in popular perception, as the more song-oriented collection which preceded it started to rise in critics' estimation. *Revolver* certainly seemed to spend most of the nineties climbing ever higher in both critics' and readers' polls, until it topped both 1998 and 2000 editions of Colin Larkin's Guinness-and-smorgasbord Album polls.

Actually, the advent of the twenty-first century suggested that the 1967 album had never enjoyed greater popular favour, or a more tenuous position in its parallel stream of critical esteem. While *Revolver* seemed to consistently outperform *Pepper* in the popular polls which the Internet had made so easy to compile – and so difficult to render reliable – *Sgt. Pepper* continued to make highly creditable appearances in most public polls (notably those conducted by Guinness, *Rolling Stone*, *Mojo*, Radio Two, Channel 4 and *Q*).

In fact, the Peppered One topped Radio Two's 2006 poll, after coming second in a joint NME.com/Guinness poll (and seventh and nineteenth in contemporary polls conducted by Channel 4 and *Q*). Evidently the fans had made up their own minds, and the critics could go hang (though in Channel 4's case, the fact that its 'viewers' couldn't think of a single Dylan album to include in the fifty greatest albums of all time suggests we're dealing with the same brand of retard who considers *Star Wars* a better movie than *Citizen Kane*).

For Britain's resolute rock critics, though, *Pepper* still had something of a pariah status, even as *Revolver* was raised up to be the perfect pop album. Polls in *NME* in 2003 and 2006 (the latter confined to British albums only) excluded *Pepper* entirely, à la 1985, while placing *Revolver* at fifth and ninth respectively. *Q* went one further. Its own British Albums poll in 2004 placed *Revolver* second and *Sgt. Pepper* nowhere. Goldstein's view, as expressed back in '67, had completed its round-the-world voyage, and become the critical consensus. And academia evidently concurred with these carping critics. In 1997, when Allan Moore published an academic treatise on the album, as part of what had been a series of studies concerning classical compositions, he concluded that 'the chief legacy of *Sgt. Pepper* is . . . one of a failed striving for legitimacy, now sufficiently far distant to be looked on with benign, amused forbearance.'

Yet the popularity of the album continues undimmed, and not just with those who look back fondly on these days of incense and rose-tints. The Sergeant, as he approaches his fortieth birthday, is now indisputably iconic. Indeed, when U2 and Paul McCartney agreed to open the all-day Live 8 telecast concert in 2005, on the twentieth anniversary of Live Aid, it was the title-track to that psychedelic soundtrack which opened this concert 'to end world poverty'.

And in a perverse way there seems something rather fitting in this – the same kind of woolly thinking which convinced hippies that if they dropped enough acid, and did as little to change things as the People's Liberation Front of Judea, the world would change for the better, now led 'their' children to believe that attending a rock concert was doing something about a problem which still remains intractable two hundred years after Malthus.

Neither 'Sgt. Pepper' the song, nor Sgt. Pepper the album had anything much to say about such worldly matters. It was as inward-looking as a work of art could be – as a number of reviewers noticed back then. And yet, thirty-eight years on, it was now seen as somehow emblematic of 'caring'. Sgt. Pepper was the product of a time so remote, so shrouded in the fog of nostalgia, that it not only transcends most criticism, it has acquired a social conscience the era never actually had.

Not that anyone, young or old, in the crowd at Live 8 could use the same 'get out of jail free' card the sixties counter-culture used to trot out in times of doubt: that when the Sgt. Pepper album appeared, the drug culture adopted by The Beatles and their contemporaries was generally believed to bestow insights beneficent and beautiful (ten-page features in Life notwithstanding). As Miles explains, 'If you grow up listening to jazz records, you know how many have been addicted and how many have died through heroin, but LSD didn't seem like that kind of drug. [After all,] the thing had only just been made illegal in 1966 . . . What you [were aware of] was the danger of speed. People knew that meth[amphetamine] killed you.'

Five years after Pepper, every respecting rock fan knew that drugs – directly or indirectly, psychedelic or soporific – had claimed the lives of Brian Jones, Jimi Hendrix, Janis Joplin and Jim Morrison; and had turned the minds of the great and the good – including figures as touched with genius as Brian Wilson, Arthur Lee, Syd Barrett, Nick Drake and Peter Green – to fried plantains. Of these scarred survivors, Wilson, Lee and Green would make their way, uneasily and tentatively, back into the world, but none of them would come close to producing work like that made in the white-heat of (drug-infused) inspiration. In Wilson's and Lee's case they were obliged to spend their post-drugs dotage touring the world playing their mid-sixties masterpieces – *Pet Sounds*, *Smile* and *Forever Changes* – by rote to the adoring. Both had learned the hard way not to leave the mind dangling out there.

> **Arthur Lee:** I'm not going to elaborate on anything that would put a dent in a young person's mind. I've been out there, man.

> **Keith Altham:** [LSD] was all terribly over-rated – there were no great secrets going to be divulged by this . . . Look what happened to Brian Wilson – saddest thing I've ever seen, [him] singing in the last few years. Don't try to tell me that *that* is the Brian Wilson that used to sing with the Beach Boys, 'cause it's not.

Drake, who started dropping acid in Cambridge just as Barrett was leaving for London, would be dead by 1974, writing almost nothing in the last five years of his life (*Pink Moon* being half-written before *Bryter Later* had even appeared). Barrett – perhaps the figure who burnt brightest, but briefest – would sporadically threaten to regroup his senses, but by 1972 had surrendered to the night. When, at this time, his ex-girlfriend Jenny Fabian 'found him again living up the road from Earl's Court . . . he [was] listening over and over again to Beach Boys tapes, which I found a bit distressing. He was still exactly the same, only now he was Syd Barrett the has-been.' Something tells me it was the pre-*Smile* canon that now preoccupied 'Barrett the has-been'. (The doctor said play Beach Boys music, 'cause it seems to make him feel all right.)

Barrett's attempts to live a life of quiet desperation were occasionally interrupted by the odd affected individual who came to Cambridge in search of the Piper. Unlike his fellow revolutionaries, the only walls he was able to construct around himself were psychological, but they generally sufficed. Finally, in the spring of 2006, Barrett was spared any more intrusive visitations as he succumbed to cancer, too. Just as Tom Stoppard was unveiling his new play, *Rock & Roll*, which begins and ends with sightings of Syd, first in 1967 and then in 1991, Barrett himself finally passed from view. The outpouring of appreciation on all sides was genuinely unexpected, wholly warranted and cruelly belated.

The Beatles had always required something more solid to shut out the inevitable seekers. Sadly George Harrison became the second Beatle to be set upon by someone truly disturbed, when he was attacked in his home by a schizophrenic Scouser in December 1999. Close friends suggest he never recovered from this traumatic assault though – like both Barretts – it was ostensibly cancer which carried him off two years later. Harrison had never felt comfortable adopting that Fab persona. Hence 'When We Were Fab'. In this he shared a kinship with the ever-inspiring Dylan. Indeed, he had been the one Beatle to have retained a lasting friendship with the prophetic poet, even co-writing a couple of albums with him and his fellow Wilburys at the end of the eighties.

Back in 1966, Dylan had been the first to hide himself away, after a world tour where he had been Christ and anti-Christ rolled into one. If the fabled motorcycle accident freed him from his obligations, he too found fans beating a path to his door. In his recent unreliable memoir, *Chronicles*, he tried to communicate just how disturbing he found this form of fame even in Woodstock, where the acid-addled tracked him down:

> Moochers showed up from as far away as California on pilgrimages. Goons were breaking into our place all hours of the night. At first, it was merely the nomadic homeless making illegal entry – seemed harmless enough, but then the rogue radicals looking for the Prince

of Protest began to arrive – unaccountable-looking characters, gargoyle-looking gals, scarecrows, stragglers looking to party.

In 2005, his faithless fans finally got to see just what had frightened Dylan so much in the winter of 1967, prompting him to tune up, turn down and drop out even before *Pepper* reared its head. Months before the Sergeant took the counter-culture into the mainstream and christened it cool, Dylan sat and watched hours and hours of 16 mm colour footage his friend Howard Alk and documentary-maker DA Pennebaker had shot on that May 1966 trip, including the entire sequence in the back of a car with a loaded Lennon; and he knew that he wanted *out*.

The release of almost an hour of this 'lost' footage, wrapped in a pretentious four-hour masterclass in how not to tell a tale – Martin Scorsese's *No Direction Home* – reinforced just how great a risk Dylan's leap into the life electric had represented. At every turn on that fateful tour, he had encountered folk who wanted him to show them the way. By 1967, he had renounced that role – at much the same time Brian and Syd abnegated it – leaving *Sgt. Pepper* free and clear to flick the switch on the lysergic light.

As the generation affected so strongly by Britpop reached the cusp of adulthood, and wanted to put away childish things in order to release the inner child, The Beatles were perfect envoys of the new pop, one that would raise Rock up by its bootstraps and say, 'This is serious – in intent and execution.' Some of those caught in their slipstream fell by the wayside, but such were the risks when entering the unknown. Rimbaud knew this. As did Dylan. Lennon even broadcast his own warning, loud and clear, in verse one of *Pepper*'s most perfect paean: 'He blew his mind out in a car.'

Unfortunately, the gesture itself – made by the most powerful pop band on the planet – proved so seismic that the artifact itself became frozen in the moment; that 'contact high' of which MacDonald wrote – shortly before his own suicide – becoming cryogenically stored in the sounds of the Sergeant. Hence why, for so many, it remains an album that cannot be separated from its milieu. Even McCartney, asked recently about the impact of the album, seemed a little overwhelmed by its enduring resonance, as he gamely tried to explain what he'd had in mind, back when it was just a way to escape the straitjacket of Beatlemania, and not an idealistic introduction to a brave new world:

> **Paul McCartney:** In terms of significance, you can't go on making *Pepper* all your life . . . It hit the right notes, the right moment in time. It was strange. It was weird. It was hugely popular . . . In terms of impact, it hit the whole world across the back of the head with a plank of wood . . . It was always going to be impossible to top . . . It was an album that marked the times and summed up the times . . . There was an absolute inevitability to something like *Pepper*. It just had to happen. When it finally happened, it was apocalyptic . . . It was a party that had to happen because of all the Victorian thinking we'd grown up with. [2004]

NOTES

Chapter 2: The Pendulum Swings

1. A number of 'authoritative' Dylan discographies have dated the release of *Blonde on Blonde* to late May, somewhat unlikely given that the final overdub on '4th Time Around' wasn't done until the second week of June. The album charted the last week in July, so a release date on or around 14 July seems most likely.

Chapter 4: Living Is Easy

1. Interestingly, Lennon seems to be remembering the song's original starting point. 'No-one I think is in my tree' comes some way into the song as released.

Chapter 5: Into Overdrive

1. The Stones undertook a month-long European tour in March–April 1967, but were otherwise off the road from the end of 1966 till November 1969.
2. The acetate for 'Lucy Leave', now in the possession of an American collector, is clearly credited to The Pink Floyd (not The Pink Floyd Sound), which suggests it was cut in 1966, even if the songs date from 1965. The retention of 'Lucy Leave' in the set as late as October 1966 suggests they still considered the song representative of their sound.
3. According to the most reliable Floyd chronology (see Hodges, Nick in Bibliography), the last Spontaneous Happening was April 7th. In fact, Richard Wright says they were 'playing a private affair at The Marquee' when they met Jenner. Jenner has consistently insisted it was at a time when he was marking 'finals', i.e. June, which probably means Wright is right.

Chapter 6: Still Single-Minded

1. Rowe, it has to be said, has been unfairly maligned for failing to sign The Beatles on the basis of their less than impressive Decca audition tape. He did go on to sign The Rolling Stones and Them on the basis of their altogether better demo tapes.

Chapter 7: In The Life Of . . .

1. Sixteen-track would be the true hiss-receptacle because of the 50% reduction in track-width since it used the same width of tape as eight-track.
2. The guide vocal loses its way when McCartney blows the line about having a smoke, and audibly exclaims, 'Shit!' Fans of this kind of vocal faux pas should also check out Elvis's 'In The Ghetto' take one, an almost perfect performance until he mucks up the last verse, and delivers a similar exclamation of frustration.
3. The Massed Alberts were a novelty group from Lennon's youth who regularly bastardised familiar standards for laughs – or not. Also produced by George Martin.

Chapter 8: Games For May

1. The complicated (not to say cross-collateralised) production/publishing umbrella deal Boyd offered to subsequent Witchseason acts would create financial fall-out for decades, see my Sandy Denny biography, *Sad Refrains* (Helter-Skelter, 2001).
2. The full recordings of 'Interstellar Overdrive' and 'Nick's Boogie' would not appear until 1990, when See For Miles issued an expanded CD version of the original soundtrack LP.

Chapter 9: Take A Trip

1. 'This Side of Paradise'.
2. The Beatles' English albums to date had all featured fourteen tracks,

save for *A Hard Day's Night*, which had thirteen; so twelve tracks would have seemed short shrift. Not so in America, where the first six Beatles albums would have fit on to a double CD (try it!).

3. Presumably Smith was considering The N'Betweens as another band to A&R for EMI. However, these recordings have yet to see the light of day. By 1969 the band would have evolved into (Ambrose) Slade.

4. According to McCartney, he was horrified to discover the snippets played backwards sounded like, 'We'll fuck you like Superman'. Still, at least it wasn't 'Mars shall invade us', a message AJ Weberman accused Dylan of hiding on *New Morning*.

Chapter 10: Needing Help

1. The song appears on a handwritten track-listing Wilson provided to Capitol around December 1966. The full listing read as follows: Do You Like Worms. Wind Chimes. Heroes & Villains. Surf's Up. Good Vibrations. Cabin Essence. Wonderful. I'm In Great Shape. Child is Father of The Man. The Elements. Vega-Tables. The Old Master Painter.

2. The four songs were 'Heroes & Villains', 'Vegatables', 'Wind Chimes' and 'Wonderful'.

Chapter 11: Turning The World On

1. In the case of 'She's Leaving Home', this extends to releasing the song at the 'right' speed, whereas the stereo version has been speeded up by approximately 2%.

Chapter 12: Scream Thy Last Scream

1. The exchange in question appeared in the 4 August issue of *Go!* Syd told the journalist, 'I'm beginning to think less now. It's getting better'. The journalist replied that if he stopped thinking entirely, he 'might as well be a vegetable.' Barrett just replies, 'Yeah.'

2. Barrett's one billed performance as a solo artist was with Jerry Shirley

and Dave Gilmour, also at Olympia, in June 1970, part of the four-day *Extravaganza '70*. His set, announced at the last minute, lasted just three songs: 'Gigolo Aunt', 'Effervescing Elephant' and 'Octopus'.

3. Apparently released in the week after Christmas in the States, the album was not given a UK release until the following February.

4. Subsequent editions of the album have airbrushed The Beatles out; but they're *definitely* there on any first pressing.

Chapter 13: Nothing To Get Hung About

1. Meredith Hunter was the coloured gentleman knifed by a Hell's Angel after waving an empty gun around at Altamont Speedway on 6 December, 1969.

2. The 1979 UK Tour would be the last time McCartney devoted so little of any tour set to The Beatles. In 1989 the Beatle-count was fifteen–sixteen songs, and in 1993, eighteen–nineteen songs, including this trio of set-closers: 'Fixing A Hole', 'Penny Lane' and 'Sgt. Pepper'.

Chapter 14: Revolving

1. CDs mastered at Abbey Road have for a number of years been criticised for their lack of 'top end', apparently the direct result of 'rolling off' the higher frequencies (presumably to obviate any background hiss). A simple test is to play an Abbey Road version of, say, a British Island CD and turn the treble up on the amp. Negligible difference means it has had the 'Abbey Road Roll Off'.

2. Essentially the period of copyright protection afforded to live recordings (and some studio recordings) varied from country to country prior to a Europe-wide agreement in the mid-nineties; and so a 'protection gap' existed for a while that was exploited by a number of European labels. For a full discussion, see my *Bootleg! The Rise & Fall of the Secret Recording Industry* (Omnibus Press, 2003).

3. Some bands leave an open mike in the studio, and run a continuous tape of sessions. Though this practice was rare prior to the digital era

because of the cost of tape, it was adopted for the Twickenham sessions in January 1969, from which the bulk of the *Let It Be* film was culled.

4. The recording of the May 1960 rehearsal used on *Anthology 1* was clearly derived from a commercial bootleg, and not from one of the superior dubs circulating among collectors at the time. It's called tape research, guys.

5. Secret Trax were in fact issuing 'real' CD versions of titles originating from West Coast CD-R label Silent Sea, so this series represented a happy combination of American compiling and Japanese packaging.

A SELECT SOUNDTRACK
FOR EVERY SECTION

T hough almost all of the music here referenced was intended to be heard in mono, most CD editions insist on providing the songs in stereo. As such, it is assumed that the best edition is the original *UK* vinyl version, unless otherwise stated.

1. Get High With A Little Help

Bob Dylan:

Bringing It All Back Home [LP]
Highway 61 Revisited [LP]
Can You Please Crawl Out Your Window? [45-A]
Positively Fourth Street [45-A]
Guitars Kissing & The Contemporary Fix [Bootleg 2-CD set of Manchester show, 17/5/66 – mix greatly preferable to official version, issued as *The Bootleg Series vol. 4*. Acoustic set to Royal Albert Hall 27/5/66 appears on *Genuine Live 1966* 8-CD bootleg boxed-set.]

The Beatles

Rubber Soul [LP]
'Tomorrow Never Knows' on *Revolver* [LP]
'Mark One' on *Anthology 2* [2-CD]
'I Feel Fine' b/w 'She's A Woman' [45]
'Ticket To Ride' b/w 'Yes It Is' [45]
'Help' b/w 'I'm Down' [45]
'Day Tripper' b/w 'We Can Work It Out' [45]
'Paperback Writer' b/w 'Rain' [45]

2. The Pendulum Swings

Albums

Blonde on Blonde – Bob Dylan
Revolver – The Beatles
Pet Sounds – The Beach Boys
The Village Fugs – The Fugs
The Holy Modal Rounders 1+2 – Holy Modal Rounders [CD twofer]
Absolutely Free – The Mothers of Invention
The Velvet Underground & Nico [Test pressing, dated 25 April, 1966, with 'New York' versions of 'Waiting For The Man', 'Venus In Furs' and 'Heroin' – Japanese bootleg 3-CD set, *Ultimate Mono & Acetates Album*]
Peel Slowly & See – The Velvet Underground [5-CD set; first CD comprising the July 1965 acoustic demos.]

Singles

'Paint It Black' b/w 'Long, Long While'; 'Have You Seen Your Mother, Baby, Standing in the Shadow?' b/w 'Who's Driving Your Plane?' – The Rolling Stones
'Set Me Free' b/w 'I Need You'; 'Sunny Afternoon' b/w 'I'm Not Like Everybody Else'; 'Dead End Street' b/w 'Big Black Smoke' – The Kinks
'I'm A Boy' b/w 'In The City;' 'Happy Jack' b/w 'I've Been Away' – The Who
'My Mind's Eye' b/w 'I Can't Dance With You – Small Faces

3. Hey, What's That Sound?

Singles

'Eight Miles High' b/w 'Why'? – The Byrds [the alternative RCA recordings are included on the *5D* CD remaster]
'Good Vibrations' – The Beach Boys [an alternative, early studio version included on *Smiley Smile/Wild Honey* CD twofer]

Video

'Surf's Up' on *Twenty-Five Years of Good Vibrations*

4. Living Is Easy

'Strawberry Fields Forever' b/w 'Penny Lane' [45]
'When I'm 64' on *Mythology Vol.3* [4-CD bootleg boxed-set; features
the song at correct speed, in a contemporary mono mix (RM6)]
Strawberry Lane [2-CD bootleg set on Secret Trax; contains the entire
history of 'Strawberry Fields Forever' from demo to completion, plus
early alternative mixes of 'Penny Lane']

5. Into Overdrive

AMMusic – AMM [LP]
'Lucy Leave' b/w 'King Bee' [demo 45, bootlegged on *Magnesium
Proverbs* CD]; 'Interstellar Overdrive' – The Pink Floyd [October 1966
demo, bootlegged on *Last Screams* CD]
Jet Propelled Photographs [CD of eight demos from winter 1967] – The
Soft Machine

6. Still Single-Minded

Between The Buttons [LP]; 'Let's Spend The Night Together' b/w 'Ruby
Tuesday' [45] – The Rolling Stones

Singles

'I'm a Believer' b/w '(I'm Not Your) Steppin' Stone' – The Monkees
'Wrapping Paper' b/w 'Cat's Squirrel'; 'I Feel Free' b/w 'N.S.U.' –
Cream
'Hey Joe' b/w 'Stone Free'; 'Purple Haze' b/w '51st Anniversary'; 'The
Wind Cries Mary' b/w 'Highway Chile' – The Jimi Hendrix Experience
'Night of Fear' b/w 'Disturbance'; 'I Can Hear the Grass Grow' b/w

'Wave The Flag & Stop The Train' – The Move
'Arnold Layne' b/w 'Candy & A Currant Bun' – The Pink Floyd [the pre-EMI-overdubs version of b-side appears on *Rhamadam* bootleg CD]
'Love Makes Sweet Music' – The Soft Machine [45-A]
'King Midas In Reverse' – The Hollies [45-A]
'My Friend Jack' – Smoke [45-A]

7. In The Life Of . . .

The Beatles

All mono:
'A Day In The Life'
'Sgt. Pepper's Lonely Hearts Club Band'
'Good Morning'
'Being For The Benefit of Mr Kite'
'Only A Northern Song'
'Fixing A Hole'
[The mono mix of 'Northern Song' can be found on *Secret Songs In Pepperland* (Japanese bootleg CD). An acetate of take 6 of 'A Day In The Life', with McCartney's guide vocal, no orchestration and unfinished ending has been bootlegged a number of times.]

8. Games For May

The Pink Floyd

Piper At The Gates of Dawn [mono LP, issued on CD in 1997]
'Interstellar Overdrive' [French EP edit – also on *Last Screams* CD]
Joe Boyd's recordings of 'Interstellar Overdrive' and 'Nick's Boogie', both fifteen minutes, have appeared complete on the *Tonite Let's All Make Love In London . . . Plus!* 'soundtrack' CD.
'Astronomy Domine' [as performed live on *Look of the Week*, on *Magnesium Proverbs* bootleg CD]

9. Take A Trip

The Beatles

All mono:
'Lovely Rita'
'Lucy In The Sky With Diamonds'
'Getting Better'
'Within You Without You'
'She's Leaving Home'
'With A Little Help From My Friends'
'Sgt. Pepper' (reprise)

10. Needing Help

'Heroes & Villains' [*Good Vibrations* boxed-set]
'Heroes & Villains'; 'Do You Dig Worms?' [*Smile*, Japanese bootleg CD, 1989]; 'Vegatables'; 'Love To Say Da-Da' [*Smile*, Sea of Tunes bootleg CD, 1999] – The Beach Boys
'A Whiter Shade of Pale' [45-A] – Procol Harum
'See Emily Play' [45-A] – The Pink Floyd [An acetate of an earlier, superior mix of 'See Emily Play' has appeared on *Magnesium Proverbs* bootleg CD, and should be heard.]

11. Turning The World On

The *Sgt. Pepper* LP in stereo on acid.
Then in mono, with a strong cup of tea.

12. Scream Thy Last Scream

Live at the Monterey Festival:

The Byrds
The Buffalo Springfield*
The Grateful Dead*

The Jimi Hendrix Experience
The Jefferson Airplane
Janis Joplin*
Moby Grape*
The Who
[Though an impressive looking 4-CD set of the famous festival was
issued by Rhino, a number of acts refused permission to use their
performances – not surprisingly, these included The Grateful Dead.
Recourse to bootleg versions is required for those acts asterisked above,
all save the Moby Grape set appearing on Living Legends' 2-CD
Monterey Pop Festival Vol. 1. The Janis Joplin Sunday set is on the offi-
cial set, but this contains the even more incendiary Saturday set. The
Moby Grape set appears on the *Dark Magic* double-CD.]

Albums

Smiley Smile – The Beach Boys [stereo]
Butterfly – The Hollies
Mr Fantasy – Traffic [mono LP, issued on CD in the US, complete with
early singles, 'Paper Sun', 'Hole In My Shoe' and 'Here We Go 'Round
The Mulberry Bush' – also all mono]
Axis: Bold As Love – The Jimi Hendrix Experience
Move – The Move
Disraeli Gears – Cream [a de luxe 2-CD set from Universal collects all
the contemporary BBC sessions, the five so-called *Disraeli Gears* demos
and mono/stereo configurations of the album.]
John Wesley Harding – Bob Dylan [stereo]
Music From Big Pink – The Band [stereo]
Sweetheart of the Rodeo – The Byrds [stereo]
Magical Mystery Tour – The Beatles [The CD edition corresponds to
the US LP, not the original UK double EP. Also from this period are
the eight-minute 'It's All Too Much', found on *Secret Songs In
Pepperland* (bootleg CD), 'All Together Now' (*Yellow Submarine* CD),
and the six-minute 'You Know My Name' (*Anthology 2*). The nine-
minute 'Flying' appears on Secret Trax 2-CD set, *Magical Mystical Boy*.]

Their Satanic Majesties Request – The Rolling Stones [two 4-CD bootleg boxed-sets *Satanic Sessions* vols 1 & 2 provide every conceivable basic track from these sessions – hard work, but certainly revealing a certain madness-in-their-method.]

Singles

Something Else EP – The Move [Three additional tracks, and an unedited 'Sunshine Help Me' appear on the 3-CD *Movements* boxed-set.]

'Apples & Oranges' – Pink Floyd [Also essential listening are the studio versions of 'Vegetable Man' and 'Scream Thy Last Scream', on *Magnesium Proverbs* bootleg CD, and 'Jugband Blues' on *Saucerful of Secrets* CD; as is the (off-air) audio of the 20 December BBC session, again available on the *Last Screams* bootleg CD.]

Video

'Wild Thing' & 'Purple Haze' – Jimi Hendrix live in Blackpool 25/11/67 [on bootleg DVD – *Hendrix '67*]
'Jugband Blues' – Pink Floyd promotional film [on bootleg DVD *Let's Roll Another One*]

13. Nothing To Get Hung About

Get Back & 12 Other Songs – The Beatles [the best bootleg CD version has been issued on Vigotone]
Abbey Road [LP]
The Rutles [CD features six bonus tracks, as does the Rhino DVD version]

14. Revolving

The Abbey Road Show 1983 [bootleg CD]
Sessions [bootleg CD – Vigotone]
Ultra Rare Trax Vols. 1&2 [bootleg CD – Swingin' Pig]
Smile [Japanese bootleg CD of *Smile* outtakes]

Smile [bootleg CD version of a possible 'finished' *Smile* from all the session tapes – Sea of Tunes]
Good Vibrations [disc 5 of 5-CD boxed-set]
Yellow Submarine [soundtrack CD]
Let It Be . . . Naked [2-CD – the second disc is a Frisbee]

Some modern reworkings of those seminal psychedelic songs:

'Smile' [2004 version] – Brian Wilson [a pale shadow full of digital tweaks, and precious little sweet inspiration; showing if anything that there *never* was a realised record]
'Fixing A Hole' – Paul McCartney [From a 1993 soundcheck. Broadcast on his *Oobu Joobu* radio series, & rather good. Available on Yellow Dog's *Beatles Originals* bootleg CD.]
'Fourth Time Around' – Bob Dylan [Granada 18/4/99, on *Les Bons Moments* bootleg CD – stunning!]
'Arnold Layne' – David Bowie w/ Dave Gilmour [CD single, from Royal Albert Hall 2006 – also includes a version sung by Richard Wright from same location. Also recommended is the 2006 live rendition by Love Minus Zero, which can be heard on their myspace site.]

SELECT BIBLIOGRAPHY

Note:. Some of the more important sources quoted verbatim in the main text have a shorthand code in square brackets, which tallies with those found here.

Anon. 'Verdict on Pet Sounds: The Most Progressive Pop Album Ever?' *Melody Maker*, 30/7/66

——'Monkees Top Beatle Record!', *KYA Beat*, 28/1/67

——'The Move Explain', *Beat Instrumental*, February 1967

——'The Beatles Ink New Nine Year Recording Contract', *KYA Beat*, 11/3/67

——'Beatles New LP: Most Expensive Ever Produced?' *Beat Instrumental*, April 1967

——'Fantastic Beatles Album!', *Disc & Music Echo*, 20/5/67

——'Beatles Laugh Off BBC Ban', *Melody Maker*, 27/5/67

——Review of Sgt. Pepper, *International Times*, 414, 12/6/67

——'Beatles LP: Was it worth the long wait?', *Disc & Music Echo*, 3/6/67

——'Talk of the Town: Sgt. Pepper', *New Yorker*, 24/6/67

——'Pink Floyd Flake Out', *Melody Maker*, 19/8/67

——'The Messengers', *Time*, 22/9/67

——'Cream Declare War On Singles', *Melody Maker*, 18/11/67

——*The Byrds' Back Pages* (1989)

Abbott, Kingsley. *Pet Sounds: The Greatest Album of the 20th Century* (Helter Skelter, 2001)

Aldridge, Alan. 'Beatles Not All That Turned On', in *The Age of Rock*, ed. Eisen

Altham, Keith. *No More Mr Nice Guy* (Blake, 1999)

Aspinall, Neil & Evans, Mal. 'Sgt. Pepper by Mal & Neil', *Beatles Monthly*, June 1967

——'Recording with The Beatles, Then and Now', *TeenSet* Autumn Special 1967

Bangs, Lester. *Psychotic Reactions & Carburetor Dung* (Knopf, 1987)

Barrow, Tony. 'Paul McCartney in America', *KYA Beat*, 6/5/67

——'Beatle "Day" Banned', *KYA Beat*, 3/6/67

——*John, Paul, George, Ringo & Me* (Andre Deutsch, 2005)

Beatles Monthly. *Sgt. Pepper* Special, June 1967

——Letters page, July 1967

——Letters page, August 1967

Boyd, Joe. *White Bicycles: Making Music in the 1960s* (Serpent's Tail, 2005) [WB]

Brown, Tony. *Jimi Hendrix Concert Files* (Omnibus, 1999)

Cale, John. Private correspondence w/ Kate Heliczer, 1965–66

Carr, Roy *The Rolling Stones: An Illustrated Record* (New English Library, 1976)

Carroll, Lewis [ed. Martin Gardner]. *The Annotated Alice* (Bramhall House, 1960)

Cavanagh, Dwight. *The Smile File* (PTB Productions, 1994)

Cavanagh, John. *The Piper At The Gates of Dawn* (Continuum, 2003)

Chapman, Rob. 'Soft Machine: Pothead Revisited', *Mojo*, #43

——'Smile: Unfinished Symphony', *Mojo*, #99

——'Seer. Painter. Piper. Prisoner', *Mojo*, #154

Charone, Barbara. *Keith Richards: Life As A Rolling Stone* (Dolphin Books, 1982)

Christgau, Robert. *Any Old Way You Choose It* (Penguin Books, 1973)

Cohn, Nik. *Pop From The Beginning* (Weidenfeld & Nicolson, 1969)

Coleman, Ray. 'Beatles Dig Dylan', *Melody Maker*, 9/1/65

——Interviews w/ The Beatles re Sgt. Pepper, *Disc & Music Echo*, 27/5/67

Collis, Clerk. 'Fantastic Voyage: The Making of Yellow Submarine', *Mojo*, #71

Cott, Jonathan. The Rolling Stone Interview: John Lennon, *Rolling Stone*, 23/11/68

Cunningham, Mark. *Good Vibrations: A History of Record Production* (Castle Books, 1996)

Dallas, Karl. *Singers of an Empty Day: Last Sacraments for the Superstars* (Kahn & Averill, 1971)

Dalton, David [ed.] *The Rolling Stones: The First Twenty Years* (Knopf, 1981)

Davies, Hunter. *The Beatles: The Authorised Biography* (Heinemann, 1968) [HD]

DiLorenzo, Kris. 'Syd Barrett: Careening Through Life . . .', *Trouser Press*, February 1978

Doggett, Peter. *The Art & Music of John Lennon* (Omnibus, 2005)

Echols, Alice. *Scars of Sweet Paradise: The Life & Times of Janis Joplin* (Virago Press, 2000)

Eisen, Jonathan [ed.] *The Age of Rock: Sounds of the American Cultural Revolution* (Vintage, 1969)

Evans, Allen. 'Beatles LP In Full', NME, 20/5/67

Farmer, Bob. 'Och Aye . . . Scotland Goes Pink', *Disc & Music Echo*, 29/7/67

——'How The Cream Whipped Up a Fever', ibid

Frame, Pete. *The Road to Rock: A Zigzag Book of Interviews* (Charisma Books, 1974)

Freeman, Alan. Interview w/ The Move, winter 1967 [reprinted unattributed in *Shindig*, #5]

Gaines, Steven. *Heroes & Villains: The True Story of the Beach Boys* (Da Capo, 1995)

Gambaccini, Paul w/ Susan Ready. *Critics' Choice Top 200 Albums* (Omnibus, 1978; 2nd ed. Omnibus, 1987)

Gillett, Charlie. *The Sound of the City: The Rise of Rock & Roll* (Souvenir Press, 1970)

Giuliano, Geoffrey. *The Lost Beatles Interviews* (Cooper Square, 2002)

Gleason, Ralph J. *The Jefferson Airplane & the San Francisco Sound* (Ballantine, 1969)

Goldman, Albert. *Freakshow* (Atheneum, 1971)

Goldstein, Richard. 'I Blew My Cool in The New York Times', in *Goldstein's Greatest Hits* (Prentice-Hall, 1970)

Granados, Stefan. *Those Were The Days: An Unofficial History of The Beatles Apple Organisation* (Cherry Red, 2003)

Granata, Charles L. *Wouldn't It Be Nice: Brian Wilson & The Making of Pet Sounds* (A Cappella, 2003)

Green, Jonathon. *Days In The Life: Voices from the English Underground 1961–71* (Heinemann, 1988) [DITL]

——*All Dressed Up: The Sixties & the Counter-culture* (Jonathan Cape, 1998)

Green, Maureen &c. 'The New Society' &c., *Observer* supplement, 3/12/67

Harrison, George. Interview w/ . . . , *Daily Mirror*, 11/11/66

——Interview w/ . . . , *Crawdaddy*, February 1977

Hendrix, Jimi. Interview w/ . . . , 'Pop Think In', *Melody Maker*, 28/1/67

Hinman, Doug. *The Kinks: All Day And All Of The Night* (Backbeat, 2004)

Hodges, Nick & Priston, Jan. *Embryo: A Pink Floyd Chronology* (Cherry Red, 1999)

Holder, Noddy. Interview w/ . . . , *Uncut* July 2001

Hopkins, John. 'The Pink Floyd vs. Psychedelia', *International Times*, #10

Hoskyns, Barney. *Waiting For The Sun: The Story of the Los Angeles Music Scene* (Viking, 1996)

Howard, Pete. 'Master Quality Beatles Bootleg CDs Surface', *ICE*, #19

——'Beatle Bootlegs Have EMI Execs Puzzled', *ICE*, #20

Hutton, Jack. 'Beatle listen-in', *Melody Maker*, 27/5/67

Jahn, Mike. *Rock: from Elvis Presley to the Rolling Stones* (Quadrangle, 1973)

James, Frederick. 'Is Sgt. Pepper Too Advanced For The Average Pop Fan To Appreciate?', *Beatles Monthly*, August 1967

Jasper, Tony. *The Top Twenty Book* (6th ed., Blandford, 1994)

Jewell, Derek. 'The Beatles Show The Way', *The Sunday Times*, 4/6/67

Jones, Cliff. 'The Madness of Pink Floyd', *Mojo*, #34

Jones, Nick. 'Freaking Out With Pink Floyd', *Melody Maker*, 1/4/67

——Interview w/ George Harrison, *Melody Maker*, 16/12/67

——'Cream: In The Kingdom of Freakdom', *Melody Maker*, 30/12/67

Jones, Peter. 'Sgt. Pepper: Track by Track', *Record Mirror*, 27/5/67

Kent, Nick. 'The Last Beach Movie Part 2', *NME*, 28/6/75

Kroll, Jack. 'It's Getting Better . . .', *Newsweek*, 26/6/67

Ledgerwood, Mike. 'By George! The Beatles Also Have a "Shadow"', *Disc & Music Echo*, 17/6/67

Lee, Martin A. & Shlain, Bruce. *Acid Dreams: The Complete Social History of LSD* (Grove, 1992)

Leigh, Spencer. 'Sgt. Pepper – The Cover', *Record Collector*, #94

——Interview w/ Roy Wood, Radio Merseyside [transcript provided to author]

Lennon, John.   Interview w/ . . . , *NME*, 19/3/66

——Interview w/ . . . , *NME* 3/5/69

Lewisohn, Mark. *The Complete Beatles Recording Sessions* (Hamlyn, 1988)

——*The Complete Beatles Chronicle* (Hamlyn, 2000)

Logan, Nick & Finnis, Rob (ed.) *The NME Book of Rock* (Star Books, 1975)

Mabey, Richard *The Pop Process* (Hutchinson, 1969)

MacDonald, Bruno [ed.] *Pink Floyd Through The Eyes of . . .* (Da Capo, 1997)

MacDonald, Ian. *Revolution In The Head: The Beatles' Records & The Sixties* (4th Estate, 1994)

——*The People's Music* (Pimlico, 2003)

Madinger, Chip & Easter, Mark. *Eight Arms To Hold You: The Solo Beatles Compendium* (44.1 Productions, 2000)

Marcus, Greil. *Stranded: Rock & Roll for a Desert Island* (Knopf, 1979)

Marsh, Dave with Swenson, John. *The Rolling Stone Record Guide* (Rolling Stone Press, 1979)

Martin, George. 'On Sgt. Pepper', *Record Mirror*, 27/5/67

——*With A Little Help From My Friends: The Making of Sgt. Pepper* (Little, [MoSP] Brown, 1994)

Mason, Nick. *Inside Out: A Personal History of Pink Floyd* (Orion, 2005)

McCartney, Paul. Interview w/ . . . , *Street Life* 3/4/76

McDermott, John. *Jimi Hendrix Sessions: The Complete Studio Recording Sessions 1963–70* (Little, Brown 1995)

McNeill, Don. 'Report on the State of The Beatles', *Crawdaddy*, #11

McParland, Stephen J. *Our Favourite Recording Sessions: In The Studio With The Beach Boys 1961–70* (California Music, 2000)

Mellers, Wilfrid. 'Lonely Beat', *The New Statesman*, 2/6/67

——*Twilight of the Gods: The Music of The Beatles* (Viking, 1973)

Melly, George. 'The new Beatles' dazzler', *The Observer*, 4/6/67

Meltzer, Richard. 'The Stones, The Beatles & Spyder Turner's Raunch Epistemology', *Crawdaddy*, #9

Miles &c. [eds.] *International Times*, #1–17 [December 1966 to July 1967]

Miles, Barry Interview w/ Paul McCartney, *International Times*, #6

——Interview w/ Pete Townshend, *International Times*, #8

——Interview w/ George Harrison, *International Times*, #13

——*Pink Floyd: A Visual Documentary* (Omnibus, 1988)

——*Pink Floyd: The Early Years* (Omnibus, 2006)

——w/ Paul McCartney – *Many Years From Now* (Secker & Warburg, 1997) [MYFN]

Mills, Jon & Morten, Andy – 'It's Time to Meet . . . The Move', *Shindig*, #5

Milne, Tom [ed.]: *The Time Out Film Guide* (Longmans, 1989)

Mojo. Interviews w/ Paul McCartney & George Harrison [unattributed], *Mojo*, #1

Moore, Allan F. *Sgt. Pepper's Lonely Hearts Club Band* (Cambridge University Press, 1997)

Morgan, David. *Monty Python Speaks!* (Fourth Estate, 1999)

Murray, Charles Shaar. *Shots From The Hip* (Penguin, 1991)

Neil, Andy & Kent, Matt: *Anyway, Anyhow, Anywhere – The Complete Chronology of The Who* (Barnes and Noble, 2002)

Nelson, Paul. Review of *Sgt. Pepper*, *Hullabaloo*, October 1967

Neville, Richard. *Play Power* (Paladin, 1971)

New York Times, The. 'They Battle for Their Beatles', Various letters, 2/7/67

Nolan, Tom. 'The Frenzied Frontier of Pop Music', *LA Times* 27/11/66

Norman, Philip. *Shout! The True Story of The Beatles* (Corgi, 1982)

O'Mahony, Sean. 'Beatles Song Factory', *Beat Instrumental*, May 1966

Palacios, Julian. *Lost In The Woods: Syd Barrett & The Pink Floyd* (Boxtree, 1998)

Parker, David. *Random Precision: Recording The Music of Syd Barrett 1965–74* (Cherry Red, 2001)

Paytress, Mark. Interviews w/ Roy Wood & Ace Kefford, *Record Collector*, #179

Peyser, Joan. 'The Music of Sound, or, The Beatles and The Beatles', in *The Age of Rock*, ed. Eisen

Phillips, Tom 'Beatles' Sgt. Pepper: The Album as Art Form', *Village Voice* 22/6/67

Pichaske, David *The Poetry of Rock: The Golden Years* (Ellis Press, 1981)

Platt, John *Classic Rock Albums: Disraeli Gears* (Schirmer Books, 1998)

Poirer, Richard 'Learning from The Beatles', in *The Age of Rock*, ed. Eisen

Povey, Glenn & Russell, Ian. *Pink Floyd: In the Flesh* (Bloomsbury, 1997)

Priore, Dominic. *Look! Listen! Vibrate! Smile!* (Surfin' Colours, nd)

——*Smile: The Story of Brian Wilson's Lost Masterpiece* (Sanctuary Books, 2005)

Redding, Noel & Appleby, Carol. *Are You Experienced?* (Da Capo, 1996)

Rice, Tim &c. *Guinness British Hit Albums* (Guinness, 1983)

Richman, Jonathan. Writer's poll, *Fusion*, December 1969

Rimbaud, Arthur [ed. Paul Schmidt]. *Complete Works* (Harper Colophon, 1976)

Rogan, Johnny. *Timeless Flight: The Definitive Biography of the Byrds* (Square One, 1990)

Rolling Stone. 'The 100 Best Albums of the Last Twenty Years', *Rolling Stone*, #507

——Interview w/ George Harrison, *Rolling Stone*, 5/11/87

——*The Rolling Stone Record Review* (Straight Arrow, 1971)

——*The Rolling Stone Interviews 1967–80* (St Martin's Press, 1981)

Sandall, Robert. 'Pink Floyd: The Third Coming', *Mojo*, #6

Sander, Ellen. *Trips: Rock Life in the Sixties* (Scribners, 1973)

Schaffner, Nicholas. *Saucerful of Secrets: The Pink Floyd Odyssey* (Harmony Books, 1991)

Schultheiss, Tom. *The Beatles A Day In The Life: The Day-By-Day Diary 1960–70* (Perigee Books, 1981)

Sheff, David. *The Playboy Interviews w/ John Lennon & Yoko Ono* (Berkley Books, 1982)

Siegel, Jules. 'Goodbye Surfing, Hello God', *Cheetah*, October 1967

Simmons, Sylvie. 'Smile? Don't Mind If I Do . . .', *Mojo*, #124

Sims, Judith. *TeenSet*, May 1967

——'(Studio 2, EMI, London)', *TeenSet*, August 1967

Smith, Norman. Interview w/ . . . , *Studio Sound*, May 1998

——Interview w/ . . . , 'The Pink Floyd Story', Capital Radio, December 1976

Starr, Ringo. Interview w/ . . . , *Modern Drummer*, July 1997

Stoppard, Tom. *Rock'n'Roll: A New Play* (Faber, 2006)

Sutherland, Steve [ed.] NME Originals: *1960s Swinging London* (IPC, nd)

Taylor, Derek [ed. George Harrison]. *Fifty Years Adrift* (Genesis, 1984) [FYA]

——*It Was Twenty Years Ago Today: An Anniversary Celebration of 1967* (Fireside, 1987)

Thompson, Thomas. 'The New Far-Out Beatles', *Life* 16/6/67

Turner, Steve. 'The Story of Sgt. Pepper', *Q*, #9/10

——*Hard Day's Write* (Perennial, 1994)

——*The Gospel According to The Beatles* (WJK Press, 2006)

Walsh, Alan. 'The Danger Facing Pop', *Melody Maker*, 20/5/67

——Interview w/ George Harrison, *Melody Maker*, 2+9/9/67

——'Hits? The Floyd Couldn't Care Less', *Melody Maker*, 18/12/67

Watkinson, Mike & Anderson, Pete. *Crazy Diamond: Syd Barrett & the Dawn of Pink Floyd* (Omnibus, 1991)

Watts, Michael. Interview w/ Ringo Starr, *Melody Maker*, 31/7/71

Welch, Chris. 'Now let the boring controversy begin!', *Melody Maker*, 3/6/67

Welch, Chris & Dawbarn, Bob. 'Psychedelic: The New In Word', *Melody Maker*, 22/10/66

Welch, Chris & Jones, Nick. 'Who's Psychedelic Now: Spotlight on Pink Floyd & The Move', *Melody Maker*, 14/1/67

Wenner, Jann. *Lennon Remembers* (Penguin, 1972)

White, Timothy. Interview w/ George Harrison, *Musician*, July 1996

Wilde, Jon. Interview w/ Paul McCartney, *Uncut* June 2004

Williams, Paul. *Brian Wilson & The Beach Boys: Essays & Conversations* (Omnibus, 1997)

Williams, Richard. 'Produced by George Martin', *Melody Maker*, 4/9/71

Willis, Tim. *Madcap: The Half-Life of Syd Barrett* (Short Books, 2002)

Wyman, Bill w/ Coleman, Ray. *Stone Alone: The Story of a Rock'n'Roll Band* (Viking, 1990)

Yorke, Ritchie. 'A Private Talk with John', *Rolling Stone*, 7/2/70

ACKNOWLEDGMENTS

Though I ventured into well-trammelled territory with this tome, I have allowed myself the odd speculative detour in the company of some informed guides. My first thanks must therefore go to those who gave me their thoughts 'on the record', providing me with a necessary framework because of their invaluable reflections. So a tug of the forelock to Keith Altham, Kate Archard, Tony Barrow, Will Birch, Joe Boyd, Jonathan Cott, John Hopkins, Peter Jenner, Glen Matlock, Roger McGuinn, Miles, Graham Nash, John O'Neill, Jules Siegel and Pete Stampfel.

Fulsome felicitations are likewise extended to Scott Curran, Peter Doggett, Sid Griffin, John Ingham, Spencer Leigh, Bill Levenson, Andrew Sclanders, Steve Shepherd, Bob Strano and Steve Turner for providing contacts, CDs, caveats and copier-fodder for the greater cause. A lesser work it would have been without you guys. Finally, thanks to Jamie Byng at Canongate for keeping the faith; and to my hands-on editor Andy Miller, who kept me from many bushes and briars as I carried on my merry way. Thank you, boys.

INDEX